THE VIEW *BEYOND*

edited by Dave Patrick

Dave Patrick lives in Nairn, near Inverness, the Highland capital of Scotland. He is a writer and Certified Quantum-Touch® Practitioner and Instructor (www.quantumtouch.com). In May 2009 he edited *The View*: Mind Over Matter, Heart Over Mind – From Conan Doyle to Conversations With God (Polair Publishing) to mark the 150th anniversary of the birth of Sherlock Holmes' creator Sir Arthur Conan Doyle; in May 2010 he organized The Vital Message conference, planned as an annual event following the publication of *The View* (www.thevitalmessage.com).

On his journey towards compiling *The View,* he joined the White Eagle Lodge; his writing is mainly focused on spirituality and the new consciousness. A former Shell Finance executive, and a trained facilitator, he has designed innovative facilitation tools and models to help businesses and social enterprises develop using heart-centred leadership principles, incorporating psychic skills like dowsing. He is a member of the British Society of Dowsers (BSD).

In series with this title

THE VIEW
From Conan Doyle to CONVERSATIONS WITH GOD
edited by Dave Patrick

Francis Bacon
born
22 January 1560 (old style)
1 February 1561 (new style)
died
9 April 1626

THE VIEW
BEYOND

SIR FRANCIS BACON:
ALCHEMY, SCIENCE, MYSTERY

*Published for Sir Francis Bacon's
450th Birth Anniversary*

Edited by Dave Patrick

Polair Publishing **London**
www.polairpublishing.co.uk

First published January 22nd, 2011
by Polair Publishing, P O Box 34886, London W8 6YR

British Library Cataloguing-in-Publication Data
A catalogue record for this book is
available from the British Library

ISBN 978-1-905398-22-5

Set in Monotype Dante by the Publisher and
printed in Great Britain by Cambridge University Press

CONTENTS

PREFACE

UNTIL THE dawn of the twentieth century, scientists were not uniquely scientists: men of single-minded concentration on observation, measurement, and calculation. They were 'philosophers': lovers of wisdom; individuals whose purview encompassed the knowable world, together with the conceivable one. Francis Bacon was one of them, and one of the greatest.

Bacon's thought opened the door to the modern conception of science, without he himself having followed the path through that door. The same as with Newton, Bacon's followers were more Baconian than he himself. They emphasized only a part of his heritage: the part that suited them best. The part that looked at science as an enterprise *in sui generis*, distinct from spirituality, from religion and from all forms of humanism.

Yet Bacon, like Newton, was a deeply spiritual person. The one-sided emphasis placed on his intellectual heritage did great harm to science in the twentieth century by drawing a radical separation between science – pure, untainted by emotion and by anything but the most rational elements of human experience – and the rest of the rich gamut of experiences that makes up the woof and warp of the consciousness of human beings. In our day we attempt to recover some of the fullness of human experience also in the context of science, recognizing that overall context is more important than abstract detail. The essays published in this volume perform great service in this regard, for they recognize Bacon in his human and intellectual complexity, and not just the purified embodiments of so-called scientific reason dictated by the equally famous 'method' that he had founded.

Anyone quoting Bacon the great rationalist will do well to take cognizance of the Bacon presented on these pages, and recall that science is a part of human experience, more exactly, a part of the experience of human beings who are themselves part of the great and miraculous web of life that evolved on this planet. We still understand but a small portion of that miracle, and science as a purely intellectual purified endeavour will never encompass all of it. Bacon, if not his followers, was aware of some of the rest of this mystery and the readers of this volume will become aware of it as well – for their own personal benefit, as well as the edification of our naively and exaggeratedly science-minded civilization.

Ervin Laszlo

Editor's Preface

Following the publication of *The View* in May 2009 to mark Sir Arthur Conan Doyle's 150th anniversary, the invitation from Colum Hayward of Polair Publishing to edit *The View Beyond* and write a chapter on Sir Francis Bacon, for his 450th, was compelling, and one I was delighted to accept – despite my limited knowledge of Bacon at the time.

Writing a meaningful chapter about Bacon was going to be challenging, as I had already studied Conan Doyle's life and works to a reasonable depth before *The View* was written; having taken a Sherlock Holmes-style investigative approach in composing my chapter for this book's predecessor, I decided to adopt it again here. Almost magically, another mystery unfolded!

The opportunity of working on this project with a wonderful team of contributors has been extremely rewarding; the synthesis of the material contained in *The View Beyond* has, in the opinion of one who has had to move swiftly up the learning curve concerning all things Bacon, enabled a near holographic picture of the man and his philosophy to be built up. Perhaps this is an example of the alchemical process at work?

Sir Arthur Conan Doyle was considered to be a man before his time, a highly-principled man of vision and action, aware of a deeper reality beyond the physical, and who fought for Truth and Justice for all; yet he was widely misunderstood and misrepresented, in his own lifetime and now. Could not the same be said about Sir Francis Bacon?

Having been a prominent figure in *The View*, in that she had channelled Conan Doyle from the afterlife in a series of sittings during 1931 and 1932 (after his passing in 1930) with the help of her spirit guide White Eagle and the mysterious French Polaire Brotherhood, I am pleased that we have been able to include one of Grace Cooke's narratives, The Master 'R', here.

We welcome you to the pages of *The View Beyond*.

SECTION I · PROLOGUES : 1

GIVE ME A DEEP-CROWN'D BOWL

ON LORD BACON'S BIRTHDAY

> Hail, happy Genius of this ancient pile!
> How comes it all things so about thee smile?
> The fire, the wine, the men! And in the midst
> Thou stand'st as if some mystery thou didst!
> Pardon, I read it in thy face, the day
> For whose returns, and many, all these pray;
> And so do I. This is the sixtieth year,
> Since Bacon, and thy lord was born, and here;
> Son to the grave wise Keeper of the Seal,
> Fame and foundation of the English weal.
> What then his father was, that since is he,
> Now with a title more to the degree;
> England's high Chancellor: the destin'd heir,
> in his soft cradle, to his father's chair:
> Whose even thread the fates spin round and full,
> Out of their choicest and their whitest wool.
> 'Tis a brave cause of joy, let it be known,
> For 'twere a narrow gladness, kept thine own.
> Give me a deep-crown'd bowl, that I may sing
> In raising him, the wisdom of my King.
>
> *Composed and read by Ben Jonson, January 1621, at a*
> *banquet celebrating Francis Bacon's sixtieth birthday.*

TODAY, the typical floor space of a chicken cage is less than a sheet of printed paper: sixty-seven square inches. In some windowless sheds

in Japan the cages are stacked eighteen tiers high. But not all chickens have
to endure battery cages. The science of genetic engineering has much improved the works of factory farming. There are now two chickens bred to
feed man. *Broilers* are bred for flesh and pass their six weeks of life in less
than a single square foot of space. It's the *Layers* who have gone high-rise
cage. Females of course – their brothers, whom man has not designed for
meat and nature has not designed to lay eggs, 250 million a year in the
USA, serve no function, and are destroyed – destroyed? (Picture a wood-
chipper filled with new born chicks, or ingenious suction pipes leading to
an electric plate.)

Sir Francis Bacon apparently died from a cold he caught on his wintry
way home after jumping from his carriage to explore his latest idea, frozen
chicken. He sentenced his reputation to death many times since when he
wrote that we must 'torture' nature to reveal her secrets and from these
secrets create good works for the benefit of man. 'Torture?', I would ask
him if I only could. Four hundred and fifty years after the birth of Francis Bacon, five billion chickens are 'tortured' annually in 'good works' to
reveal their protein secrets for the benefit of man. It's a matter of agricultural science. 'Torture?', you ask. Depends on your definition of torture?
How much suffering will you tolerate for your food? Everything must die.

What did Francis mean? William Blake certainly understood him and,
because of his understanding, despised him as the father of Newtonian
Science; Urizen, soulless persecutor of nature, enemy of imagination, the
eternal Captain Hook to our natural spirit Pan. Even recently the inspired
English poet, Kathleen Raine, would not remain on a speaker's platform
when she realized a fellow speaker actually admired Bacon.

That speaker is one of the contributors to this book and once tried to
explain Bacon's specific use of the word 'torture' to me. In its pure sense,
'torture' means to stretch; to determine the strength, the tort, the nature
of an assertion. To try one's theories. To prove them through experiment
without bias. Perhaps Bacon is simply repeating his call that our ideas and
assertions about nature must be grounded in a proper observation of nature, not only in Academic logic: 'How many angels can you fit on the tip
of a pin?'. It's possible. Samuel Johnson wrote of Bacon's Essays that 'their
excellence and their value consisted in being the observations of a strong
mind operating on life.' I have always understood Bacon's contribution to
my craft as an actor, primarily of the best plays of his time, to be this: to

recreate them and act in them with a strong observation of life. For this I am eternally grateful to him.

Archbishop Tenison tells us in 1679 that Mr. Ben Jonson (the learned and judicious poet) helped Bacon with writing work. When Bacon died, Jonson wrote of him:

'...he who hath filled up all numbers,
and performed that in our tongue,
which may be compared or preferred
either to insolent Greece, or haughty Rome.'
('Numbers' refers to poetic lines.)

An extraordinary example of Jonsonian laziness, complimentary comparison, or what? For he eulogized thus his fellow playwright, in the 1623 Shakespeare Folio:

'...or when thy socks were on,
Leave thee alone, for the comparison
Of all, that insolent Greece or haughty Rome
sent forth, or since did from their ashes come.'

High praise indeed for both poets from the poet laureate of the day. For Bacon was a poet, as Jonson insists, as Percy Bysshe Shelley once wrote, and even such scholarly refined minds as our own day's Brian Vickers have agreed, 'it would be a dull reader who would not grant him that title. 'A concealed poet' is the tantalizing phrase that comes down to us from Bacon's time.

Be that as it may. Jonson continues:

'In short, within his [Bacon's] view, and about his times were all the wits born that could honour a language, or help study. Now things daily fall: wits grow downward, and Eloquence grows backward: so that he may be named and stand as the mark and acme of our language.'

Perhaps my favourite among Jonson's descriptions of his friend, though, is one I don't have at hand just now – but if my memory serves me right, he recalls that men would take notebooks to Bacon's dinner table to write down his words and refrain from coughing lest they miss something; that Francis was the gravest speaker he ever heard, 'when he could resist a jest.'

What a different image of Sir Francis Bacon this conjures up from the common conceit: Father of Newtonian Science; Ambitious Machiavellian Political Intriguer; or, worst of all, Corrupt Judge.

Sir Francis Bacon has been someone I read for guidance and pleasure. I agree with his insight that the proper subject of our enquiry into human nature should be the cause of human actions ... man's affections, his appetites and desires. I hope the theatre can be the appropriate medium for such an enquiry. I delight in his wit and I have learnt much from his advice on methods of learning, *The Advancement of Learning*, especially in regard to Nature. I am sad that he is known in some places only as a father of modern science's tendency towards a domination of nature. He writes elsewhere that to master nature we must serve nature. If only this were a requisite phrase in every corporate mission statement! It has been a guiding principle for me, particularly in my work in the theatre. Indeed, I found many passages of *Novum Organum* quite applicable to the creation of 'works', as he says, in the theatre, though I'm not sure he is referring to the theatre.

Theatre is a term he uses quite regularly and Francis clearly loved the theatre, presenting two Shakespeare plays himself at Gray's Inn and Whitehall – which only adds to the extremely puzzling silence in Bacon's writing about the other truly remarkable author of his lifetime, a man with whom he shared many common interests and words, William Shakespeare. Which of the two men would I prefer to meet if I was given the opportunity of time travel? Perhaps I would meet them both. Wouldn't that be delightful!

I look forward immensely to learning more of this friend who found it hard to resist a jest. I will have my notebook at hand.

Mark Rylance

THAT LARGE HEART OF HIS

FRANCIS Bacon has always been a strong presence in my life. I was brought up by a mother who admired him greatly and was unwavering in her belief that he was the real author of the Shakespeare works, and then I married a man with similar views and an extensive library on the subject. So it would be surprising if I had not developed at least a passing interest.

Once you start looking into Bacon's life and works, it's difficult not to become fascinated. Able to read and write Latin and Greek, and familiar with countless classical texts, Bacon was also fluent in French, Italian and Spanish; he had a deep knowledge of philosophy, law and the natural sciences, and was an essayist, author, MP, diplomat and Queen's Counsel. He was one of the most influential men of his time, having been involved with the highest affairs of state from an early age. Queen Elizabeth sought his advice, and King James I honoured him with a series of appointments culminating in Lord Chancellor.

That is impressive, but if you add to this the possibility that he also wrote the Shakespeare plays and poetry, it is extraordinary. I know it's romantic to think of the simple agricultural worker, with the family name of Shaksper, from Stratford-upon-Avon, with no known education, library or papers (his daughter was illiterate, and no books, letters or papers were found when he died), pitching up in London and writing and acting in the most brilliant plays ever produced. But I do think it's worth entertaining the thought that the author could have been Francis Bacon. When you look, with an open mind, at the settings of the plays, the circumstances, the words and phrases, and the dates when they were written and published, there are some very interesting coincidences.

Henry IV Part 1, for instance, has scenes set in the very provinces of France which formed Bacon's first experience of that country. While there he came into contact with an idealistic group called the *Pléiade*, who were reforming French literature, science, art and philosophy on the lines of Greek thought, and a similar enterprise became the main plot behind *Love's Labour Lost*. Likewise, letters from his brother, Anthony, over a ten-year sojourn in France and Italy could have provided the inspiration for the setting of *The Two Gentlemen of Verona*. Then again, in about 1609 the Virginia Company sent a number of ships to America. The main ship was blown off course and finished up on the island of Bermuda, where the crew stayed for several months until the boat could be mended and sailed back to Newfoundland. Bacon was the legal advisor to the company and so would have been very aware of the events. It is thought that they influenced his writing of *The New Atlantis* and also his final, and very powerful play, *The Tempest*.

Bacon lived frugally and temperately but was frequently short of money, his father having neglected to make allowance for him in his Will before his sudden death. As a result, Bacon often had to take out loans in order to live. On one occasion he was imprisoned on account of the early withdrawal of a bond by a Jewish lender. He was very upset and embarrassed about these events which were quite unnecessary and it looks as though he took his anger out in the creation of Shylock, immortalizing the Jew, in *The Merchant of Venice*, a little while later.

Like any writer, Francis was constantly making notes and jottings. During one three-year period he kept a notebook which he called his *Promus*. Here we find about 1594 words, phrases and dialogues from many sources, English and foreign. These crop up about three thousand times in the Shakespeare plays and poems, as well as in Bacon's other writing, sometimes literally and sometimes adapted. For instance, in *King Lear*, a new phrase 'Good Dawning', is used, and in *Romeo and Juliet* seven phrases that are close together in the *Promus* occur in eleven consecutive lines of the play. Devoted students of the works of Shakespeare and Bacon have found hundreds of identical or similar expressions: words, metaphors, opinions, quotations, and even identical errors.

The author of the plays added many thousands of new words to the English language. The vocabulary of Shakespeare's writings extends to over 31,000 words, many never used before or since, some invented scholastically, going to the roots of the classical and European languages. Francis Bacon had about the same number of words in his prose works. Milton only demonstrated an eight thousand-word vocabulary and, for comparison, a Stratford villager would only have a four-hundred-word vocabulary.

When considering the authorship of the Shakespeare plays, there are some interesting issues of timing. In *Coriolanus*, one of the plays never heard of until 1623, there is a remarkable passage (Act 1, sc 1) indicating that the author was aware of the circulation of the blood. Harvey discovered this in 1619, three years after Shaksper died. Similarly, in the play *Henry VIII*, a historical fact is deliberately altered as follows. When Wolsey fell from grace he was relieved of the Great Seal by two peers, Norfolk and Suffolk. When the same thing happened to Francis Bacon, four peers were sent to demand the Great Seal. And in the play, *Henry VIII*, four peers wait on Wolsey instead of two, and they bear the same titles and names as those who waited on Francis Bacon. This is another incident that happened after Shaksper (and Oxford, another favoured by some for the Shakespeare authorship) were both dead.

Likewise, when the First Folio appeared in 1623, Shaksper had been dead for seven years and the Earl of Oxford for seventeen. But of the thirty-six plays contained in the Folio, only sixteen had previously been published, and most of these had been thoroughly revized. Fourteen were published for the first time but were known to exist, while six of them – *The Taming of the Shrew, Henry VIII, All's Well that Ends Well, Timon of Athens, Coriolanus* and *Julius Caesar* – had never been printed or heard of before. *Othello* had been published in 1622, but when it appeared a year later in the Folio, 160 lines, in the true Shakespeare style, had been added, carefully worked into the text.

Bacon had a friend called Sir Tobie Matthew who corresponded with him for many years. In his letters, Bacon would refer to the manuscripts he was working on as 'the works of my recreation', or 'my other works'. On one occasion, when he was returning a manuscript to Bacon, Sir Tobie wrote to Bacon: 'I will not promise to return you weight for weight but *Measure for Measure*'. Bacon wrote to Sir Tobie on another occasion: 'Methought you were willing to hear *Julius Caesar* rather than Queen Elizabeth commended....' These two plays first appeared in the 1623 Folio but the two friends had prior knowledge of them. After the publication of the 1623 Folio, Sir Tobie again wrote to Sir Francis: 'the most prodigious Wit that ever I knew of my nation on this side of the sea, is of your Lordship's name, *though he be known by another...*'

Bacon also referred to his wished anonymity in a greeting he sent via

Sir John Davies to King James I, on the King's arrival in England, asking him 'to be good to concealed poets'. But why did Bacon want to keep his identity secret? In his day it was normal for a nobleman to write anonymously, and when the plays were first published they were not attributed to any author. In addition to this, Bacon might have wished to keep his authorship secret – to protect his reputation. The theatre had a very bad name in the circles in which he moved. He might also have wanted to keep peace with his mother, Lady Anne Bacon, an exceptionally talented woman with strong Puritan views who, according to one authority, 'ruled her sons with a tight hand and treated them as little boys when they were men of forty'. Lady Anne became very upset when her son Anthony took lodgings next to a theatre! Anonymity also enabled Bacon to make political points in the plays, as, for instance, in Richard II, without fear of prosecution for treason: he lived in dangerous times. Perhaps too it suited him to keep his more philosophical work separate from anything connected with the theatre.

We do know that Bacon, with his background of court affairs and intrigue, was no stranger to subterfuge, and that he was fascinated by cryptology and even described how text could be put into code using a system he had designed that is similar to our modern binary code. In view of that, it seems very likely that Bacon left typographic clues to his authorship in the Shakespearean works, but some of the wilder claims that he encrypted his personal history in the plays are certainly not proven.

It is almost certain that Bacon's authorship of the plays was known to his circle of close friends and it is thought by some that he did make a public claim too, though as always, an enigmatic one. In his scheme for his Great Instauration, a project he conceived to bring about the illumination of humankind and the restoration of paradise on earth, there are six parts, parts 1, 2 and 3 to be published openly and parts 4, 5 and 6 privately. Part 4 was about psychology, as Bacon explains:

'The Fourth Part is to set forth examples of … Invention according to my Method.…choosing such Subjects as are at once the most Noble.… and the most different from one another … that there might be an Example of every kind.… I mean Actual Types and Models by which the entire process of the Mind and the whole Fabric and Order of Invention [invention meant poetry and drama] from the beginning to the end [from the first act to the last], in certain subjects and those various and remarkable, should be set as it were BEFORE THE EYES [i.e., set on stage]'. (Spedding, *Works of Francis Bacon*, edited by Robertson.)

That particular work of examples of 'Actual Types and Models' has never been found. It does not appear in Bacon's open works at all. But what are the Shakespeare plays if not examples of human nature and behaviour held up for all to see? Perhaps in the words above Bacon did in fact lay claim to the plays.

There are of course many more aspects to Bacon's life and work, expounded and described in this book, that are relevant and educational today. His scientific method, called 'induction', in which he counsels us to find truth by a process of deduction in systematic and methodical steps and to clear our mind of 'idols' or preconceived ideas and prejudices, is particularly valuable and underlies much of his scientific and philosophical writing.

Perhaps, however, the quality above all others that comes through Bacon's works is his kindness and generosity of spirit. It is completely contrary to the picture that emerges in Macaulay's unpleasant and misleading essay on him, as has been countered and explained in the two books, *Evenings with a Reviewer*, by Spedding. It is true that Bacon was accused of taking bribes and that this led to his downfall as Lord Chancellor. But bribes were commonplace in the legal process in the seventeenth century; sometimes people had to wait as long as five years to get a court hearing, and gifts were given in order to speed their progress. Bacon did not like this behaviour and tried to reform the system. There is no evidence that Bacon took bribes in order to prejudice the verdicts, and that would have been completely inconsistent with such a moral man.

Although he suffered the indignity of being removed from office, we have the greater gifts of having the complete Shakespeare works and Bacon's philosophical works, both of which were published in 1623; if Bacon had stayed in office these would never have reached the printers before he died in 1626.

Many warm and complimentary words were written about Bacon by his friends and contemporaries. For instance, Sir Tobie Matthew, writing in 1618 to the Grand Duke of Tuscany, gives some account of Bacon's career and position, and a description of his immense intellectual powers. He goes on to say that the praise applies not only to the qualities of the intellect, but as well to those 'which are rather of the heart, the will, and the moral virtue; being a man most sweet in his conversation and ways, grave in his judgments, invariable in his fortunes, splendid in his expenses; a friend unalterable to his friends; an enemy to no man, a most hearty and indefatigable servant to the king, and a most earnest lover of the public – having all the thoughts of that large heart of his set upon adorning the age in which he lives and benefitting, as far as possible, the whole human race.'

I hope that something of this spirit will come to you through these words, and that in reading this book you will be inspired by the words and philosophy of possibly the greatest writer who ever lived.

Rose Elliot

THE GREAT INSTAURATION

Peter Dawkins

IN TRIBUTES by those who knew him, Francis Bacon is referred to as Apollo, the Day Star and leader of the Muses, and as Pallas Athena, the Tenth Muse and Spearshaker. He is spoken of as a concealed poet who filled the world with his writings, and who rescued and renewed Philosophy in the socks of comedy and buskins of tragedy. He is also referred to as the Chancellor of Parnassus (Apollo and Athena's mountain of poetry and inspiration, containing the Delphic oracle), and as Solomon, and as the third Plato (the first Plato was the Greek philosopher, the second Plato was Ficino). Ben Jonson reverenced Bacon as 'one of the greatest men, and most worthy of admiration, that had been in many ages,' and as 'he who

---

Peter is a philosopher, seer, geomancer, historian, author, lecturer, workshop leader and teacher, who practised as an architect for ten years in both England and Scotland before devoting himself full-time to research and educational work in connection with the world's wisdom traditions. He has travelled widely and has become a specialist in landscape temples and sacred space; in this connection he is founder-director of Zoence Academy. A special area of research has been into Francis Bacon, Shakespeare and the Rosicrucians, and to this end The Francis Bacon Research Trust was founded in 1979, of which Peter is the founder-director. He has acted as an advisor to actors and directors, including at the Shakespeare Globe theatre in London. In 2008 he received an award for distinguished scholarship in Shakespeare Authorship Studies from Concordia University, Portland, Oregon, USA.

Peter is the author of many books, including *The Shakespeare Enigma*, which demonstrates how Bacon and his group were responsible for the Shakespeare plays and the deliberate treasure trail set up by Bacon as a training in his 'art of discovery', whilst its complementary book, *Building Paradise*, describes what the Baconian-Rosicrucian method and work actually is.

hath filled up all numbers, and performed that in our tongue, which may be compared or preferred either to insolent Greece or haughty Rome'. All these descriptions give a hint of the true and hidden nature of Bacon and his work—a work that he called 'The Great Instauration'.[1]

The word 'Instauration' is derived from Latin *instauratio*, meaning (1) repair, renewal, restoration; (2) an act of founding or establishing something. It is famously used in the Latin Vulgate Bible (2 Kings 12 : 4-16) where it refers to the repair and restoration of Solomon's Temple in the reign of King Joash of Judah (ninth century BCE). The word also refers to spiritual edification or illumination, wherein Solomon's Temple signifies the 'temple of light' that is the illumined human mind or soul, including humanity's world soul.

Bacon chose this name carefully, for his immense scheme is none other than the universal and general reformation of the whole wide world through the regeneration or renewal of all arts and sciences, so that humankind might know and practise truth, and thereby recreate a paradise on earth—a golden age of wisdom, peace and prosperity.

To Bacon, truth is love or goodness, and the harmony, order, stability, friendship, peace and illumination that it brings. His *New Atlantis* allegory, like the *instauratio* reference to the repair and restoration of Solomon's Temple, is another way of describing the purpose of the Great Instauration, wherein the golden age of the previous Atlantis is restored, howbeit in a new and more enlightened way. The other analogy that Bacon uses is that of the biblical Eden from which mankind has fallen, and our restoration or redemption to a new Eden through the practice of Christian charity. Bacon's particular point is that charity, for it to be truly useful and good, requires knowledge and gives rise to new knowledge, which is illuminating, and also that, besides the practice of love, the purpose of man is to know that truth which is love.

Other names that Bacon gave to the Great Instauration were 'The Six Days' Work', 'The Greatest Birth of Time', 'The Most Virile Birth of Time', 'The Great Renewal of the Empire of Man over the Universe', and, more simply, 'The Advancement and Proficience of Learning'. The early seventeenth-century Rosicrucian manifestos, which described Bacon's Great Instauration in terms of yet another allegory, referred to it as 'The Universal and General Reformation of the Whole Wide World'.

Francis Bacon was, according to his own personal chaplain and confessor, Dr William Rawley, not only a deep philosopher but also a religious person and able to render a reason of the hope which was in him.[2] It is not surprising then that Bacon's writings are infused with quotations from, comments on and interpretations of scriptural teachings. In a prayer filled with Freemasonic symbolism and written later in his life, Bacon declared that the Scriptures had been his principal books of study and knowledge, and that it was in God's temples that he had found God: 'Most Gracious Lord God, my merciful Father, from my youth up, my Creator, my Redeemer, my Comforter. Thou (O Lord) soundest and searchest the depths and secrets of all hearts; thou knowledgest the upright of heart, thou judgest the hypocrite, thou ponderest men's thoughts and doings as in a balance, thou measurest their intentions as with a line, vanity and crooked ways cannot be hid from thee.... Thy creatures have been my books, but thy Scriptures much more. I have sought thee in the courts, fields, and gardens, but I have found thee in thy temples.'[3]

To a large extent Bacon patterned himself on King Solomon, in the sense that the latter was renowned for building the great temple at Jerusalem, known as Solomon's Temple, for forming a Masonic fraternity to design and construct it, for writing a book of wisdom and a book of natural history, and for being a master of Cabala. All this Bacon set out to be and do, and his mastery of Cabala can be seen in his design of the Great Instauration, which is based on fundamental cabalistic principles. One of the foundations of Cabala is an understanding and knowledge of the deeper meanings of Genesis. This is why, in his *New Atlantis*, Bacon referred to his *Great Instauration* as 'The Work of Six Days', as he designed it in imitation of the biblical Six Days' Work of Creation that leads to the Seventh Day of Rest and Illumination.[4]

Bacon took Solomon's wisdom to heart, such as the book of Proverbs, and in particular took seriously Solomon's statement that 'the glory of God is to conceal a thing, but the glory of a king is to find it out'.[5] He saw this as referring to 'that innocent and affectionate play of children' known as hide and seek, in which 'the Divine Majesty took delight to hide his works' so that we might find them out, and therefore we could not have 'greater honour than to be God's play-fellows in that game'.[6] Bacon also took seriously the biblical statement that man was made in the image or likeness of God,[7] which he took as meaning that our purpose was to imitate God as far as is humanly possible—God being, according to Bacon, the All-Good whose nature is goodness and love. For this reason the Great Instauration is dedicated to good works, or charity, as well as to the glory of God, and much of what Bacon discovered, did or thought, including the key parts of his method, was purposely hidden by him, but in such a way that we might discover it.

This game of concealing and revealing, which is also a fundamental cabalistic precept, is an integral part of Bacon's method. It is one of the keys that Bacon veiled but which we can discover if we look carefully and follow the clues. Another key is strife and friendship, which Bacon describes as 'the spurs of motion and the keys of works'. What he is referring to is the marriage of the two, so that we strive together in friendship to perform good works and discover the truth. A third key is imagination, which Bacon describes as playing a pivotal role as messenger between sense and reason, and again between reason and action, and even more importantly as Janus, the creator, initiator and hierophant of the mysteries. A further very important key is time, involving knowledge of time sequences, cycles and power points. On the title page of *The New Atlantis*, time is depicted bringing forth the hidden truth. There is a special connection between time and imagination.

Like Solomon, Bacon set out to compile a book of wisdom and a natural history, and to construct a temple of light in the human mind, which he symbolized as a Pyramid of Philosophy.[8] He also, in his own words, 'rang the bell that called the wits together' and established a 'fraternity in learning and illumination'[9] to assist him and carry on the good work—a fraternity intended to be a worldwide association or society of like minds and hearts, on which the sun never sets. The original model for this society was sketched out in Bacon's *New Atlantis* and called the College of the Six Days' Work. It was first manifested as the group of wits that gathered around Bacon to assist him, referred to in the Gray's Inn revels of 1594 as the Honourable Order of the Knights of the Helmet,[10] and in the early seventeenth-century Rosicrucian manifestos as the Fraternity of the Rosy Cross.

The science that Bacon sought to develop is an ethical one. He explained that its ultimate purpose is to discover the summary law of nature, which he identified as the law of love. By nature he meant the nature of all things—the nature of the natural world, the human world and the spiritual or divine world. These are the three 'worlds' as defined in the Hermetic and cabalistic teachings as well as the Christian teachings (i.e., body, soul and spirit).

Bacon further described the summary law in biblical terms as 'the work that God worketh from beginning to end', showing that he understood it as love in action. To discover this law we have to practise it, or at least whatever we can understand of it at any time. He doubted that we would ever know it in its fullness but nevertheless we should try, gradually ascending to that knowledge as if climbing a ladder, from knowledge of the lesser laws to knowledge of the greater laws, from physics to metaphysics, from natural laws to spiritual laws. Bacon didn't leave out the natural world as we understand it, as he saw that all laws are descended from and aspects of the one summary law of love. In other words, the nature of God, which is love, is in everything, but in varying degrees and proportions, and is the truth waiting and wanting to be discovered.

Such knowledge Bacon saw as sacred and therefore should not be sought 'either for pleasure of the mind, or for contention, or for superiority to others, or for profit, or fame, or power, or any of those inferior things; but for the benefit and use of life.'[11] This, of course, is not knowledge as normally understood and used, which Bacon well recognized, and thus he explained that his science was different to normal or mainstream science and was designed to run side-by-side with the latter. But it would be the science that would bring the greatest benefits to humankind and the world, and usher in a paradisal golden age.

This work, as conceived by Bacon, is nothing more or less than a labour of love. It requires labourers who are philosophers (i.e., 'lovers of wisdom'), who can work charitably, or philanthropically. Bacon refers to such dedicated people as the *filii sapientiae*, 'the sons of wisdom' or 'sons of science'. He also refers to them as his successors—those to whom what is already known, secret or otherwise, has been passed down or who have 'wits of such sharpness and discernment that they can of themselves pierce the veil'. In the latter case, Bacon is referring to both the veil that he and others like him have erected and also the veil of nature erected by God. It is also a reference to the veils of initiation.

In his method of transmission Bacon uses both what he calls the magisterial method and the initiative method; also what he calls the exoteric method and the acroamatic or enigmatical method. As he explains: 'The magisterial method teaches; the *initiative* intimates. The magisterial requires that what is told should be believed; the initiative that it should be examined. The one transmits knowledge to the crowd of learners; the other to the sons, as it were, of science. The end of the one is the use of knowledges, as they now are; of the other the continuation and further progression of them.' He further explains that he borrows the term initiative from 'the sacred ceremonies' (i.e., as practised in the mystery schools), 'which discloses and lays bare the very mysteries of the sciences'.[12] These sacred ceremonies of initiation were known as mysteries, each one being a sacred drama that helped the initiates progressively to discover truths and new truths by means of direct experience and revelation.[13]

Bacon stated that his plan is that his 'teaching should quietly enter into souls fit and capable of it', and therefore what he published was written and printed purposely in such a way that it would 'not be to the capacity or taste of all' but rather 'single out and adopt his reader'.[15]

What is important to grasp, but is often completely missed by modern commentators, is that Bacon recognized 'a double emanation of virtue from God; the one referring more properly to Power, the other to Wisdom; the one expressed in making the subsistence of the matter, and the other in disposing the beauty of the form.'[16] Quoting the words of Jesus, 'You do err, not knowing the Scriptures, nor the power of God,'[17] Bacon identifies two books, metaphorically speaking, that we should study—the Book of God's Word and the Book of God's Works. The former he refers to as the Scriptures, revealing the will of God, and the latter as the creatures expressing God's power. The study and knowledge of these two 'books' he calls Divinity and Philosophy, the former being associated with faith and religion, or sacred theology, and the latter with philosophy and human learning. Moreover, he considers the latter to be 'a key unto the former; not only opening our understanding to conceive the true sense of the Scriptures, by the general notions of reason and rules of speech; but chiefly opening our belief, in drawing us into a due meditation of the omnipotency of God, which is chiefly signed and engraven upon His works.'[18]

Besides representing Divinity and Philosophy as two books in which we should learn to read, Bacon also symbolized them as two temples or pyramids—the Pyramid of Divinity and the Pyramid of Philosophy. They can be understood as standing together like the Pillars of Hercules or Great Pillars of Solomon's Temple, another symbolism that he uses.

Of these two, Bacon saw it as his particular mission to set in motion

the instauration or renovation of Philosophy, although he makes it clear—
and it is certainly clear in his writings—that he does not neglect Divinity.
He also warns us that we should be careful not to confuse the two, and
that the divine things or mysteries of God cannot be attained by contemplation of God's works; rather, they can only be sought through the means
of divine grace, as a revelation from God inspired into our hearts. He emphasizes that of the two, Sacred Divinity is the chief and is like the mistress
who is served and helped by her wise servant and humble handmaiden,
Moral Philosophy. In this description of Philosophy as being moral and
the servant to Divinity, we can probably most easily see Bacon's overall
intention for and purpose of the science that he set in motion and hoped
would develop in future ages, after the period of gross materialism, which
he foresaw (and which he prayed would not be too severe), had passed.

In more detail, the intention is to erect, metaphorically speaking, a
Pyramid of Science or Philosophy, which science can then be put into action or 'art' that is charitable. This Pyramid has three faces, each face representing one of the three basic knowledges or aspects of Philosophy—
divine, human and natural. These are called Divine Philosophy, Human
Philosophy and Natural Philosophy. The names of the operative or artistic
counterparts are, respectively, Ecclesiastical Prudence, Human Prudence
and Natural Prudence.

Besides being three-faced, the Pyramid of Philosophy is also three-
tiered, the base or first stage being History, the second or middle stage being Physics, and the third and final stage being Metaphysics. The first stage,
constituting the foundations of the Pyramid, comprises well-ordered and
digested experience, the second stage comprises the science of material
and efficient causes, and the third stage comprises the science of formal
and final causes. The capstone or vertical point of the Pyramid signifies
what Bacon refers to as the knowledge or science of the Summary Law of
Nature.

Divine Philosophy, therefore, is constructed of Ecclesiastical History,
Divine Physics and Divine Metaphysics; Human Philosophy is built up
of Civil History (i.e., human experience), Human Physics and Human
Metaphysics; and Natural Philosophy has Natural History, Natural Physics and Natural Metaphysics for its stages. In operative terms, the art of
each knowledge (Ecclesiastical Prudence, Human Prudence and Natural
Prudence) is put into practice in three corresponding ways: Experimental,

Mechanical and Magical.

Bacon was enough of a realist to know that a pyramid, like any build-ing, has to be built from the ground upwards and has to have good foun-dations. One of his major criticisms of past and current philosophies was that they were too airy and not sufficiently well grounded, and that their methodology was not good enough. He saw that any true and lasting phi-losophy would need a much better method to build it than was so far avail-able, and foundations that were sufficiently strong, wide and deep to form a basis for an all-embracing philosophy.

Bacon referred to his new method as 'The Art of Interpreting Nature', or 'A Perfect Method of all Arts', or 'The Art of Discovery'. He considered this as his special gift to mankind. He published part of this method—but not all of it—in his *Novum Organum* (1620). The book was intended to have three parts but was only published with two. Bacon 'reserved' the third and most important part: that is to say, he veiled it. What he did publish, he did in order to set in motion as soon as possible the collection of a *Natural and Experimental History*, gathered from the facts of nature and experience of all kinds, to form a foundation upon which a temple of true philosophy could be raised.

Bacon also realized that it was necessary to develop an accurate sci-ence of physics before being able to rise higher with any real certainty. However, he pointed out that the highest aim of man's researches should be to try to discover not only the metaphysical laws—the 'forms' or causes of the more physical laws and phenomena—but also to try to seek out an understanding of the supreme or summary law of all nature, that of love itself, the cause of causes.

Bacon's understanding of this was that not only should we seek the highest truth, which also means practising it or living it, but also that the higher laws control the lower ones; therefore it might be possible through knowledge of the higher laws to adjust the operations of the lower laws in order to produce what humankind generally calls miracles. But all this should only ever be done with true humility and according to the will of God, and should be entirely charitable. Bacon realized what great things were possible—the great exemplar in this case being Jesus, who said that we could do the same as him and more[19]—but that we should take care, 'first, that we do not so place our felicity in knowledge, as we forget our mortality; the second, that we make application of our knowledge, to give ourselves repose and contentment, and not distaste or repining; the third, that we do not presume by the contemplation of nature to attain to the mysteries of God.'[20]

Bacon's method incorporates a plan involving six major stages by means of which the Pyramid of Philosophy can be built. The six major stages he called the Six Days' Work, referring to the Six Days' Work of divine Creation and recognizing that 'Day', in terms of the divine Eternity and Infinity, is not a day as we commonly understand, but rather a symbol of a stage in the process of creation. 'The Six Days' Work', in other words, are six stages in the creative process, leading to the 'Seventh Day' or seventh stage of completion and enjoyment of what has been created. This forms the divine archetype or law for all genuine creativity.

In respect of creating a pyramid or body of science concerning truth, how long each stage takes in terms of time is partly up to us and the effort we put into it, and partly dependent on divine grace and the working of the laws of the universe, which laws include the law of time, time cycles and power points in time in respect of our world. However, as in all things, we do not have to complete the whole of the first stage before starting on the second, and we do not have to complete the whole of the second stage before starting on the third. But the order of working is important.

Making use of analogy, Bacon presents his scheme to us as if he were an architect creating a building—not just any building but 'a holy temple in the human intellect, on the model of the universe'.[21] In explanation of this universality, he says, 'For whatever is worthy of existence is worthy of knowledge—which is the image (or echo) of existence.'[22]

The six stages of the Great Instauration can be summarized as (1) a survey and appraisal of the terrain (i.e. state) of the sciences together with a plan of action, (2) the discovery, acquirement and development of a method of building, (3) the collection of a history—a data bank—on which to draw, which will form the foundations or first stage of the building, (4) the presentation of the data 'to the eyes', (5) the drawing out of temporary axioms or ideas of truth derived from the presented examples, and (6) the development of final axioms or certainties as a result of putting the ideas into action successfully—the test being that 'truth prints goodness'. These final axioms form the second and third stages of the building, the capstone being knowledge of the summary law of nature.

Drawing on various places where Bacon describes these six parts and various translations of his Latin versions, we find that Bacon termed them as follows:

Part 1: The Divisions of the Sciences, or a Summary Survey and Partition of Sciences;

Part 2: The New Method, or Well-grounded Information concerning the Interpretation of Nature, or True Directions for the Interpretation of Nature, or A True Guide to the Interpretation of Nature;

Part 3: The Phenomena of the Universe, or History Natural and Experimental for the building up of Philosophy, or a Natural and Experimental History with regard to an Ordered Philosophy, or a Natural and Experimental History for the foundation of Philosophy;

Part 4: The Ladder of the Intellect, or The Thread of the Labyrinth, or The Method of the Mind in the Comprehension of Things Exemplified, or the Intellectual Sphere rectified to the Globe of the World;

Part 5: Forerunners, or Anticipations of the Second (or New) Philosophy;

Part 6: The Second (or New) Philosophy, or Active Philosophy from intimate converse with Nature, or Active Science, or Knowledge in Action.

Of the six parts, the fourth part is particularly difficult to understand both from the extraordinary selection of names that Bacon chooses to give to it and also from how he explains it, which is somewhat enigmatic. However, elsewhere he provides a clue when talking about the three faculties of the mind—Memory, Imagination and Reason. He equates memory with history, imagination with poetry, and reason with philosophy. He further explains that it is the role of imagination to present the experiences of sense to the reason, and likewise to present the ideas and understandings of reason to action, acting as a messenger between the two. Sense is associated with experience and the gathering of data, therefore with history, and action produces further experience.

This is a powerful clue as to what Bacon means when he describes the fourth part in terms of the example that he provides for us. He states that these are 'things which it seems necessary to premise, partly for convenience of explanation, partly for present use.' Of these, he says, 'the first is to set forth examples of inquiry and invention according to my method, exhibited by anticipation in some particular subjects; choosing such subjects as are at once the most noble in themselves among those under enquiry, and most different one from another; that there may be an example in every kind.' He then goes on to say that he means by this 'actual types and models, by which the entire process of the mind and the whole fabric and order of invention from the beginning to the end, in certain subjects, and those various and remarkable, should be set as it were before the eyes.'[23]

When reading this statement, we need to remember that he states elsewhere that his intention, which is the intention of the Great Instauration, is to study all nature—divine, human and natural—and, moreover, that 'the principles, fountains, causes, and forms of motions, that is, the appetites and passions of every kind of matter, are the proper objects of philosophy'.[24] He then goes on to say that 'I form a history and tables of discovery for anger, fear, shame, and the like: for matter political; and again for the mental operations of memory, composition and division, judgment and the rest; not less than for heat and cold, or light, or vegetation, or the like.'[25] He is clearly talking about human nature, and the best place to see such a history and tables of discovery set before the eyes, in the way that he describes, is the theatre. That is to say, at least concerning the study of human nature, the fourth part of the Great Instauration uses poetry in the form of drama, whereas the laboratory is more appropriate for the study of nature's nature, and the temple is more appropriate for the study of divine nature.

Bacon thought very highly of poetry, as he did of the imagination, and of poetry he said that 'it appeareth that poesy serveth and conferreth to magnanimity, morality, and to delectation,' and 'therefore it was ever thought to have some participation of divineness, because it doth raise and erect the mind, by submitting the shows of things to the desires of the mind; whereas reason doth buckle and bow the mind into the nature of things.'[26]

All good teachers practise what they teach, and so Bacon left not just an idea for posterity but also practical examples, working models for the rest of us to study, learn from and, if necessary and wherever possible, develop further. He tried to provide us with examples of each of the individual parts of the Great Instauration, which he symbolized as individual volumes or books, seven in all. In some instances there is one particular original volume published for the part of the Great Instauration it illustrates, such as the 1623 *De Augmentis Scientiarum* to illustrate Part 1, the 1620 *Novum Organum* to illustrate Part 2, and, it is believed by some, the 1623 *Folio of Shakespeare's Comedies, Histories and Tragedies* to illustrate Part

4; but for Part 3 several publications comprise Bacon's example of a natural history, and not all of them were published in his lifetime. The most famous of them was *Sylva Sylvarum*, published in 1626/27 together with *The New Atlantis*. The temporary axioms of Part 5 can be found presented in various of his printed works. The final axioms of Part 6 that Bacon provided as his contribution to the new philosophy are also there to be found, scattered as truths throughout his works.

Footnotes

[1] Ben Jonson, Discoveries (1641).

[2] William Rawley, 'The Life of the Honourable Author', prefixed to Resuscitatio, Or, Bringing into Publick Light severall Pieces of the Works…of the Right Honourable Francis Bacon (1657).

[3] Found among Bacon's papers: Birch MSS, 4263, f.110, copy in contemporary hand, published in James Spedding's The Letters and the Life of Francis Bacon, Vol. VII, p 229.

[4] Genesis 1: 3-31; Genesis 2:1-3.

[5] Proverbs 25: 2.

[6] Francis Bacon, *Advancement of Learning*, Bk I (1605): 'For he [Solomon] sayeth expressly, the glory of God is to conceal a thing, but the glory of a King is to find it out; as if according to that innocent and affectionate play of children, the Divine Majesty took delight to hide his works, to the end to have them found out; and as if Kings could not obtain greater honour, than to be God's play-fellows in that game; specially considering the great command they have of wits and means, whereby the investigation of all things may be perfected.'

[7] Genesis 1: 28.

[8] Francis Bacon, *Novum Organum* (1620), Aph. 120: 'I am not raising a capitol or pyramid to the pride of man, but laying a foundation in the human understanding for a holy temple after the model of the world.'

[9] Francis Bacon, *The Advancement of Learning*, Bk II (1605).' And surely, as nature createth brotherhood in families, and arts mechanical contract brotherhoods in commonalities, and the anointment of God superinduceth a brotherhood in kings and bishops; so in like manner there cannot but be a fraternity in learning and illumination, relating to that paternity which is attributed to God, who is called the Father of illuminations or lights.'

[10] Title used in 'The Honourable Order of the Knights of the Helmet'—an entertainment written and directed by Francis Bacon for the Grays Inn Christmas Revels (Gesta Graiorum), performed on Friday 3rd January 1594.

[11] 'Praefatio Generalis', *De Dignitate & Augmentis Scientiarum* (1623).

[12] Francis Bacon, *De Augmentis Scientiarum*, Bk VI, Ch 6.

[13] Francis Bacon, *De Augmentis Scientiarum*, Bk VI, Ch 6.

[14] Francis Bacon, *Novum Organum* (1620).

[15] Francis Bacon, *Valerius Terminus*.

[16] Francis Bacon, *The Advancement of Learning*, Bk II (1605).

[17] Matthew 22: 29.

[18] Francis Bacon, *The Advancement of Learning*, Bk II (1605).

[19] John 14: 12.

[20] Francis Bacon, *The Advancement of Learning*, Bk II (1605).

[21] Francis Bacon, *The Advancement of Learning*, Bk II (1605): I have held up a light in the obscurity of Philosophy, which will be seen centuries after I am dead. It will be seen amidst the erection of Tombs, Theatres, Foundations, Temples, of Orders and Fraternities for nobility and obedience — the establishment of good laws as an example to the World. For I am not raising a Capitol or Pyramid to the Pride of men, but laying a foundation in the human understanding for a holy Temple after the model of the World. For my memory I leave it to Men's charitable speeches, to foreign Nations and the next Ages, and to my own Country after some Time has elapsed.

[22] Francis Bacon, *Novum Organum*, Bk I, Aph.120.

[23] Francis Bacon, *The Great Instauration*, Plan of the Work: transl. from *Instauratio Magna* (1623), 'Distributio Operis'.

[24] Francis Bacon, *Thoughts on the Nature of Things*.

[25] Spedding, IV, 112: transl. of Francis Bacon's *Novum Organum* (1620), I, cxxvii.

[26] *The Advancement of Learning* (1605).

THE EXOTERIC AND THE ESOTERIC: FRANCIS BACON'S TWO PHILOSOPHIES OF NATURE

John Henry

IN THIS chapter I want to draw attention to, and briefly indicate, the nature of Francis Bacon's tentative beliefs about the natural world, how it is organized, and how it works. I call this Bacon's esoteric philosophy, because for the most part he kept it to himself, writing about it only in works that remained unpublished during his lifetime. It is important to study Bacon's esoteric philosophy not just because it is intrinsically interesting, and adds to our understanding of Bacon as an innovative thinker, but also because the very existence of this hidden philosophy seems to undermine everything that Bacon is usually held to stand for. At first, the existence of Bacon's esoteric philosophy might seem to suggest that he could not have been sincere about his more public, exoteric philosophy. After more considered reflection, however, I believe that the existence of Bacon's esoteric philosophy, comparatively successful in its own terms, in fact shows that he was fully committed to the exoteric philosophy which was undoubtedly his greatest achievement.

In order to bring out the significance of the esoteric philosophy, then,

John Henry is Professor of the History of Science at the University of Edinburgh. Specializing in the history of Renaissance and early modern science, he is all too aware of the role magical worldviews played in the origins of modern science and much of his work has been devoted to demonstrating this—both to academic and wider audiences. His publications include: *Moving Heaven and Earth: Copernicus and the Solar System* (Icon Books, Cambridge, 2001); *Knowledge is Power: Francis Bacon and the Method of Science* (Icon Books, Cambridge, 2002); (with John M. Forrester) *Jean Fernel's On the Hidden Causes of Things: Forms, Souls, and Occult Diseases in Renaissance Medicine* (Leiden: E. J. Brill, 2005); and *The Scientific Revolution and the Origins of Modern Science*, third edition, revised (Basingstoke and New York: Palgrave Macmillan, 2008).

it is important to be clear about what is *usually* taken to be Bacon's philosophy of nature, the one that he did discuss openly in print, and the one which has earned him his place as one of the most powerful and innovative contributors to the so-called Scientific Revolution. Only when we are clear about his publicly expressed philosophy can we fully appreciate the significance of the fact that he actually harboured a secret philosophy.

Bacon's Exoteric Natural Philosophy

In brief, Bacon is famous in the history of science not because he made any new discoveries or new inventions, but because he developed and promoted a *new method* of doing science. Rather than focussing on trying to make a specific discovery, or a particular invention, Bacon believed that he could contribute more to the benefit of humankind, if he could show the most efficient way to make such discoveries and inventions. Consequently, he put all his emphasis upon developing a general method or approach for arriving at scientific truths. We can see this in a number of early comments he made, for example:

> ...above all, if a man could succeed, not in striking out some particular invention, however useful, but in kindling a light in nature a light which should in its very rising touch and illuminate all the border-regions that confine upon the circle of our present knowledge; and so, spreading further and further should presently disclose and bring into sight all that is most hidden and secret in the world that man (I thought) would be the benefactor indeed of the human race...
>
> (Proemium, Of the Interpretation of Nature, 1603)

Bacon saw this enterprise as even more important than the three great innovations of the Renaissance, the printing press, gunpowder, and the magnetic compass, even though, as he clearly acknowledged,

> ...these three have changed the whole face and state of things throughout the world; the first in learning, the second in warfare, the third in navigation; whence have followed innumerable changes; insomuch that no empire, no sect, no star seems to have exerted greater power and influence in human affairs than these changes.
>
> (*New Organon*, I, Aphorism 129.)

It is evident, therefore, that Bacon believed his new method of doing natural philosophy would also change the world, and essentially he was right about that. In brief, the main features of Bacon's new method were experimentalism, an emphasis upon *inductive* logic, which went hand in hand with experimentalism (and replaced the logic of syllogistic *deduction* which characterized the method of the prevailing Aristotelian natural philosophy), and an emphasis upon the practical usefulness of knowledge of nature (as opposed to the 'ivory tower' contemplative nature of knowledge emphasized in scholastic Aristotelianism). These Baconian emphases led to the development of modern science and, eventually to the science-technology complex, and remain crucial aspects of modern science. So, there is no denying that Bacon did change the face of our world.

Bacon himself could not have predicted the science–technology complex which began to emerge after the Industrial Revolution, but what he foresaw was something he called the Great Instauration (or *Instauratio Magna*). He mapped this out in six parts:

1. The Divisions of the Sciences.

2. The New Organon; or, Directions concerning the Interpretation of Nature. Published in an incomplete form as *Novum Organum*, in 1620 (Bacon's most important work in natural philosophy).

3. The Phenomena of the Universe; or a Natural and Experimental History for the foundation of Philosophy. Published in incomplete form in *Parasceve ad historiam naturalem et experimentalem* (1620), and *Historia naturalis et experimentalis* (1622). Also found in various unpublished and incomplete works, such as, *Sylva Sylvarum* (1624, published posthumously in 1626).

4. The Ladder of the Intellect.

5. The Forerunners; or Anticipations of the New Philosophy.

6. The New Philosophy; or, Active Science.

The culmination of the Great Instauration was to be the establishment, the instauration, of this New Philosophy, referred to in Part 6. But this point would only be reached, *could* only be reached, Bacon believed, after completing the other stages, and in particular, stages 2 and 3. And we can see from Bacon's publications that he never succeeded in completing even these stages. But, essentially, what he envizaged was a process of fact-gathering in an extensive collaborative enterprise to be undertaken by many people. The aim was to build up what we would now call a comprehensive data base, a comprehensive survey of empirically grounded facts, which would then serve as a reliable basis upon which to base our interpretations about the underlying nature of the world. Stage 2 was concerned with showing precisely how to deal with, and analyse, the information in the data base to arrive at reliable and certain conclusions.

Due to the hugely ambitious nature of his enterprise, Bacon never managed to complete even one part of his Great Instauration. This was not simply because he never succeeded in persuading King James I to provide him with the army of civil servants he required to gather the data to fulfil Part 3. Bacon himself would not be rushed, and he always insisted that we must avoid *premature* attempts to establish any new philosophy.

Bacon was living at a time when the Aristotelian system of philosophy, which had dominated Western European intellectual life since the thirteenth century, was looking increasingly untenable. The ultimate aim of the Great Instauration was to find a replacement system of philosophy, capable of replacing the comprehensive system of Aristotle, lock, stock and barrel. But Bacon was all too aware that others had tried to find replacement philosophies, and that all of them were deeply flawed, and therefore unacceptable. Bacon didn't want to make the same mistake, and end up with nothing. This is why he stuck to his plan for the Great Instauration and, refusing to jump to any conclusions, he concentrated on developing his method in the *Novum Organum*, and on increasing his stock of knowledge by slowly working towards his would-be complete database.

We can see his concern to avoid jumping to what he calls 'rash and premature' conclusions in the opening words of his preface to the *New Organon*, and elsewhere:

> Those who have taken upon them to lay down the law of nature as a thing already searched out and understood, whether they have spoken in simple assurance or professional affectation, have therein done philosophy and the sciences great injury. For as they have been successful in inducing belief, so they have been effective in quenching and stopping inquiry; and have done more harm by spoiling and putting an end to other men's efforts than good by their own.
>
> (Preface, *Novum Organum*, 1620)

The understanding must not, however, be allowed to jump and fly

from particulars to axioms remote and of almost the highest general-
ity (such as the first principles, as they are called, of arts and things),
and taking stand upon them as truths that cannot be shaken ... The
understanding must not therefore be supplied with wings, but rather
hung with weights, to keep it from leaping and flying. Now this has
never yet been done; when it is done, we may entertain better hopes
of the sciences. (*Novum Organum*, I, Aphorism 104)

Furthermore, Bacon explicitly stated that his ambition to achieve the
sixth part of the Great Instauration, the anticipated 'New Philosophy', was
far from completion:

The sixth part of my work for which the rest are but the preparation,
will reveal the philosophy which is the product of that legitimate,
chaste, and severe mode of enquiry which I have taught and prepared.
But to perfect this last part is a thing both above my strength and beyond my expectation. What I have been able to do is to give it, as I
hope, a not contemptible start. The destiny of the human race will
supply the issue...
                     (Plan of the Great Instauration, *Novum Organum*, 1620)

In view of this kind of talk, often repeated, it was always assumed
that Bacon did not have a system of philosophy of his own devizing, but
was content to suppose that his method, his 'legitimate, chaste, and severe
mode of enquiry', would eventually lead subsequent generations of human beings to establish the New Philosophy.

We now know, however, thanks largely to the researches of Graham
Rees (late professor of English at Queen Mary, University of London) that
Bacon did have his own philosophy, but that he tended to keep it secret.
He did allude to his esoteric philosophy, here and there, in his published
writings, but he never fully expounded it. Consider, for example, Apho-
risms 116 and 117 of the first part of the *Novum Organum* (I have added the
emphases):

But for my part I do not trouble myself with any such speculative and
withal unprofitable matters. My purpose, on the contrary, is to try
whether I cannot in very fact lay more firmly the foundations and ex-

tend more widely the limits of the power and greatness of man. *And although on some special subjects and in an incomplete form I am in possession of results which I take to be far more true and more certain and withal more fruitful than those now received (and these I have collected into the fifth part of my Instauration),* yet I have no entire or universal theory to propound. For it does not seem that the time is come for such an attempt.

(*Novum Organum*, I, Aphorism 116)

Still I candidly confess that *the natural history which I now have, whether collected from books or from my own investigations, is neither sufficiently copious nor verified with sufficient accuracy to serve the purposes of legitimate interpretation.* Accordingly, if there be anyone more apt and better prepared for mechanical pursuits... let him by all means use his industry to gather from my history and tables many things by the way, and apply them to the production of works... But for myself, aiming as I do at greater things, I condemn all unseasonable and premature tarrying over such things as these....

(*Novum Organum*, I, Aphorism 117)

The reference in Aphorism 116 to the 'fifth part of my Instauration' is especially interesting. In Bacon's 'Plan of the Great Instauration', Part 5 is designated for 'Forerunners; or Anticipations of the New Philosophy', but he also says it is for 'his own discoveries'. And here, as we can see, he says he has actually collected these into the fifth part of his Great Instauration. In fact, Bacon never did do this, or, if he did, the fifth part was never made public and was soon lost. Effectively, therefore, Bacon continued to keep his own discoveries hidden.

Bacon's Esoteric Natural Philosophy

Before turning to look at the details of Bacon's esoteric philosophy, it is worth pondering why Bacon kept it so secret. The first thing to say is that, to be true to his *exoteric* system, Bacon was obliged to keep his own 'premature' system secret. If he had published it, it might well have persuaded his readers that the system of nature was now understood, and so, as Bacon wrote in the Preface to his *Novum Organum* (quoted above), Bacon would have 'done more harm by spoiling and putting an end to other men's efforts than good by [his] own.'

But there's more to be said about Bacon's secrecy. Bacon's own system, as we'll see shortly, was essentially an alchemical system based on alchemical precepts, theories, and practices. Now, alchemists always had a reputation for being highly secretive, but there's something markedly different about Bacon's secretiveness compared with that of other alchemists.

Alchemists were certainly secretive about their techniques and procedures, and often about their results. It is all too evident, therefore, that they vehemently maintained their trade secrets. But they were not usually secretive about the fact that they were alchemists. Contemporaries knew perfectly well who was an alchemist, or claimed to be one, and who was not. In the generations after Bacon's, for example, everyone who knew Robert Boyle would have known he was an alchemist, and Newton's colleagues in Cambridge could hardly have failed to notice that he spent most of his time in pursuit of alchemical secrets.

The remarkable thing about Bacon, however, is that, although he developed an alchemical philosophy, and must, like Boyle and Newton, have spent considerable amounts of time performing alchemical experiments, this went unnoticed by his contemporaries. Nobody ever remarked upon it, and it was not mentioned in early biographies, nor for that matter in any of the more recent biographies of Bacon. So, here we have someone who was not only secretive about his alchemical procedures and results, but who was also secretive about the very fact that he was an alchemist.

Now, it's possible that Bacon kept this part of his life secret simply to avoid possible scandal if it was known that one of James's chief ministers was dabbling in alchemy. This might, after all, have led to fears that the result might be a catastrophic devaluation of the currency. I believe Bacon hints at this in *The New Atlantis* (1626) where the leading sage in Salomon's House, the major scientific research centre on the imagined Utopian island, says:

> And this we do also: we have consultations, which of the inventions and experiences which we have discovered shall be published, and which not; and take all an oath of secrecy for the concealing of those which we think fit to keep secret; though some of those we do reveal sometime to the State, and some not. (*The New Atlantis*, 1626)

Now, if we accept that the head of this research institute is an imaginative representation of Bacon himself, then here we have Bacon suggesting that there are some discoveries which even he, as a leading minister of the State, would withhold from the State. Some Bacon scholars have tended to see this as an anticipation by Bacon that some technologies are too dangerous to reveal to the state (thinking perhaps of Einstein's regret that he urged Roosevelt to build the atomic bomb), but it's much more likely that Bacon was not thinking of destructive technologies but of the alchemical dream of converting lead into gold. Anyway, whatever the reason for Bacon's secrecy, it is truly remarkable that he was able to practise alchemy for many years, performing many experiments, and eventually developing an all-encompassing alchemically-inspired philosophy of nature, without any of his contemporaries ever remarking upon this fact.

But, when I say that Bacon practised alchemy, I don't mean to say that he engaged himself in trying to create gold. In Bacon's day alchemy covered everything that we now think of as chemistry, and the evidence in Bacon's works suggests that he saw alchemy as the best way to reveal the secrets of the universe. So, although Bacon did offer advice on the best way of creating gold, in accordance with his own system of alchemical philosophy, it was clearly not the most important aspect of his alchemical work, and very far from being its *raison d'être*. Indeed, it is obvious from his writings that Bacon was much more concerned with the other alchemical dream, namely, the manufacture of a universal panacea, an alkahest, capable of curing all disease and prolonging life. But even this could hardly be said to be the sole focus of Bacon's alchemy.

We know that Bacon must have spent many hours doing alchemical experiments because of the scattered references in his writings to experiments he had carried out. These are often given in sufficient detail that it is clear Bacon carried them out himself, and in many cases he simply recounts the experiments in the first person, telling us exactly what he did. Often it is easy to see how these experiments might have related to Bacon's attempts to establish the details of his secret alchemical philosophy. He spent a lot of time, for example, comparing the weights of equal amounts of various substances. Having done this, he then uses the figures he arrived at to establish what volumes of different substances would be equal to a given weight of gold. The volume occupied by an ounce of spirits of wine, he calculates, would be twenty-one times greater than the volume occupied by an ounce of gold.

As we read on it becomes apparent that the purpose of these experiments is to distinguish between *two different sorts of matter* which Bacon believes to constitute all things. Consider, for example, this extract from his unpublished *History of Dense and Rare* (1624):

> But as for the degree of *pneumatic matter's* expansion compared with that of *tangible matter*, though it be a difficult thing to find out, I have still not abandoned any care in its investigation. Now it seemed to me the most certain test would be that if any *tangible body* (its bulk having been taken and measured before hand) could be altogether turned into a *pneumatic one*, after which the bulk of the pneumatic would likewise be noted down, so that the multiplication of dimension that had taken place could be clearly demonstrated by comparing the values before and after. (*Historia densi et rari,* 1624).

To understand what Bacon means by pneumatic matter and tangible matter, which he takes for granted here, we need to look at his secret philosophy.

Bacon's secret philosophy took its starting point from a traditional assumption of the alchemists, namely that all material substances derived from the interactions of two fundamental active material principles, mercury and sulphur. This alchemical belief no doubt owed its origins to the fact that both mercury and sulphur are extremely reactive and, because of that, they were frequently used as the starting point for many alchemical experiments. What's more, over the ages, these two became representative principles of two opposing kinds of substances. Sulphur represented, and constituted, all oily and inflammable substances, and even fire itself, while mercury represented water, and all watery and non-inflammable substances, and even, through a standard association in the four-element theory, air (air and water seemed to be interchangeable into one another in the hydrologic cycle). Sulphur, similarly, was associated not only with fire but also with earth, the source of subterranean fire as seen in volcanoes. So, just as the four elements were said to be combined in different ways to give rise to every natural thing, and to account for that thing's properties, so mercury and sulphur were seen in the alchemical tradition as combining to give rise to all things.

Now, the most successful promoters of this alchemical world view during Bacon's lifetime were the Paracelsians, followers of the Swiss medical and religious reformer, Paracelsus (c. 1493–1541). And Paracelsus, notoriously, had gone so far as to suggest that the whole world system was a giant alchemical experiment, and God was the supreme alchemist. According to Paracelsus and his followers, where it says in the book of Genesis that 'the Spirit of God moved upon the face of the waters', this means that God acted as an alchemist, working changes on one of his solutions. And where it said 'God divided the light from the darkness', and 'God made the firmament, and divided the waters which were under the firmament from the waters which were above the firmament', these were again best understood as alchemical separations, in which a previously unknown light substance might be separated out from a dark substance, and so on.

Now, Bacon was not a Paracelsian, far from it; he seemed to despise Paracelsus with a passion. He referred to Paracelsus as 'the adopted son of the family of asses', and his system of philosophy was nothing more than a collection of 'detestable falsehoods', 'specious allures', and 'empty delusions'. Even so, there are definite similarities between the Paracelsian worldview and Bacon's own secret philosophy, because both of them were based on earlier alchemical traditions (the late Graham Rees referred to Bacon's natural philosophy as 'semi-Paracelsian'). But what seems to have been completely original to Bacon is the distinction which we have just come across, between pneumatic and tangible matter.

Essentially, Bacon divides natural phenomena into what Graham Rees called two 'quaternions', or 'great tribes' as Bacon himself sometimes calls them, characterized by mercury or sulphur, and his two kinds of matter, tangible and pneumatic, manifest themselves in different ways in each quaternion. The following table sums up the main categories.

	SULPHUR QUATERNION	MERCURY QUATERNION
Tangible substances	Sulphur (subterranean)	Mercury (subterranean)
(with enclosed spirits)	Oil and oily, inflammable substances (terrestrial)	Water and "crude" non-inflammable substances (terrestrial)
Pneumatic substances	Terrestrial fire (sublunar)	Air (sublunar)
	Sidereal fire (the matter of the heavenly bodies)	Ether (the medium through which the heavenly bodies move)

According to Bacon, the interior of the Earth is made up of dense, passive, tangible matter, while the rest of the universe is filled with weightless, invisible, active, pneumatic matter. Between these two, there is a boundary zone, extending a few miles below the Earth's surface, and up to the sphere of the Moon, where tangible matter and pneumatic matter are mixed together, and give rise to all earthly phenomena. Clearly, this closely relates to the older alchemical idea that all earthly substances are constituted of a mixture of sulphur and mercury. Bacon's system would have seemed somewhat familiar to contemporary alchemists (and therefore supported by their theories, and their experimental results), while at the same time being recognizably different.

The two family groups, or quaternions, are seen as essentially antithetical to one another, but still capable of mixing to give rise to all the different substances we see in the universe. In subterranean regions, *tangible* forms of sulphur and mercury combine in different ways to give rise to all the varieties of minerals. Between the surface of the earth and the boundary created by the heavenly sphere of the moon, sulphur and mercury combine to form organic beings. The varieties here are considered to be so extensive that another set of variations is called upon to account for all the different things—so called 'attached spirits'. Some attached spirits are inanimate and merely endow a body with volatility or transparency, or some similar physical quality; others are animate and endow a body with life, whether plant or animal life. These spirits derive from the combination of *pneumatic* (or spiritual) forms of sulphur and mercury. In terrestrial regions these pneumatic forms of sulphur and mercury manifest themselves as fire and air respectively. Above the sphere of the Moon, in the region of the heavens, pneumatic forms of sulphur and mercury take over completely and provide on the one hand the matter of which the stars are made (from pneumatic sulphur), and on the other the aetherial medium through which the stars move (from pneumatic mercury). Other heavenly phenomena arise from combinations of sulphur and mercury, and inanimate and animate spirits—the former being sufficient to account for various astronomical phenomena, and the latter being required for animate beings such as angels.

Bacon's system, therefore, allowed him to understand (at least in principle), and offer theories about, inanimate substances, whether they be tangible or intangible; that is to say, whether they are solids, liquids or gases (so this covers all the things that might be subjected to alchemical manipulation). He could also claim to understand, or at least offer theories about, animals and plants, which are tangible but must also contain attached spirits, because only pneumatic matter can bestow life or vitality; and about animate spirits (again, in principle at least), such as human souls and angels, even though they are intangible or pneumatic (we would say 'spiritual'). And finally, he can also understand, or offer theories about, the workings of the heavens.

Generally speaking, pneumatic matter is perpetually active and, as such, provides a continual driving force. In our sublunar world, for example, virtually everything is made of a combination of tangible and pneumatic matter. The pneumatic matter combined with terrestrial matter constitutes what Bacon calls 'attached spirits', and these are always struggling to break free of the tangible matter to become pure, unattached or free spirits. It is this perpetual struggle within even seemingly inert bodies which accounts for the activities of those bodies and for all the changes that are continually happening all around us.

In short, Bacon's fundamentally alchemical system has led him to a comprehensive system covering all aspects of the physical world, from inanimate minerals, through plants and animals to the heavens. The system even allows him, for example, to explain why the dream of converting base metal into gold is so difficult. Gold is too heavy and dense for the base metals to be easily converted into it. Because of the innate activity of pneumatic matter, rarefaction (or spontaneous diffusion) tends to prevail over condensation or compaction, and so alchemical transmutation has to work against the natural trend, compacting lighter metals into denser gold. But this is just one example. Bacon's system is extremely versatile, being able to account in a seemingly plausible way for many everyday phenomena. It is because of this, and its universal scope from the mundane to the astronomical, that Bacon believed that he might have discovered the true system of the world, the true philosophy, which perhaps would in due course be established in Part 6 of the Instauration.

But it wasn't just a question of universal scope; after all, there were plenty of new systems of philosophy which had been developed by various of Bacon's contemporaries as replacements for the Aristotelian system. Any new system worth its salt had to be a complete and comprehensive system; because that is what Aristotelianism had long seemed to offer.

There were plenty of these new sects in philosophy; in the *Novum Organum*, for example, Bacon explicitly alluded to those of Bernardino Telesio (*De rerum natura iuxta propria principia* of 1586), Francesco Patrizi (*Nova de universis philosophia* of 1591), and Petrus Severinus (*Idea medicinae* of 1571). There were others, such as those offered by the Rosicrucians, by Tommaso Campanella (*Philosophia sensibus demonstrata* of 1591), and even by Bacon's fellow countryman, William Gilbert (*De mundo nostro sublunari philosophia nova*, written before 1603, first published posthumously in 1651 but known to Bacon in manuscript). But it is important to note that Bacon had good reasons to believe that his system was superior to any of these. It seems to me that Bacon was perfectly justified in writing in Aphorism 116 that 'I am in possession of results which I take to be far more true and more certain and withal more fruitful than those now received'.

This is not to say, of course, that Bacon's system was true or correct. Clearly, it was not—his system was very similar to traditional alchemical theories, but it is not in the least like modern scientific theories. The important question is how good Bacon's system was in comparison with those of his peer group, so to speak; that is to say, in comparison with other contemporary systems of natural philosophy. The simple answer to this question is that Bacon's system fared very well indeed, and genuinely did seem 'to be far more true and more certain and withal more fruitful than those' rival systems. In the light of this, it is easy to understand why Bacon was so committed to his own esoteric system of philosophy, in spite of the fact that it went against his own cautions against jumping to rash and premature conclusions. The simple fact was that it did seem to work so well in a number of areas.

In the rest of this chapter, I want to illustrate this with just one example. This example relates to an area of the physical sciences for which Bacon is not renowned—indeed far from it. Our example is planetary astronomy, and this is usually mentioned by students of Bacon only as a cautionary tale. It is well known that Bacon always rejected the new Copernican system, in which the Earth was said to be in motion around the Sun, and this is usually seen as an embarrassing lack of acuity on Bacon's part. It is important, however, not to judge Bacon from our perspective, but from his own. It is all too often assumed that Bacon simply dismissed the Copernican theory because he was ignorant of astronomy. In fact, as we shall see, he had an astronomy of his own, which derived from his esoteric alchemical philosophy, and it was this which led him to reject Copernicus. Although we can tell with our twenty-twenty hindsight that Bacon was wrong, it is hardly surprising, when we look at the details of Bacon's astronomy, that he favoured it over the highly counter-intuitive (and downright implausible) suggestion that the Earth is moving through space at an unimaginably high speed.

Bacon's Alchemical Cosmology

Bacon would have been particularly aware of the Copernican theory because England was one of the strongholds of Copernican theory. Historians of astronomy have managed to establish that before 1600, only *ten* astronomers in Europe believed in the truth of the Copernican theory; of those ten, *three* were English.

Now, astronomy had been in crisis long before Copernicus. Indeed, Copernicus came up with the drastic solution of putting the Earth in motion precisely because astronomy was in crisis and desperate times seemed

This Renaissance depiction of the Aristotelian universe, published in
1539, shows a Christianized view of the system, with the abode of God
outside the heavenly spheres that feature in astronomy. The important thing
to note here, however, is that the system is neatly spherical, with all the
astronomical spheres being centred on the Earth.

to him to require desperate measures. But there were other possible ways to reform astronomy, and one which attracted a number of sixteenth-century thinkers, was known as the theory of homocentric spheres. The Aristotelian world picture is neatly homocentric (with all the heavenly spheres centred upon a single point) but this was very hard to reconcile with actual astronomical observations. Consider the phenomenon of retrograde motion when a planet seems to stop its normal course, and temporarily move back the way it has come.

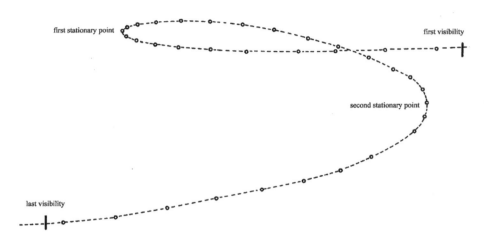

Retrograde motion is the term used to denote the temporary backwards motion of a planet, contrary to its usual progress across the sky. We now know this is an illusion caused when the Earth overtakes the planet, but this explanation was not available to pre-Copernican astronomers.

We now know that this is merely an illusion caused when the Earth overtakes the planet, but how was it explained by those who did not know the Earth was moving? Similar problems were caused by the fact that the planets do not move in perfect circles, as the Greeks supposed, but in ellipses, and do not move with constant speeds, as the Greeks also supposed, but are continually slowing down and accelerating in accordance with gravitational forces.

What was to become the received solution to all these problems was achieved by the Ancient Greek astronomer, Claudius Ptolemy (90–168 AD). Ptolemy used different centres of rotation for the orbit of each planet, and (to explain retrograde motion) even put planets in rotation on epicycles which rotated around the main orbit. In doing so, however, he had to deviate from homocentricity and to have different planets rotating around different centres, and even to have planets rotating around points which were rotating around other circles. Even when Copernicus offered his alternative solution to the problems of astronomy, he also had to resort to multiple circles and centres. The following schematic representation gives a rough idea.

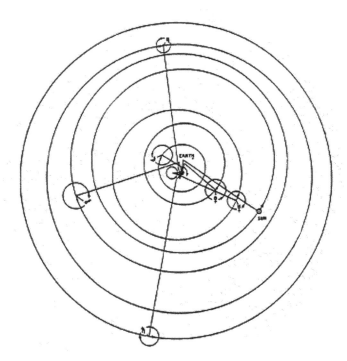

The Ptolemaic System

Now, the Ptolemaic system worked surprisingly well, but by the sixteenth century, ongoing attempts to patch over its increasingly gaping discrepancies from astronomical observations were recognized as nothing more than temporary fixes. It became apparent that a much more fundamental revision of astronomy was required. One of the most attractive alternatives to Ptolemy was a return to the homocentric system first developed by the Ancient astronomer, Eudoxus (408–355 BC).

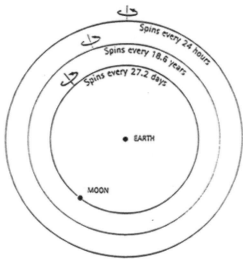

Eudoxus could account for the complex motions of the Moon by
supposing it was carried on three connected spheres, each with a different
period of rotation, and a different axis of rotation. Similar combinations of
spheres were required for each individual planet, so the System as a whole
had far more spheres than the ten envisioned in the Aristotleian universe.
The important feature, however, was that all the spheres had a single centre
of rotation, at the centre of the Earth.

The homocentric system was never as successful as the Ptolemaic at
actually tracking, and being able to predict, precise planetary movements,
but by having spheres rotating inside other spheres on different axes of
rotation, but always with the same centre, Eudoxus was able to account
pretty well for complex movements, including the retrograde motion (this
is demonstrated by a moving diagram on the internet: 'The Universe according to Eudoxus', http://hsci.ou.edu/images/applets/hippopede.
html but it is still difficult to believe). Thinkers like Girolamo Fracastoro
(1483–1553), and Bernardino Telesio (1509–1588) tried to improve on the
ancient homocentric system. Their starting point was not the scanty reports of the Eudoxan system available in Ancient Greek writings, but the
homocentric system which had been developed in the Middle Ages by the
Andalusian astronomer, Al-Bitruji, known to the Latin West as Alpetragius
(d. 1204). His system, translated into Latin as *De motibus coelorum* (On the
motions of the heavens), had been printed for the first time in 1531 and so
became more accessible to Renaissance philosophers.

Although the theory of homocentric spheres was never quite as successful at calculating planetary movements as Ptolemy's had been, it seemed to have one clear advantage over the Ptolemaic system. In the Ptolemaic system it was assumed that all the heavenly spheres moved westward around the Earth once every twenty-four hours (this was actually due to the eastward motion of the Earth on its axis), at the same time as they were moving about the Earth *eastwards* at different rates (Saturn, the outermost, taking thirty years to circle the Earth in an easterly direction, Mars two years, Mercury eighty-eight days, etc.).

Alpetragius suggested that there were *only westward motions*: the *primum mobile* (the outermost sphere) and the fixed stars moving right around once every twenty-four hours, and then each successive heavenly sphere moving more slowly, the further it was from the *primum mobile*. Accordingly, Saturn (the outermost planet) moved westward every twenty-four hours just short of a complete circle. The accumulated shortfalls each day, compared to the complete circuit made by the fixed stars, amounted to what looked like a complete eastward circulation once every thirty years. Similarly Jupiter's daily failures to complete a full westward circuit, resulted in an apparent eastward rotation around the Earth once every twelve years, and Mars once in two years (and so on: the Sun in one year, Venus in nine months, Mercury in just under three months). The slowest mover of all, compared to the fixed stars, was the Moon, which had a shortfall of about one hour each night, and so took twenty-five hours to make a complete circuit of the Earth, even though it was travelling a much shorter distance than any of the other planets.

It should be clear that Alpetragius's account of planetary movement seemed simpler, and much more plausible, than the Ptolemaic assumption that everything was moving eastwards at different rates, and on top of that, everything also moved right around the circuit of the heavens once every twenty-four hours in completely the opposite direction.

One thing Alpetragius never tried to do, however, was to explain why the planets moved successively slower, depending on their increasing distance from the fixed stars, or their increasing proximity to the Earth. But for Bacon these successively slower celestial motions were actually *a necessary consequence of his alchemical world picture.*

In the heavens, the two opposing principles of the two quaternions are represented by ether and sidereal fire. But ether is seen as an attenuated form of air and is at its strongest near the Earth, and becomes successively weaker as it gets further away from the Earth. For fire, it is the other way around: terrestrial fire is surrounded by air, which is associated with water, and as such is an enemy of fire. So terrestrial fire struggles to burn, and needs a constant supply of fuel to keep going. The further fire is from the Earth, however, and therefore from its associated air, the stronger fire becomes. Sidereal fire is the pure form of fire, Bacon supposes, and can burn incessantly without any need for fuel. Fire is also the most mobile and active substance and so sidereal fire, being the purest form of fire, must be in perpetual vigorous motion. At its strongest furthest from the Earth, sidereal fire in the *primum mobile* and the sphere of fixed stars moves constantly around the Earth once every twenty-four hours. Because Saturn is closer to Earth, it is affected by ether, which is slightly more powerful than it is at the sphere of fixed stars, and so more capable of slowing the motion of the sidereal fire surrounding Saturn; and so on for the other planets. The Moon moves slowest of all because, as Bacon said, it is only the 'first rudiment' of sidereal fire when looked at from the centre, or is the 'last sediment' of sidereal fire, when looked at from the *primum mobile*.

It seems likely that Bacon became excited about the power and all-purposeful nature of his system, when he noticed that a theory which he had developed out of his work in alchemy just happened to fit the Alpetragian system of astronomy like a glove. No other alchemical system accomplished this. Although Paracelsus had written a work entitled *Astronomia magna*, it accomplished nothing like this. Ostensibly about astronomy, Paracelsuus's work was actually nothing more than a reiteration of the age-old idea of the macrocosm and the microcosm, the notion that the human being was a 'little world', a miniature model of the whole universe (or vice versa). The closest Paracelsus came to discussing the actual movements of the heavenly bodies was when he recounted some astrological lore in support of the macrocosm-microcosm analogy. This was a far cry from what Bacon believed he had achieved with his system.

So, Bacon's system was not merely compatible with Alpetragian astronomical theory, it actually improved on the theory by explaining why the planets slowed successively the nearer they were to the Earth.

Given that Bacon had a secret alchemical philosophy that seemed to offer strong support to a geocentric system of astronomy, it is hardly surprising that he should reject the unproven and intrinsically implausible and unfeasible Copernican system. In rejecting Copernicus, Bacon was not simply being obtuse; he was defending a genuinely plausible astronomical alternative. Bacon failed to follow this through, of course, and did not try to develop Alpetragius's astronomy into a fully working system to satisfy the most technically-minded among professional astronomers. This was beyond Bacon himself, but at a time when few people believed the real solution to astronomy's difficulties lay in a moving Earth, he had every right to believe that a technically successful Alpetragian astronomy would one day be developed by others.

What's more, Bacon was able to extend these ideas even further. He used the same reasoning to explain the fact that the prevailing winds were nearly always, like the motions of the heavenly spheres, westerly. But the motion of the air was far more feeble than that of the sidereal fire, and so much, much slower. Similarly, the motions of the waters in the oceans, he suggested, had an overall westerly motion, but because of the interference of land masses, the result was not a continual slow circulation around the earth, but the ebb and flow of the tides. The westward motion of Atlantic waters, for example, caused a pile up of water along the eastern seaboard of the Americas. The rebound, due to gravity, was sufficient to overcome the westward motion and sent waters back to cause high tides along the shores of Europe and Africa, which were then countered by the natural western movement; and so the cycle of the tides continued.

It should be seen, even from this brief outline, that there really was a great deal to be said in favour of Bacon's system. The major systems of natural philosophy, such as those by Telesio, Patrizi, Severinus, Campanella, Gilbert, and the Rosicrucians, had nothing like the same scope, and could not match what must have looked to Bacon like genuine explanatory power. Small wonder that Bacon thought he was on to something special.

Conclusion

It would hardly have been surprising, therefore, if Bacon *had* gone public with this system, and published it. Perhaps he did indeed intend to publish it as Part 5 of the Great Instauration. He might even have won many followers, at least initially; perhaps persuading many Paracelsians to convert to his alchemical philosophy, or winning over those few who had been persuaded by Telesio, or Patrizi, or Campanella. If he had chosen to try to win converts to his own system of philosophy, however, it would not have lasted. By now, Bacon would simply be remembered alongside Telesio and the others, as another thinker who came up with an ingenious and imaginative, but wrong, system of philosophy to replace Aristotelianism.

But clearly Bacon was cleverer than that. Although he continued to work in secret, trying to establish the truth of his system by experiment, and writing numerous works expounding the details of his system, on the winds, on tides, on the differences between animate and inanimate, and between tangible and pneumatic matter, he was evidently never fully satisfied with his own system. When he did go into print with his philosophy, therefore, it was not with this philosophy, but with his philosophy about the correct *method* to use to establish the true philosophy, whatever it might be. It is perhaps worth saying, therefore, that the fact that Bacon was not seduced by his own alchemical philosophy, in spite of its apparent success in homocentric cosmology and elsewhere, is further testimony to his genius.

And this brings us to a final point. Nobody has ever managed to explain how Bacon was able to come up with his highly original methodological programme for the sciences. Why did he recognize the experimental method as the best approach? What led him to try to codify an improved kind of inductive logic? These and other aspects of Bacon's methodology have always seemed the kind of critical refinements that could only occur to a practising scientist, and yet Bacon has always been seen as someone who did not practise science, but showed others how to practise it (which is a bit like somebody who can't play the trumpet teaching others how to do it). So, how could he have known that the methodological principles he expounded were the best ones?

I like to think that it was while he was trying to establish the truth of his alchemical philosophy, in which experiment was necessarily involved, that he hit upon the most reliable methods for establishing scientific truths. In other words, his own repeated efforts to establish his alchemical philosophy, and his critical acuity in deciding which of his results were reliable and which perhaps only illusory, led him eventually to see what the best method of science should be. So, in spite of appearances, we could say that it was his esoteric system of philosophy which (by helping him to see the best methods to use to establish scientific truth), indirectly, secured his place in the history of philosophy.

TECHNOLOGY, STATECRAFT AND THE SOUL: THEMES EMERGING IN FRANCIS BACON'S
THE NEW ATLANTIS

Nick Lambert

'We of this island of Bensalem have this; that by means of our solitary situation; and of the laws of secrecy, which we have for our travellers, and our rare admission of strangers; we know well most part of the habitable world, and are ourselves unknown. Therefore because he that knoweth least is fittest to ask questions, it is more reason, for the entertainment of the time, that ye ask me questions, than that I ask you.'
The Governor of the House of Strangers, in *The New Atlantis*

THE MAJORITY of Francis Bacon's surviving works are lengthy documents, ranging from surveys of human thought, to histories, to his famous discourse on *The Advancement of Learning*. However *The New Atlantis,* a mere sixteen thousand words long and (apparently) incomplete, is at once the most accessible, the most discussed and in many respects the most mysterious of his texts.

Taking the form of an evocative journey to a distant island in the Antipodes, a world away from Jacobean England in a place only recently explored by sailors, Bacon develops the tale of Bensalem as a successor to the fabled Atlantis that has overcome society's ills through the application of science, and now sits in seclusion far from the envy of other states. Its

Dr Nick Lambert lectures in Digital Art at Birkbeck College, University of London. His areas of research include art and technology, contemporary digital art and the use of digital technologies in the history of art. He recently led a major AHRC funded research project, Computer Art & Technocultures, that was held jointly with the Victoria & Albert Museum. Outside this role, he has an extensive interest in Renaissance *ars memoriae*, esoteric works and the history of Hermetic thought.

signal achievement is not territorial conquest but a great college of learned men called Salomon's (i.e., Solomon's) House, where all aspects of the natural world are investigated and new inventions developed.

As Bacon's fortunes as a philosopher have risen and fallen in concert with the intellectual tides, so *The New Atlantis* has taken on different complexions: a purely Utopian fable, a vision of future perfectibility, a sinister picture of a secularized society governed by technology, a Freemasonic allusion and so on. Each of these readings depends partly on abstracting and interpreting sections of the tale and partly upon a wider reading of Bacon's bibliography, in particular *Valerius Terminus* and *Sylva Sylvarum*, together with identifications of his sources and inspirations. In recent years, Bacon's possible Hermetic influences and also his religious leanings have come more to the fore. Whilst he inveighed against superstition, idolatry and magic in his *Advancement of Learning* and *Great Instauration* (taking particular aim at the Paracelsans), Bacon was still very influenced by a Hermetic conception of the universe that owes much to Ficino and Agrippa von Nettesheim.

The latter's careful observation of mechanical processes, and praise for the applied industrial arts, also seems to have impacted on Bacon's influential ideas about the study of technological innovations. But what has often been overlooked is that Bacon also found justification for this mastery over Nature in the Bible, in the writings of certain Church Fathers and in his understanding of pre-Socratic Greek Philosophy. As a prophet of the Age of Discovery, Bacon is also deeply the product of the Age of Re-discovery, which was spearheaded by the likes of Erasmus and Isaac Casaubon and their translations and analyses of ancient texts.

It is worth considering the opening section of *The New Atlantis* in the context of the Age of Discovery that was unfolding during Bacon's youth. In 'Japan and the "New Atlantis"', D.W. Thompson argues that Bacon's account of the sailor's discovery of *The New Atlantis* differed from both More's *Utopia* and Campanella's *Civitas Solis* by its realistic evocation of a sea voyage and the careful geographical setting given for the island of Bensalem.

This Thompson traces to the account given by William Adams, the first Englishman to settle in Japan, whose experiences of landing there and becoming a resident closely resemble aspects of Bacon's narrative. Even the Christian element is present, except that this was brought by Jesuits (whose envious attempts to harm Adams led to his recommendation to the Japanese authorities that they be expelled, an ironic reversal of the situation in Bensalem!). Adams arrived around 1604 and thus his narrative, in the form of several letters home to his wife and friends, was widely known in England through his contacts in the East India Company, whose chairman Sir Thomas Smythe was acquainted with Bacon. Indeed, Smythe's proposed 'insider trading', taking advantage of Bacon's official connections, was a factor in Bacon's later fall from grace.

It may be that feudal Japan's status as an effectively closed nation, carefully screening potentially undesirable foreign influences in the period before the country was entirely cut off to foreign trade in 1638, is reflected in Bensalem's attitude to other nations. Its position on the other side of the world gave Japan the requisite distance and exoticism to serve as an imaginary territory in Bacon's mind, and the notion that there might be a Christian country in the Far East had been an element of the Western imagination since medieval travellers sent back reports of Prester John. Also Japan, unlike the Americas or indeed China, was at the periphery of Spanish and Portuguese influence.

Japan, then, was an extant country with a Christian element, cut off from the world but accessible to English sailors, whose traditions enabled Bacon to construct a utopia with some distant connection to fact as seen through the eyes of his countryman Adams.

When Francis Bacon wrote about a New Atlantis, he was consciously referring back to a theme that had previously been expressed visually on the frontispiece of his *Instauratio Magna*, the Great Instauration. A ship can be seen sailing beyond the Pillars of Hercules, the location traditionally attributed to Atlantis since Plato's *Timaeus*, and an apposite Biblical text was inserted below. It was a quotation from the Book of Daniel: *Multi pertransibunt et augebitur scientia*: 'Many will pass through and knowledge will be the greater'. Bacon had referred to this in his *Advancement of Learning* thus:

And this proficience in navigation and discoveries may plant also an expectation of the further proficience and augmentation of all sciences; because it may seem they are ordained by God to be coevals, that is, to meet in one age. For so the prophet Daniel speaking of the latter times foretelleth, **Plurimi pertransibunt, et multiplex erit scientia**: as if the openness and through-passage of the world and the increase of knowledge were appointed to be in the same ages; [p. 80]

The early seventeenth century was marked by a great expectancy of imminent change, even of the Apocalypse as foretold by Daniel and the Book of Revelation. The discovery of new countries beyond the former bounds of European knowledge and the emergence of transformative technologies lent great impetus to the view that history itself was speeding up and the End was not far off. Bacon himself seized on the technological innovations in his famous statement in the *Novum Organum*:

> Printing, gunpowder and the compass: These three have changed the whole face and state of things throughout the world; the first in literature, the second in warfare, the third in navigation; whence have followed innumerable changes, in so much that no empire, no sect, no star seems to have exerted greater power and influence in human affairs than these mechanical discoveries.
>
> [*Novum Organum*, Book I, CXXIX]

These references are neatly summarized in Bacon's frontispiece, which might be approached in several ways. Firstly, the Classical device of the Pillars of Hercules – usually synonymous with the Straits of Gibraltar although other Pillars existed to mark coastal boundaries – featured on the coats of arms of several Spanish cities such as Cadiz. From these Atlantic ports the first explorers, and conquerors, of the New World set off into uncharted territories and brought their wealth back to Spain and Portugal.

Bacon's ship is embarking for this new territory in both a literal and figurative sense, for the *Great Instauration* continued his exploration of the new terrain of knowledge and learning that formed the core of his published works. In this respect he was keen to shatter the boundaries of the ancient world, and especially the philosophy and scientific theories of Aristotle that had been upheld almost unquestioned since the fall of Rome. Passing the Pillars could be seen as a passing beyond the learning of classical times into new waters.

Secondly, the Biblical phrase links not only to this concept but to the title of Bacon's books. The idea of an 'Instauration' is that knowledge is being recovered, and rediscovered, rather than learnt anew. Consonant with the Four Ages of Greek mythology, the world was held to have declined since the Flood when the antediluvian civilizations were destroyed save for Noah (and his analogues *Deucalion* et al). The context for the quote from

Title page for *Instauratio Magna*

the Book of Daniel is that in the days before the End of the World, this lost knowledge would be recovered and men given a glimpse of the universe before God terminated the whole of creation.

Professor Allan Chapman discusses the meaning of this quote:

> That little Latin text is from the twelfth book of Daniel in the Old Testament, verse four, translated into English: 'Many shall run to and fro and knowledge shall be increased.' This was part of Daniel's prophecies for the coming of the end of the world, the visionary times of the end. 'Many shall run to and fro,' the great geographical discoveries, and 'knowledge shall be increased,' learn more and more and more. In other words, was all of the insight part of a sort of recapitulatory flash that God would give us before literally wrapping up the world like a carpet and hence the end?
>
> [from http://www.gresham.ac.uk/printtranscript.asp?EventId=251]

Chapman's fascinating lecture entitled 'The Jacobean Space Programme – Wings, springs and gunpowder: flying to the moon from 17th century England' deals with the multiple currents of scientific exploration and experiment current in Bacon's time and afterwards. The title is drawn from the tract *The Discovery of a World in the Moone* published in 1638 by the Bishop of Chester, Dr John Wilkins, that the Moon was inhabited and that it might be possible to construct a vehicle to get there. Having quoted Bacon approvingly earlier in the text, Wilkins says:

> So, perhaps, there may be some other meanes invented for a conveyance to the Moone, and though it may seeme a terrible and impossible thing ever to passe through the vaste spaces of the aire, yet no question there would be some men who durst venture this as well as the other.
>
> [From Wilkins, *The Discovery of a World in the Moone Or, A Discourse Tending To Prove That 'Tis Probable There May Be Another Habitable World In That Planet*, London 1638]

This was in the context of general excitement occasioned by the telescopes of Galileo and those of the English scientist Thomas Hariot (often overlooked as a pioneer of optics), and of course the microscopic worlds investigated by Robert Hooke. Although obviously later than Bacon, the formation of the Royal Society by Wilkins, Hooke, Boyle and their brethren drew heavily upon his legacy and speculations. Indeed, even before Sprat placed Bacon on the cover of his *History of the Royal Society*, its members had often referred to it as the realization of Salomon's House.

Today Bacon is usually seen as a progenitor of the Royal Society's scientific approach to knowledge, but there is an increasing recognition of the role played by his spiritual and philosophical outlook. In retrospect, we may be applying too strict a delineation between the worlds of scientific and religio-philosophical thought; and even though Bacon himself did much to make such divisions (and had good reasons to do so), neither he nor his immediate successors can be divorced from the context of contemporary mysticism.

The New Atlantis is commonly seen as a utopian fable, of a piece with the *Utopia* of Thomas More, Campanella's revolutionary *Civitas Solis* and the lesser-known Christianopolis by Johannes Andreae. Of these roughly contemporary works it has something in common with Campanella, in that both writers extol the pursuit of knowledge as an essential task of their respective fictional states, but otherwise Bacon diverges considerably from the idealized communism of the earlier Spanish author. Indeed, Eleanor Blodgett holds that he responded to specific aspects of Campanella's work with rebuttals of his own:

If Bacon read the *Civitas Solis* shortly after its publication, we may, with not unreasonable imagination, trace in *The New Atlantis* a part of his possible reaction to the setting up of this type of commonwealth as an ideal. Bacon had neither the tyranny of oppression nor the haven of convent life to influence his choice of an ideal state. He saw no reason why his fictitious country of Bensalem should not be a kingdom ruled by a wise monarch. Loyal to the faith of the English church, he wanted no such doubtful substitute for Christianity as Campanella had offered. And with true English veneration for the family as a unit, he had no sympathy with Campanella's institution of communism with its various ramifications. [p. 769]

[from 'Bacon's New Atlantis and Campanella's Civitas Solis: A Study in Relationships' by Eleanor Dickinson Blodgett: *PMLA*, Vol. 46, No. 3 (Sept., 1931), pp. 763–80]

It is sometimes overlooked that *The New Atlantis* is not a utopian republic but rather a monarchy with a state religion, in contrast to More's tolerant Utopia (which is mentioned in *The New Atlantis* too). This political undertone could be read as Bacon's direct opposition to Campanella's vision, as Dickinson suggests, by refuting specific aspects of Campanella's state; or as a nod to its achievability in the 'real world' of the seventeenth century, where Bacon hoped that King James might have sponsored a Salomon's House of his own. Bacon was making notes as early as 1608, proposing to establish a

'college for Inventors [including] 2 Galeries wth [statues] for Inventors past and spaces or Bases for Inventors to come And a Library and an Inginary.'

He envizaged input from the best educational establishments of his day: the schools at Eton, Winchester and Westminster, plus Magdalen College Oxford and Trinity and St John's at Cambridge. Amongst the rules governing his College, he included 'praescripts touching Secrecy, tradition and publication', directly foreshadowing the setup of Salomon's House. [see Blodgett] When such support was not forthcoming and the old Universities proved uninterested in his vision of practical research, Bacon directed more energy into his philosophical and political activities.

The other contemporary utopian fable, Johannes Andreae's *Chris-*

tianopolis, was published in 1619, when Andreae was still a young deacon in the Lutheran church at Vaihingen, near Stuttgart. As a Lutheran of a mystical disposition, and greatly interested in church reform, Andreae adapted some of the concepts of Campanella's religious republic to his own ends. Christianopolis, unlike the *Civitas Solis*, is not a great country but rather a small island in the middle of the ocean where the principal character finds himself shipwrecked. As its name indicates, it is a Christian religious community, founded by refugees from religious persecution, and takes the form of a concentric fortress with a great tower at its centre. Andreae invests the tale with much charm, and through the eyes of his shipwrecked sailor we are introduced to the structure and beliefs of this *collegium*. Some flavour can be gained from this extract:

> Work, or as they prefer to call it, 'the exercise of the hands' is done to a plan and everything that is produced is taken to a common store. [...] For the community is as it were all one single workshop, albeit with all sorts of different crafts in it. [...] If there is an ample supply of things for the common store, the craftsmen may indulge their creative impulses and experiment with new inventions. No-one has any money, and it has no private use among them, although the community has a treasury.
>
> [p. 175, *Christianopolis*, ed. Edward H Thompson, 1999, pub. Kluwer)

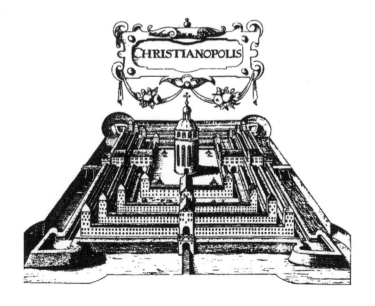

Thompson says that Andreae aimed to ameliorate the failings of human life by addressing the terror of childhood, the error of youth and the horror of old age; these were removed by the benevolent social structure of Christianopolis and its use of work and learning (including an appreciation of the sciences) to augment the benefits of reformed religion.

With Andreae we come closer to the intriguing intersection between Bacon's fable and that famously shadowy organization that manifested itself in the early seventeenth century in Protestant Germany and in France, the Rosicrucians. Andreae is the author of the key Rosicrucian parable *The Chymical Wedding of Christian Rosenkreutz* and the suspected (though unproven) writer of the *Fama Fraternitatis*, and the *Confessio Fraternitatis*, the documents that established the concept of the Rosicrucians in the early seventeenth-century imagination.

It was Frances Yates who placed Bacon's *New Atlantis* in a Rosicrucian context using clues in the text, though she was also guided by the later rewriting of the tale by the alchemist John Heydon in his *Holy Guide* of 1662. Although Heydon made explicit Rosicrucian references within Bacon's original text (and was accused by Elias Ashmole of being an 'ignoramus and a cheat' for extensively plagiarizing contemporaries like Sir Thomas Browne), Yates considered him to have simply expanded on inferences already present in Bacon's work:

> Though the name Rose Cross is nowhere mentioned by Bacon in *The New Atlantis*, it is abundantly clear that [...] New Atlantis was governed by R.C. Brothers, invisibly travelling as 'merchants of light' in the outside world from their invisible college or centre, now called Salomon's House, and following the rules of the R.C. Fraternity to heals the sick free of charge, to wear no special dress. Moreover the 'cherubim's wings' seal the scroll brought from New Atlantis.
>
> [*The Rosicrucian Enlightenment*, p. 127]

There are other potentially Rosicrucian concepts within Bacon's text, not least in the name of the College of the Six Days' Work, and the six-day allegory of Andreae's *Chymical Wedding*. The activities of the Bensalemite 'merchants of light' going out into the world unobtrusively to bring back the inventions and ideas of other nations recall the Fraternity of the Rosy Cross's avowed invisibility; and their Strangers' House 'heals the sick, and that gratis' just as the Rosicrucians' own founding articles require.

However the merchants' mission is more one of practical espionage than spiritual enlightenment, and the Strangers' House serves an important function for the Bensalemite state. Moreover, Saloman's House was in no way an 'invisible college' in the Rosicrucian sense. This dissimilarity has been noted before. Brian Vickers took very specific aim at Yates's arguments concerning Bacon in his extensive article 'Frances Yates and the Writing of History', a closely-argued deconstruction of *The Rosicrucian Enlightenment*. Vickers was concerned to expose certain assumptions underlying Yates's portrait of Rosicrucian influences, and none more so than those surrounding *The New Atlantis*. One of the central points concerns the tone and approach of Bacon's treatise:

> If we were to compare it in a free and open manner with the Rosicrucian manifestos we would observe some general parallels, such as the notion of philanthropy common to them both-and to innumerable other works of the Christian Renaissance – and some clear differences. In place of the Rosicrucian Hermeticism and mysteries, everything in Bacon's community is designed to be communicated; and whereas the accounts of science in the Fama and Confessio are vague in the extreme, with the usual alchemists' prevarications [...] Bacon offers an extremely particularized thumbnail sketch of a high-powered scientific research institute.
>
> [Vickers, 'Frances Yates and the Writing of History',
> *The Journal of Modern History*, Vol. 51, No. 2,
> Technology and War (Jun., 1979), p. 310]

Thus a major difference between the institution of the Rosicrucians as a fraternity and Bacon's Salomon's House is that the former is a free-floating brotherhood that takes pains to conceal itself within societies, and the latter is an arm of the State, in fact the major social achievement of Bensalem.

The famous graphic depiction of the Rosicrucian brotherhood moving through the land, Theophilus Schweighardt's *Speculum sophicum rhodostauroticum*, contains certain commonalities with Bacon's organization (not least the emblem of Jehovah's wings at the top, which Yates uses as a major plank of her argument). Visible on a distant mountaintop is Noah's

[Daniel Mögling], Speculum sophicum Rhodostauroticum. [Frankfurt], s.n., 1618, from http://www.ritmanlibrary.nl/c/p/h/bel_29.html

Ark, symbolic of the antiquity of the Hermetic doctrine, and the new stars in the sky are the supernova seen by Kepler in the constellation Ophiucus (the serpent) in 1604 and a variable star seen in Cygnus in 1600. Schweighardt, the pseudonym of Daniel Mögling, wrote an account of the Rosicrucian *collegium* that was

> a great building lacking windows and doors, a princely, aye imperial palace, everywhere visible, but hidden from the eyes of men, adorned with all kinds of divine and natural things, the contemplation of which in theory and practice is granted to every man free of charge and remuneration, but heeded by few because the building appears as bad, little worth, old and well-known to the mind of the mob [...] This is the Collegium ad Speculum Sophicum of the Rosicrucian Brotherhood.
>
> [From the 'Speculum sophicum rhodostauroticum' – The 'Mirror

of Wisdom' of Theophilus Schweighardt, trans. by Donald Mclean
http://www.levity.com/alchemy/schweig.html]

The engraving might seem comical to modern eyes, not least because
so much action is happening around the Collegium itself. It offers illumination to one man, guides a traveller to its door, rescues another from the
well of bad opinion, whilst trumpets blast, the drawbridge clatters and an
unlucky fellow topples off a cliff. It offers a wealth of symbolism in the
tradition of the Renaissance emblem book, as adapted to the Rosicrucian
cause by Michael Maier and Robert Fludd. Via these emblems, it suggests
a link from the Invisible College of the Rosicrucians, through Bacon's Saloman's House, to both the Royal Society and later Freemasonry.

However, in responding to a theory that Bacon's Salomon's House pre-
figured the Solomonic mythology that is central to Freemasonry, Thomas
De Quincey made the very cogent point that Salomon's House is a place
of exoteric scientific research, supported by the State, and that contrary to
the Masonic mysteries, 'The book of the Six Days is studied as a book that
lies open before every man's eyes.' He amplifies this a little later, saying:

And in fact the *exoterici*, at whose head Bacon stood, and who afterwards composed the Royal Society of London, were the antagonist
part of the Theosophists, Cabbalists, and Alchemists, at the head of
whom stood Fludd , and from whom Free-masonry took its rise.
[De Quincey, 'Historico-Critical Inquiry into the Origin
of the Rosicrucians and the Freemasons,' in the *London
Magazine* in 1824, pp. 388-9 and p. 390]

It was De Quincey's contention that the Rosicrucians had given rise
to Freemasonry; whilst this is arguable, he was right to identify Robert
Fludd as the key figure in English Rosicrucian-influenced circles though
Fludd never succeeded in becoming a member of this invisible movement.
But the differences between Fludd's approach and Bacon's are instructive:
Fludd's epic *Utriusque Cosmi maioris salicet et minoris metaphysica* of 1617–19
was a compendium of Hermetic and Paracelsan knowledge, quixotically
addressed to King James I, which was the polar opposite of Bacon's sober
treatises.

Where Bacon argued for a new rationality, Fludd used evocative and

Baroque imagery that sought to unify the Renaissance sciences and arts in a magical whole. Looking for the underlying secrets of the Universe in the microcosm and macrocosm of traditionalist Hermeticism, Fludd engaged in an exchange of letters with Johannes Kepler about the value of Hermetic knowledge versus science, and later had to defend himself against Marin Mersenne's accusations that he was a magician and an atheist. Fludd was in some respects a generation too late: he lived to see Hermetic thought start to wane against the influence of the new rationalism. Yet one cannot doubt Frances Yates' original contention that Hermetic philosophy was not only an exciting development of the early seventeenth century but that it spurred a variety of scientific as well as magical outcomes. After all, Fludd was the first to champion the idea of the circulation of the blood through the body, even though he did so for reasons connected with the macrocosm and microcosm.

It is interesting that there was a late flowering of interest in alchemical thought in England around the 1650s, when Elias Ashmole was especially active and Thomas Vaughan was translating key alchemical texts. In some respects certain founders of the Royal Society linked this alchemical activity with the scientific thrust of the society, hence the statement that it was the Invisible College and Saloman's House. Isaac Newton's recently uncovered interest in biblical prophecy and his long-known interests in alchemical experiment are the major example of this continuation of Renaissance thought. However the Society focused on empirical science to such a degree that alchemical practitioners were unwelcome and even Newton's alchemical papers went unpublished in the early eighteenth century. Rosicrucianism and alchemy found another outlet in the more esoteric branches of Freemasonry, from which they went on to provide the impetus for the occult revival in nineteenth century France.

If we can say with certainty that Bacon was not a Rosicrucian and was largely antithetical to their worldview, there is at least some common influence that comes from shared theological and philosophical sources. In his recent doctoral thesis, Stephen Matthews acknowledges that Bacon had at least some grounding in Hermetic ideas, not least because he traced his theological stance back to some of the earliest Church Fathers who themselves drank from the Neoplatonic spring that watered the watered the Hermetic flora of the *Corpus Hermeticum*. Sometimes this emerges in his early plan for a fraternity of fellow-workers towards a scientific goal:

In the second book of *The Advancement of Learning* Bacon argued that there must necessarily be a fraternity of those dedicated to learning, as a consequence of its holy source: 'And surely as nature createth brotherhood in families, and arts mechanical contract brotherhoods in communalties, and the anointment of God superinduceth a brotherhood in kings and bishops; so in like manner there cannot but be a fraternity in learning and illumination, relating to that paternity which is attributed to God, who is called the Father of illuminations or lights.' [Matthews, quoting Bacon's second book of *The Advancement of Learning*, p. 347]

Note the description of God as the Father of Lights, which also appears in the *Chymical Wedding*. The theological ideas of the earliest Church Fathers were compatible with several aspects of the Hermetic texts and indeed they sometimes quoted them approvingly. They were also products of the same, or similar, Neoplatonic thoughts that also inspired Hermeticism. A range of sixteenth-century thinkers, especially Giordano Bruno and Marcelio Ficino, saw in the *Corpus Hermeticum* a single, ancient theology that underlay all religions and came from God in deepest antiquity via 'Thrice Greatest Hermes'. This was the *priscia theologia*, and it gave great impetus to the efforts of Bruno and others to re-integrate aspects of pagan and magical thought into Christian Europe around the time of the Reformation.

But in 1614, Isaac Casaubon published *De rebus sacris et ecclesiasticis exercitationes XVI* that examined the Greek text of the *Corpus Hermeticum*. Using linguistic and chronological references, he dated it no earlier than 300AD, causing it to lose the aura of great antiquity that had clung to it ever since it was brought back from Constantinople in the late fifteenth century. By the third decade of the 1600s, the *Corpus Hermeticum* was no longer seen as an ancient prequel to the Bible but a parallel development of the Neoplatonic movement in Late Antiquity.

When Bacon sought his religious justification in Patristic theology, he was also able to consider certain aspects of Hermeticism. The only one he explicitly rejected – and the very one espoused by Paracelsus and his followers – was that of a divine universe, where the very creation itself was divine. He criticized those who used the Book of Nature to comprehend the mind of God, rather than see it as a means towards greater understanding and eventual control over the conditions of the Fall.

[…]in keeping with Bacon's Christian understanding of the Deus Absconditus, God Himself cannot be known via natural philosophy, but His power and attributes can. [p. 378]

In this regard, it is important to note that Bacon's Bensalem received its knowledge of Christianity direct from the source, as it were, through the miraculous provision of original Biblical texts by the Apostle Bartholomew some twenty years after the Crucifixion. Following the appearance of a pillar of cloud on the ocean, a wise man from the islands found a small ark floating on the water that contained canonical books of the Old and New Testaments. Stephen McKnight finds in this evidence that Bacon was very concerned to bring about a Christian state inspired by the founding principles of the religion and untainted by doctrinal disputes that were tearing Europe apart in the seventeenth century:

Moreover, the Bensalemites have evidently been able to preserve the purity of the Christian *kerygma* and have founded a true Christian kingdom: one that the Europeans likened to Heaven and its inhabitants to angels. Again, the purity of religion in Bensalem stands in contrast to the degenerated Christianity of Europe, where doctrinal disputes and ecclesiastical corruption have contaminated the lifeblood of the faith. [Stephen McKnight, 'Francis Bacon's God', *The New Atlantis* Spring 2005, http://www.thenewatlantis.com/publications/francis-bacons-god]

This is the key to Bensalem's civic happiness and its pursuit of science for the improvement of the human condition. The exploration of nature and its mastery is of a piece with Solomon's own wise investigations, hence the name of Salomon's House, and it is complementary to the religious underpinnings of Bensalem. As McKnight puts it:

The description of Solomon's House makes it clear that its first pursuit is light. Light as enlightenment is a basic religious motif, and Bacon never changes its religious connotation.

[McKnight, ibid]

McKnight is keen to emphasize this Christian foundation of Bacon's thought in *The New Atlantis* that derives form from his reading of the Church Fathers and the Biblical texts relating to the recovery of knowledge. He also challenges the more cynical interpretations of *The New At-*

lantis which give Bacon's religion a Machiavellian edge, that cloaks secular power in a religious garb and supposedly distorts Christianity's fundamental tenets. In fact, McKnight argues, the very reason that Bensalem has survived and the old Atlantis perished is because it has remained true to its Christian precepts and not indulged in empire-building:

> Atlantis is destroyed by the gods because of its drive to expand its empire through conquest and world domination. This *libido dominandi* stands in stark contrast to Bensalem, which is characterized as an embodiment of the cardinal Christian virtues of faith, charity, peace, and justice. Even after the series of natural disasters, which weakened or destroyed other civilizations, Bensalem does not seize the opportunity to invade lands and enslave their inhabitants. Instead, it chooses to withdraw in order to live in peace.

McKnight is trying to redress the balance against modern critiques of *The New Atlantis* that see it as the prototype for a purely scientistic worldview that proposes to conquer Nature and disregard all previous philosophies and religion as superstition. Since his effective canonization as the guiding spirit behind the Royal Society, with the prominence accorded to him in the frontispiece to Sprat's *History*, Bacon has been irrevocably associated with the foundation of empirical science.

As a symbol and presiding genius of modern Western society's technological progress, he has been subject to paeans of praise from Abraham Cowley onwards (reaching a crescendo in the early nineteenth century) and also to extraordinary vilification, especially in recent times, in this role as figurehead. In *Peace Among The Willows*, Howard B White's influential study of Bacon's political opinions, the statesman is shouldered with the responsibility of our civilization's inherent flaws:

> Once Prometheus has given us the fire, every sporting sophist, every petty despot, can light a match. To a generation already drowned in superlatives, no words can paint the terror, the death in life, that is modernity.... Modern man is lost in a labyrinth.... It was, in my opinion, Francis Bacon who led us into the labyrinth, who stole the fire from the gods.
>
> [White, pp. 12-13]

White argues that in his rejection of the ancients, Bacon laid a foundation for a science without ethics or morals, guided only by the concept of what could be achieved by human endeavour with little underlying sense of restraint. This thesis, whilst persuasive, is best seen in a tradition of post-World War II American conservatism that aimed to curb the social results of the perceived excesses of technology. It ignores the strong foundational influence of Reformed Christianity, and aspects of Calvinism in particular, on Bacon's thought. Indeed, some commentators such as Robert Faulkner posit that Bacon subtly disguises a new faith in science with a veneer of Christian charity, to sugar-coat this particular pill for a religiously-oriented audience:

> The New Atlantis is Bacon's supremely politic mix of transformed familiarity with veiled novelty. The common reader is to be converted by appearances, as most Christian Europeans are in the story are converted by sights of progress that masquerade as acts of Christian charity [...] A Christian theme of conversion to Christ is reconstituted into faith in progress.
>
> [Robert K. Faulkner, in *Polity*, Vol. 21, No. 1
> (Autumn, 1988), pp. 111-136 p118]

It also makes Bacon solely responsible for the directions taken by military and mercantile enterprises armed with advanced technology that paid no heed to Bacon's own reservations about what such technologies might achieve in the wrong hands. I think this is almost as egregious as blaming Wagner for the crimes of the Third Reich, and perhaps shows the dangers of simply inverting the idea of a peculiar 'Baconian genius' and taking him out of the context of his century. And it is not only social conservatives who want to hold Bacon responsible for a scientistic and materialistic culture: Horkheimer and Adorno also criticise him for promising an Enlightenment that was in fact founded on the domination of nature and other peoples; the colonization of the mind as well as the planet's resources. This theme has since become quite established in studies of the rise of technology and imperialism.

Even as Bacon the political philosopher and prophet of the dominance of technology was being attacked for the ills generated by a technological society, historians and philosophers of science began to doubt his position as a scientific pioneer. Bacon's concept of induction through experiment was rendered irrelevant by later scientists, and moreover he did not engage with some of the major theories of his day, not least Galileo's heliocentric cosmos. His contributions to scientific knowledge were negligible too. Paolo Rossi, whose study *Francis Bacon: From Magic to Science* established Bacon's relation to Renaissance and late Medieval scientific thought, pithily summarized this dual challenge to Bacon's posterity:

> According to the philosophers of our century who extolled scientific knowledge against the nonsensical propositions of metaphysicians, Bacon has nothing to do with science. According to the Continental philosophers who criticized or blamed scientific knowledge for its many sins, Bacon is the very essence of science. Being at disagreement over every philosophical problem, the two philosophical parties [...] completely agree on rejecting Bacon's idea of science and Bacon's philosophy but for completely opposite reasons. Once again, Bacon was reduced to a symbol.
>
> [Rossi, *The Cambridge Companion to Bacon*, p44]

However, if Bacon is seen in terms of his own era, some of these paradoxes can be resolved. It was entirely possible in his time to be a deeply Christian thinker yet take on elements of Hermetic thought by reference to the supposed antiquity of Hermeticism; yet still oppose some of its more extreme manifestations. One could also accommodate the newer discoveries of natural philosophy and the mechanical arts without these undermining the basic tenets of Christian belief, and indeed incorporate them into a framework where they were part of a general Instauration that would enable the renovation of the world prior to the coming of the Millennium. As Matthews states:

> It was not by striking out on their own that human beings would hold up their end in the Instauration event, but by embracing their divine destiny, and rising to a level of cooperation with God, which had become possible through the Incarnation. The Instauration was to be a period of human agency, but the paradigm for human action was the divine action of creation itself. [p. 392]

Crucially, Bacon could foresee a newer kind of rationality that would, in advancing the material and spiritual state of humans, also bring them closer to the prelapsarian state of perfection they had enjoyed before the Fall, before the Flood and before the fall of Atlantis. These concepts were not mutually exclusive and *The New Atlantis* is an attempt to summarize all these threads in narrative form, perhaps to illustrate for Bacon's own benefit that one could join Christianity and science in a socially harmonious island state. It is neither a 'utopia' in the strict sense, nor a simple satire or allegory, but rather an expression of Bacon's hopes for overcoming the many widening divisions of his own century.

In many respects *The New Atlantis* is not prophetic as such; it also looks back, and not merely to Biblical and Classical analogues. The Baconian voyage to Bensalem comes at the end of a long tradition of Renaissance magical voyages that perhaps began with the *Hypnerotomachia Polyphili* and continued throughout the sixteenth and early seventeenth centuries. Henceforth the voyages would either be wholly fantastical, like Cyrano's journey to the Moon, or grounded in the real world like Selkirk and Defoe, satirical like Gulliver or purely instructional, as the *Pilgrim's Progress*. Bacon marks a cultural transition and that is perhaps the main reason he is both lionized and vilified according to critical taste. Only by delving more deeply into his complexities can a fuller picture emerge, and *The New Atlantis* be brought into clearer focus.

THE SONS OF FRANCIS

Colum Hayward

THIS CHAPTER is an attempt to understand a little of how the Baconian temper persisted in England after Sir Francis Bacon's death – an essay primarily about a quality of mind, much more than about the categories of Bacon's preoccupations, be they scientific, political or even esoteric. It is not an attempt to discover the work of Bacon's immediate loyal followers – men like William Rawley (c. 1588–1667), his secretary, literary executor and biographer, or Thomas Bushell, his servant and pupil (1594–1674).

One famous friend of Bacon's, who survived him by fifty years, was the philosopher, Thomas Hobbes (1588–1679). We know this from John Aubrey, a close friend: it was from Hobbes that Aubrey had the famous 'chicken' story of Bacon's death, which Rawley tells us occurred on 9 April 1626. If all of Aubrey's information came from Hobbes himself, the philosopher was very confident of his place in Bacon's estimation, since Aubrey goes so far as to tell us that Bacon 'better liked Mr Hobbes's taking his thoughts, than any of the others, because he understood what he wrote, which the others not understanding, [Bacon] would many times have a hard task to make sense of what they wrote'. Yet we have come to see that there was real continuity of thought between Bacon and the younger Hobbes. There are even minor treatises that might be by Bacon, by Hobbes, or by Hobbes' patron William Cavendish, such is the closeness

Colum Hayward was a double contributor to this book's predecessor, *The View,* and is the compiler of another article in this one (below, pp. 253–64). He completed a PhD at the University of Cambridge and has written a number of articles on seventeenth-century studies. He is a practised meditation teacher and has been associated all his life with the White Eagle Lodge, for whom he wrote *Eyes of the Spirit: working with a spiritual teacher,* in 1997. He declares an interest in a having a healthy mind within a healthy, spiritual body.

of thought and phrase.[1] Hobbes was 38 and Bacon 65 at the latter's death.

An overview of the relation between Hobbes and Bacon would reasonably be that they shared a general contention that philosophy might itself be a true science and thus a practical utility. Hobbes turned his attention primarily but by no means exclusively to the concept of the State, and his great work, *Leviathan*, appeared in 1651, right in the middle of the Interregnum. It is, however, built on a view of human nature that in turn owes to a view of the way in which humans perceive things, such as how they see. His famous statement, *homo homini lupus est*, 'every man is a wolf to every other man', is typical of his attempts to build political philosophy on simple reductive observations. He rejected Aristotelianism, like Bacon, and sought a complete return to first principles in matters of philosophy. He believed that intellectual, moral and political life could all be the object of a mathematical model of calculation.

Bacon had another famous amanuensis besides Hobbes, however, and one who actually lived with him at Gorhambury for a while. Ben Jonson, the playwright and poet, is listed among Bacon's household in 1618 as Chief Gentleman Usher. He assisted in the Latin translation of Bacon's works, and is the source of one of the most famous of contemporary tributes to Bacon, recorded in *Timber, or Discoveries*: 'I have, and doe reverence him for the greatnesse, that was onely proper to himselfe, in that hee seem'd to mee ever, by his worke, one of the greatest men, and most worthy of admiration, that had been in many Ages'. Jonson favoured Bacon's promoting 'the Common-wealth of Learning' without specific comment on the programme Bacon set out. At the human level, Jonson speaks at the same time of praying for the Chancellor in his time of adversity.[2] This encomium of Bacon may actually have been delivered at Gresham College, sometimes seen as a progenitor of the Royal Society.[3]

Though there are some similarities, Jonson and Hobbes also represent opposite extremes: the first pre-eminently humanist, and therefore moralist, a strong judge of character, and the second a materialist quite ready to reduce human nature to a catch-all formula. That might be how Jonson would have seen Hobbes as his philosophy developed, but to a limited extent it is also what Jonson did in his Humours plays, except that we know that the sense of individuality of character always prevailed over theory in the end. Jonson was too much of the street and the city to sacrifice that. His *Epigrammes*, short poems primarily about people, are the best antidote to Hobbes-style reductionism in his oeuvre.

Does mention of Jonson and Bacon together give a sense of extremes, even contradiction, in Bacon's work? It may now, but it's unlikely that it did at the time. Jonson looked over Hobbes' preface to his translation of Thucydides for him. The Earl of Newcastle is said to have regarded Jonson as the star of his literary world, and yet was to be the patron of Hobbes' attempts to uncover a mechanical basis for human passions. And among Jonson's own following in the next generation, those that are known as the Sons of Ben, was one who shared Jonson's humanism, but probably made Hobbes equally welcome at his house. This was Sir Lucius Cary (1609 or 10–43, Second Viscount Falkland from 1633): known to posterity as one of Charles I's Secretaries of State at the outbreak of the Civil War, but more conspicuously as the host of a remarkable coterie of intellectuals who came to his home at Great Tew, or sometimes Burford Abbey, both in Oxfordshire. He was called by one of his biographers 'the most faithful and discerning of the Sons of Ben'.

The evidence that he entertained Hobbes is from John Aubrey again. To be precise, what Aubrey says is that Falkland was Hobbes' 'great friend and admirer'. Hobbes was a friend of other members of Falkland's circle, too: the poet Sidney Godolphin (1610–43), the Anglican theologian and disputant William Chillingworth (1602–44), the poet Edmund Waller (1606–87), and the jurist John Selden (1584–1654, although Selden told Aubrey that he knew Hobbes much later). He also knew Edward Hyde (1609–74, knighted by Charles I and later created Earl of Clarendon by Charles II), who is our principal source in understanding the character of what is often simply referred to as 'Great Tew'. Noel Malcolm, a contemporary biographer of Hobbes, suggests that 1634 is a year Hobbes might have actually visited Great Tew; Sir Leslie Stephen believed it happened later.[4]

Bacon, Hobbes, Jonson ... and now Falkland. Before explaining my reason for connecting the four men in this chapter, let us just take a moment to consider the nature of Falkland and his circle, for they are going to be crucial in the story. Here is the most famous passage written about Falkland, from Clarendon's *History of the Rebellion and Civil Wars in England*.

In this time, his house being within ten miles of Oxford, he contracted familiarity and friendship with the most polite and accurate men of that university; who found such an immenseness of wit and such a solidity of judgment in him, so infinite a fancy bound in by a most logical ratiocination, such a vast knowledge that he was not ignorant in any thing, yet such an excessive humility as if he had known nothing, that they frequently resorted and dwelt with him, as in a college situated in a purer air; so that his house was a university bound in a lesser volume, whither they came not so much for repose as study, and to examine and refine those grosser propositions which laziness and consent made current in vulgar conversation.   [*History, III, vii, 220*]

Although Clarendon elsewhere speaks of the great size of Falkland's library, he here makes it clear that it was the character of Falkland, and the quality of the establishment he had created, that enticed the wits of the university to Great Tew or Burford (whichever of Falkland's houses was the current choice). I might add that Clarendon elsewhere comments that Falkland kept such an open house that often he did not discover who he was entertaining until he saw them at the dinner table. Even without their host they had the company of each other, and to the short list of friends that I have already given as friends of Hobbes, Clarendon adds Sir Francis Wenman (d. 1640, one of Falkland's Oxfordshire neighbours), Gilbert Sheldon (1598–1677, then Warden of All Souls), George Morley (1597–1681, a Canon of Christ Church), John Earle (c. 1601–65, Fellow of Merton College and chaplain to the Earl of Pembroke) and John Hales (1584–1656, sometime Regius Professor of Greek and later Fellow of Eton). Henry Hammond (1605–60, divine, Fellow of Magdalen College), Thomas Triplet, Robert Payne and George Eglionby may further be added, and also George Sandys (1577–1644, the traveller and translator of Ovid), and Dudley Digges (c. 1583–1639, MP and diplomat son of the mathematician Thomas Digges). Hyde himself was a rising lawyer. Antony Wood, the chronicler of intellectuals of the period, confirms the talent Falkland had for friendship when he says that when Falkland visited his brother Lorenzo Cary at Exeter College, Oxford, in 1628 or just after, 'His chamber was the rendezvous of all the eminent wits, divines, philosophers, lawyers, historians and politicians of that time'.[5]

Although many of the names I have given require explanation nearly four centuries later, many of the men I have mentioned went on to be influential in a whole number of different fields; it sounds as though both the Cary brothers were talented in their recognition of ingenuity. As to where that talent came from, the obvious example is the experience he had as a young man, finding himself taken into Ben Jonson's circle, maybe contrasting it to his experience in Ireland (the place of his youth, on account of his father's position there). He later described London as 'the place he loved most of all the world' and there has to be a reason for that affection, when Clarendon's account of the Tew circle makes us think, somewhat falsely, of him being embedded in Oxfordshire. In fact, he simply made a promise to himself not to taste the joys of London until he had fully mastered Greek, and that means that Oxfordshire was something of an exile for him.

Falkland had a poetic exchange with Jonson over the loss of the supreme friend of his later teens, Sir Henry Morison, a friend from Ireland and a fellow officer there. Morison died of smallpox in 1629, and Falkland wrote a poem in his memory, and another on the anniversary of his death. Jonson responded with a poem that stands out among other poems he wrote, the ode 'To the immortal memorie, and friendship of that noble paire, Sir Lvcivs Cary, and Sir H. Morison.', which is a celebration of their friendship. There is however another poem that may tell us more about Falkland's place in Jonson's affection if (as a nineteenth-century editor suggested, and which seems eminently likely) the previous poem in Jonson's collection *Underwoods* is addressed to Falkland:

> Sonne, and my Friend, I had not call'd you so
> To mee; or had beene the same to you; if show,
> Profit, or Chance had made us: But I know
> What, by that name, wee each to other owe,
> Freedome, and Truth; with love from those begot:
> Wise-craft, on which the flatterer ventures not....
> Though now of flattery, as of picture, are
> More subtle worked, and finer pieces farre,
> Then knew the former ages: yet to life,
> All is but web, and painting; be the strife
> Never so great to get them: and the ends,
> Rather to boast rich hangings, then rare friends.
>
> [*Underwoods, lxix, ll. 1–6,21–26*]

To summarize, life has an art to it, the reward of which is friendship: Jonson conceives life in terms of how it may be made good. Here is the optimism of the humanist (contrasting with the pessimism about people in general); the belief that human behaviour can be changed by guiding principle, and by seeing life in its wholeness. Throughout his poetry, Jonson's favourite metaphor about life is that of the circle.

One of the striking things about Falkland is that in the 1630s, although he had a seat and from 1633 a title, he was surrounded by men of academic and other distinction, but had none himself, except the accomplishment of having learned Greek and the passport of being a 'Son of Ben'. And there is another circle for the youthful Falkland that we cannot ignore, which is that of his mother. Although his father held a good position at Court, that of Lord Deputy for Ireland, it was undoubtedly his mother who was the bookish and intellectually creative influence among his parents. She was gregarious, too. The poet John Donne was her onetime neighbour in Drury Lane, and Falkland later claimed to have known him. One of the daughters of Elizabeth Cary, Lady Falkland, wrote a posthumous biography of her, and as a reminder of the central subject of this chapter we can say right away that one of the authors she is credited with reading (in a list of classical and European moralists) is Francis Bacon.

Lady Falkland had an effect on her son that was to steer his intellectual preoccupations in the direction of theological controversy, with them frequently taking opposing sides. Maybe this choice is a pity, but it may have been exactly the place where the largeness of his mind and the gentleness of his temper were most needed.[6] The defining phrase about that mind, and the circle of friends influenced by it, is one we have already met in the quotation from Clarendon's *History of the Rebellion*:

> they came not so much for repose as study, and to examine and refine those grosser propositions which laziness and consent made current in vulgar conversation.

In short, the endeavour of Great Tew was not just a rational but a critical one. The models for this are generally looked for in the humanism of Vives (an author Falkland frequently cites), More and Erasmus, mediated by Jonson, but there are some closer parallels. One is apparently Hobbes, who used remarkably similar language to describe people's intellectual habits thus, in his investigations in political philosophy:

> The reason whereof is no other, than that in their writings and discourses they take for principles those opinions which are already vul-

garly received, whether true or false; being for the most part false.

[*Elements of Law*, I, xiii, 3]

For the moment, though, let us concentrate on Bacon's list of the four Idols in the *Novum Organum*, the things which confuse human thinking, namely

- the idols of the tribe, which are our prejudices that arise from human nature
- the idols of the cave, which are our psychological distortions
- the idols of the marketplace, our linguistic distortions, arising out of social relationships
- the idols of the theatre, which are our ideological prejudices.

The indebtedness of the Falkland circle to Bacon has been little commented upon, because it has been all too easy to see the humanist model behind the so-called Tew circle as though that were an altogether different area, but when we consider *The New Atlantis*, and think in terms of Salomon's House, the moment we think about it being not about content (i.e., research) but about method, it is Great Tew we turn to as the immediate attempt to further Bacon's programme. This does not mean that Falkland ever saw Great Tew in an institutional light – far from it – but rather that the critical component of the Baconian endeavour fired Falkland with a sense of purpose.

Or, it fired Clarendon. We simply don't know how far 'the Tew circle' was the almost accidental creation of Falkland's talent for friendship, or whether it was Clarendon who regarded it as a unitary thing, defined by the house itself, or alternatively as a programme, designed systematically to 'examine and refine' the language of debate. However, the poet Abraham Cowley somewhat backed up Clarendon's view of Falkland's universal grasp, albeit in the context of Falkland's integration of learning rather than his critical abilities, when speaking of his mind thus:

There all the Sciences together meet,
And every Art does all her kindred greet,
Yet justle not, nor quarrel but as well
Agree as in some Common Principle.

['To the Lord Falkland', ll. 7–10, in *Poems*, 1905, p. 19]

It was certainly Clarendon who referred to *The Advancement of Learning* as 'never enough admired', but it was Falkland himself who spoke in his *Reply* to an *Answer* to his *Discourse of Infallibility* of

> The Oraculous Truth of my great Lord Bacon's observation, that un-
> lesse men in the beginning of their disputes agree about the meaning
> of their tearmes, they must end about words, where they ought to
> have begun.   [*Reply*, 1651, p. 209]

At one level, this is simply a point in argument; at another, it is Falkland's
attachment of his colours to a complete programme for the reformation of
learning. Clarendon may have wanted Great Tew to feel like a college, but
the attachment of Falkland to the Baconian idea was surely there already.
Falkland did not, in his short life, find any opportunity to pursue Baconian
science and probably did not have the disposition to do so. What he was interested in was Baconian methodology, and he responded to this in the best
way he knew, which was to make his home and his library resources – as
well as his conversation – available to as many scholars as possible.

A name to compare with Falkland and his circle here is that of Samuel Hartlib (c. 1600–62). Whereas Falkland had links to the Court, the
polymathic Hartlib was distinctly of an anti-Court party and sided with
Cromwell. Known as 'the great intelligencer of Europe, he conducted an
enormous correspondence, and his education was a Baconian one. He
sought to broaden the availability of knowledge, and it was associates of
his that were the first appointments at New College, Durham, set up as a
deliberate counterbalance to Oxford and Cambridge by Cromwell and the
Parliament. He sued unsuccessfully for funding for a research college, on
the lines of Salomon's House. Later, as history turned towards the foundation of the Royal Society, all Hartlib's work was formative; but there
were a number of different groups all moving towards the same end. If
Falkland had a link with Hartlib's circle, it was through Lady Ranelagh
and her brother Robert Boyle. There was an Irish connection between his
family and the Boyles, and after the Restoration Sir Peter Pett claimed to
have had recollections of him both from Boyle and his sister (who seems
to have had a significant friendship with Falkland). Brother and sister lived
together for much of their respective lives, and shared the same circle of
friends. Sheldon and Hammond knew her too, in the 1650s. Deep analysis of Hartlib's enormous correspondence has been deemed outside the
scope of this chapter, however, so there may be more to discover.[7]

It is much easier to link Falkland's friends with the Oxford circle, who were equally instrumental in the founding of the Royal Society, and indeed crucially so after the political turnaround in 1660. Let us first garner some details about them. We have some knowledge of the library lists of members of the Great Tew circle, and these and divers written testaments indicate the currency of Baconian example among members of the circle. Thus George Sandys called Bacon 'the Crowne of modern authors', while Sheldon praised Bacon as early as 1622, sending a friend a copy of the *History of Henry VII*. Among the library lists, none of them complete, we may note George Morley's copies of the *Henry VII*, *Instauratio Magna* (1620), and *De Augmentis Scientiarum* (1623); at the other end of his life he seems to have added a *Natural History* (1676) and Rawley's *Lord Bacon's Remains* (1661). A 1640 *Advancement of Learning* seems to have been among Clarendon's books, but it is only one of a long list and, much more interestingly, among his papers there are twelve pages of notes in folio from the *Advancement*, and in his first exile (1646–60) he wrote out another four pages of notes under a heading, 'Cursory and occasionall considerations'.[8]

I have mentioned the Spanish humanist J. L. Vives as one of Falkland's mentors and models, alongside More and Erasmus, as though this was something he had from Jonson. That may be true, but it needs to be said that Bacon also admired Vives. An enemy of a certain type of humanism, that which led men 'to hunt more after words than matter; and more after the choiceness of the phrase, and the round and clean composition of the sentence, and the sweet falling of the clauses ... than after the weight of matter'[9], Bacon found in Vives one who attacked the cult of style just as much as he did. In stressing the proximity of Bacon and Jonson, I have sought to show on the one side that Bacon was no stranger to a modernized humanism, and on the other that there is a modernity to Jonson's humanism, and particularly so in the way it was mediated to the next generation by Falkland and his circle.

This is most crucially demonstrated in Falkland's rationalism with regard to religion. 'Rationalism' can be argued to be a relative term, but it is manifestly and distinctively present at Great Tew. John Hales wrote a tract *Of Schism* which fell foul of Archbishop Laud and which is full of irony about the level of human ignorance that the Church, over the years, had managed to institutionalize; while Falkland wrote of the doctrine of the Church's infallibility, that 'unlesse it be manifest which is the Church, God hath not attained his end'. Of the perpetrators of religious persecution, he ruefully observed, 'I doe not believe all to be damned whom they damne, but I conceive all to be killed whom they kill' [*Discourse of Infalllibilitie*, 3, 26].

However, although the rationalism of the circle was to lead to latitude in the Church, and Chillingworth's *Religion of Protestants* had an unlikely influence on the development of probability theory, its modernity shows up most of all in some connections to science that were long ignored.

Scholarship was able to show only recently that Laudian Oxford was a nursery for mathematical philosophy and scientific experiment.[10] Although the intellectuals who rode out to Great Tew possibly did so *instead* of conducting experiments, it does not mean that they were shut off from those who did. Gilbert Sheldon was a close and lasting correspondent of the scientist Robert Payne, of whom more later, and had further close friendships with two mathematicians: Seth Ward (1617–89), author of *Idea Trigonometriae*, and John Pell (1611–85), a pupil of Hartlib and one of the great names in algebra. Sheldon's correspondence with Henry Hammond during the Interregnum is revealing of a philosophical interest in the scientific programme: Hammond makes comments on Gassendus, an English translation of Descartes, and Gassarel's *Curiosities* (without actually liking the last two). Both Sheldon and Hammond were friends of Thomas Willis (1621–75), who pioneered research into the anatomy of the brain and nervous system. Morley had five of Willis's books in his library, and many other scientific works beside – along with those of alchemists and astrologers. Clarendon in his library seems to have had not only the classics of pre-Baconian science, but also Napier's *Logarithms* (1614), Henry Power's *Experimental Philosophy* (1664), Boyle 'on Spring and Weight' (of the air, 1662) and *Experimental Philosophy* (1663), and Ward's *Astronomica Geometrica* (1656). Among continental writers represented are Galileo's *Discorsi* (1638), Lefebvre's *Chemistry* in French (1660) and English (1664), Vossius' *De Motu Marium et Ventorum*, Schooten's *De Organica* and the controversy between Schooten and Descartes over geometry (1649). Medical works included three by Willis, Whitaker's *De Sanguine Uvae* (1655), Charleton's *Exercitationes Pathologicae* (1661) and Redi, *De Infectis* (1671). He too had works by Gassendus and Descartes, as well as Sorbière.

With so many of these volumes carrying post-Restoration dates, it might well be argued that such volumes might be the equipment, maybe unread, of every intelligent gentleman, but the allusions in earlier correspondence give the lie to this. Sometimes there was pressing personal need for medical works: Sheldon and Hammond's correspondence contains many allusions to 'receipts' for their personal ailments, and yet Sheldon asked the spy John Barwick to hunt on the continent for books by the Leipzig physician Joannes Michaelis. Scientific connections were conspicuous in preferments after the Restoration, when Sheldon was promoted to Archbishop of Canterbury.

Falkland's name has not figured in recent paragraphs, because we do not know what his library contained, one of his offspring having sold it 'for a horse and a mare', or so the story goes. I have mentioned his connection with Robert Boyle and his sister. We have, however, yet to say enough about maybe the most significant correspondent the circle had in the world of post-Baconian science. Robert Payne (1595 or 96–1651) was until recently quite a shadowy figure. He was chaplain to the Cavendish family at Welbeck Abbey, and although he was actually younger than Hobbes, Hobbes (also a Cavendish protégé) seems to have treated him as a kind of teacher in mechanical and mathematical science. Payne has no list of published works to his credit, which is why he has remained so obscure; yet recent research has shown that manuscripts at Chatsworth believed to be the work of Hobbes are in fact the work of Payne, although most of them are notes and lists.

One manuscript, however, is significant: a fair copy of a nonetheless incomplete work entitled 'A Short Tract on First Principles'. About the authorship of this there has been much controversy, but a very convincing case has been made by Noel Malcolm that the work is Payne's response to an intellectual challenge put to both Hobbes and Payne by the Earl of Newcastle, one which is possibly alluded to by Hobbes in a letter of August 1635 to Newcastle.[11] Payne was an intimate friend of Gilbert Sheldon and George Morley, and Henry Hammond received regular news of him during the period that they were all, in their own way, forced into retreat or exile. At the same time he seems to have kept regular correspondence with Hobbes throughout the latter's travels; few examples survive, but letters from and to Hobbes are frequently referred to in Payne's correspondence with Sheldon, and at certain times Payne was corresponding with Hobbes every three weeks on average. And although these friends from the era of Great Tew regarded Payne with tremendous affection (Hammond wrote to Sheldon, 'Poor R. Payn is dead, Gods will be done', and Morley wrote

'I conceiue no man hath a more particular losse in D. P. then my self'[12]),
it was not religion, pleasantries or even politics that Payne shared with
them, but news of intellectual – and largely scientific – developments on
the continent and at home.

So great is the harmony that appears to prevail among Falkland's
friends both at Great Tew in the 1630s and after Falkland's death, in 1643,
that it is quite a surprise suddenly to find a really negative comment written by one of them about another (the only other disputes that racked
Great Tew surrounded William Chillingworth's relations with Falkland's
Catholic mother). Payne's sister Martha passed his papers on to Hobbes
when he died, and Morley's letter just quoted confesses that if the recipient
'had but half y^t Modesty & honesty y^t he had, it would haue bin much better legacy for him then any writeings, wch he will but scorne, as he would
have done any though ye best Philosopher Devine y^t ever was in ye world
had bin ye author of them'.[13]

The complaint of arrogance – or let us better say 'aggressive self-confi-
dence' – against Hobbes was not a rare one. In the context in which we are
speaking, it was an ideological issue too. The ethos of Great Tew was the
convivium based on friendship, human values above all. Here is a modern
writer on the setting of More's *Utopia*:

> The ideal setting of this supreme value – good conversation on things
> that matter – is the surrounding of simple but cultivated manners exhibit
> when the civilized man invites his friends to a meal in his country house.[14]

We are talking of a humanist ethos represented post-More by Jonson's
poem, 'Inviting a friend to supper', and even by John Milton's 'To Mr Lawrence'. There are plenty of tributes from friends to Hobbes' powers of friendship, but it may be significant that those who wrote of him with the most
affection were his continental acquaintances. Aubrey's attempts to defend
Hobbes' memory in England are rarer and the more poignant in this light.[15]

To understand the difference between Hobbes' approach to knowledge and that of the other members of Falkland's circle, a single additional
quotation may perhaps suffice. This is Henry Hammond, writing of what
he calls 'the ordinary means' of understanding the Bible:

> The assistance of God's Spirit joined with the use of learning, study,

meditation, rational inference, collation of places, consulting of the Original languages ... together with unbias'd affections, and sincere desire of finding out the truth....

[Postscript', paragraph 2, to *Annotations on the New Testament*]

In short, study – however exact and rational – always needed a moral component to it. While it is not for us to judge Hobbes, it seems to be qualities of this sort that Morley and his correspondents most found lacking in the philosopher. And of course they did, for it was Hobbes' stated philosophical position to stand outside of history, reject authorities both ancient and modern, and argue everything from first principles.

The fascination of Payne, particularly if he is the author of the 'Short Tract', is that his intellectual programme, with the encouragement of his patron, was remarkably similar to Hobbes, without the downside of personality. Payne sought to discover a science of human psychology rooted in the other sciences, particularly mechanics and optics. Yet he seems to have retained a humility throughout – one which ironically has kept him out of the public eye for four centuries. Whether Hobbes succeeded and Payne failed in his analysis of human passions is an open question, but even the 'Short Tract', which Noel Malcolm believes marks a first attempt at systematizing psychology, was apparently left unfinished. Hobbes went on to publish his own work, and his *Elements of Law* (1640) may be seen as an attempt to deal with the same questions.[16]

We seem to have moved a long way from Bacon, but in certain respects we have not. The stimulus to find a mechanistic cause of human emotion begins with him; it is the Baconian question, ultimately, not Newcastle's, that Hobbes and Payne are both answering. The short passage from *The Elements of Law* that I quoted on p. 79 sounded so like Clarendon's words about Tew (and may have influenced them); actually, though, they were looking in a very different direction. In seeking a 'mechanical' explanation, Hobbes was seen by his old friends to have espoused a most unattractive determinism. Clarendon, as Sir Edward Hyde, entered into a long public debate with a philosopher he had once thought of as his friend, which apparently covered *The Elements, De Cive* and *Leviathan*, and did not end even there. Among Clarendon's papers are manuscript comments on Hobbes' *De Cive*; if they are not by Hyde himself, they show a remarkable similarity of outlook to his notes on *The Elements of Law*, and the often colloquial, first-person Latin suggests that they were intended to be seen by Hobbes.[17] Even the notes of *The Elements of Law* occasionally show Hyde trying to infuse a moral temper into Hobbes' work. The writer of the notes on *De Cive*, taking a single example, seeks to remind Hobbes that civil association proceeds not only from fear but from actual love of society, *ab amore mutui consortii*.

Given what Hyde must have known of Hobbes' scientific endeavour (again if the comments are his), remarks such as this seem a trifle bizarre until we recollect that Hyde is trying to promote a system of his own – a humanistic one in which it is difficult to generalize human affections, or to reduce them. Unlike Sheldon, Morley and Hammond, Hyde (frequently cut off from his friends) did not have Robert Payne to mediate the merits of a Hobbesian programme to him, and in any case he was ploughing an enormously risky political path throughout the Interregnum – one of simply watching and waiting for what he saw as the usurping political party to destroy itself, without missing the opportunity to act when that point was reached. In this, he could really do without Hobbes and his political philosophy – surely the reason he attacked *Leviathan,* and urged Matthew Wren to do the same in the crucial year of 1659. Hobbes had become a great enemy to the carefully-preserved values of Great Tew.

This is not a chapter about Hobbes but about what happened to Bacon's reputation. I believe that at Great Tew that reputation, Bacon's, was revered, even to the extent of Sheldon, Morley and Hammond showing real fascination with Robert Payne's Baconian programme, reading the works of Hobbes' continental correspondents, and listening to what Hobbes was doing through Payne's reports. However, whereas Payne managed it without seeming to destroy the types of human association they valued, Hobbes' self-assertion broke the rules of the *convivium* and thus seemed to put all at risk.

In mounting a defence of humanist values, they were appropriating the Jonsonian aspects of Francis Bacon against the ones Hobbes so enthusiastically took on. They are in effect saying, and the debate rages on into the pages of this book four centuries later, that science must never completely be without moral and ethical signposts around it, else it becomes monstrous. The debate between Hobbes and the other friends of Falkland is many things, but ultimately it is a fight for Bacon's soul.

Footnotes

[1] Hobbes, *Three Discourses: A Critical Modern Edition of Newly Identified Work of the Young Hobbes*, edited by Noel B. Reynolds, and Arlene W. Saxonhouse, Chicago, 1995; Fortier, John C., 'Hobbes and "A Discourse of Laws": the perils of wordprint analysis', *The Review of Politics*, 22nd September 1997.

[2] *Timber, or Discoveries*, ll. 885–947, in Jonson, *Works*, ed. C. H. Herford and Evelyn Simpson, Oxford, vol. viii.

[3] Jonson, *Works*, xi, 582-5 and Hill, C. P., *Intellectual Origins of the Puritan Revolution*.

[4] Malcolm, Noel. 'Summary Biography', in *Aspects of Hobbes* (Oxford, 2002), p. 11

[5] Wood, ii 565, citing Fuller, *Worthies of England*

[6] R. W. Serjeantson, in 'Elizabeth Cary and the Great Tew Circle', *The Literary Career and Legacy of Elizabeth Cary, 1613–1680*, ed. Heather Wolfe, London, 2007, pp. 165–82. Serjeantson takes me somewhat to task for not paying more attention to Falkland's debate with his mother in my own earlier writing on Great Tew; this is not the place to do it, and his own article fills the gap admirably.

[7] The key source for material on Hartlib is Charles Webster, *The Great Instauration* (London, 1976)

[8] For fuller information, see my own Ph. D thesis: J. C. Hayward, 'The Mores of Great Tew' (University of Cambridge, 1981)

[9] *The Advancement of Learning*, in Bacon, *Works*, iii, 282

[10] See Quinton, Anthony: *Bacon*, Oxford, 1980, p. 51; Curtis, *Oxford and Cambridge in Transition*, (Oxford, 1959) pp. 227–60, and Tyacke, 'Science and Religion in Oxford' in *Puritans and Revolutionaries*, Oxford, 1978

[11] Malcolm, Noel, 'Robert Payne, the Hobbes Manuscripts, and the "Short Tract"', in *Aspects of Hobbes*, pp. 80–145. For Hobbes' letter to Newcastle, see p. 134, citing Hobbes, *Correspondence*, I, 28–9.

[12] British Library, MS Land. 841. No. 91 and MS Harl. 6942, no.151

[13] MS Harl. 6942, *no.151*

[14] H. A. Mason, *Humanism and Poetry in the Early Tudor Period*, 1959, p. 119

[15] For both the complaints about Hobbes' self-opinion and the defences by his friends, see Malcolm, 'Hobbes and the Royal Society', in *Aspects of Hobbes*.

[16] Again see Malcolm, 'Robert Payne, the Hobbes Manuscripts and the 'Short Tract'.

[17] I analysed these notes in chapter VII of my doctoral thesis, 'The Mores of Great Tew' (see above)

FRANCIS BACON: BETWEEN SCIENCE AND THE AGELESS WISDOM

James North

Prologue: *The Ancient Wisdom Today*

> '*...there is met in Your Majesty a rare conjunction as well of divine and sacred literature as of profane and human, so as Your Majesty standeth invested of that triplicity which in great veneration was ascribed to the ancient Hermes: the power and fortune of a king, the knowledge and illumination of a priest, and the learning and universality of a philosopher*'

From the middle of the nineteenth century to the present day, a constant stream of once secret information has flowed into public awareness, one that seems to go against the grain of modern culture yet meets its deepest needs. Through the writings of Madame Blavatsky and the Theosophists, Rudolf Steiner and members of various Hermetic and magical orders, a sophisticated and consistent religious philosophy emerged as an alternative view of life.

Blavatsky defined Theosophy as a synthesis of religion, philosophy and science. This traditional philosophy and way of life has changed and

James North studied Classics at Magdalen College, Oxford, and Renaissance Philosophy at the Warburg Institute in London. During his research into early modern science and religion at the Warburg, he became aware that the standard academic view of Bacon and the origins of modern philosophy was significantly flawed. This was the beginning of a personal quest to understand Bacon's unique mind and uncover the deep spiritual roots of science.

James has worked as a musician, computer programmer and policy adviser in the public sector. In his spare time, he has given many lectures on Hermetic philosophy, kabbalah and also Sir Francis Bacon. He created a website for the Francis Bacon Society and has edited its journal, *Baconiana*, since 2007.

in some respects evolved over the millennia but overall it has remained remarkably consistent. It is often known as the Ancient Wisdom or the Ageless Wisdom. For the rest of this article, I will simply call it the Wisdom.

The main reason that publicizing the Wisdom was bound to cause controversy in the nineteenth century was that religion and science had gone their separate ways for several hundred years. Materialistic science was regarded as the domain of exact knowledge, and religion as a sphere of transcendental belief. Belief in the virtue of this separation grew under the influence of early modern scientists – physicists like Galileo and Newton, and chemists like Boyle – but its deeper philosophical foundations were defined by René Descartes and, above all, Francis Bacon.

For some thinkers, this separation arises from a real dualism in nature; for others, it refers to the need to use different methods to study different parts of one reality. If the Western academic world had really grasped the distinction between these two viewpoints, Bacon would not have been so misunderstood.

Alchemy and magic had flourished in the Renaissance. Their doctrines were religiously unorthodox, but held the promise of power over nature, which had been neglected by traditional Christian philosophy.

What many wanted was a natural science that supported rather than challenged Protestant thought, and was equally opposed to supposedly 'superstitious' beliefs like alchemy and to the un-Biblical philosophy of pagans like Aristotle, which was integral to Roman Catholic intellectuality.

The Reformation called for a return to the Bible without idolatry or pagan-influenced theology. Francis Bacon offered powerful arguments that what might be called a 'Reformed science', based on pure study of nature without intellectual idolatry and man-made pagan philosophical systems, was its secular counterpart.

The Protestant vision of science advanced by Bacon and others was like the Wisdom in promoting the equal importance of religion and science; but it was unlike it in attacking the ways of thinking that traditionally allowed these studies to be joined and bridged, such as Platonic philosophy or alchemical theory.

Yet by the nineteenth century, science itself was starting to uncover strange almost 'occult' phenomena such as electricity, hypnotism and (later) radio waves, and to develop theories such as Darwinian evolution, which had clear antecedents in esoteric traditions. In this turbulent envi-

ronment there arose the popular semi-religious movement of Spiritualism, which claimed to show verifiable psychic phenomena, opening a new
field of 'psychic studies'.

For many centuries, teachers of the Wisdom in the East and West had
kept their deepest knowledge secret, only sharing it with students who had
undertaken years of study, spiritual exercises and tests of character, like
ancient initiates of the Mysteries. They felt that those who had not purified
their bodies, minds and spirits could only suffer from the exposure to the
Wisdom. But for various reasons, members of previously secret societies
began to publish the philosophical part of the Wisdom, and the greatest
impetus to this process of publication was Blavatsky's work.

This philosophy spread and was popularized, forming the basis of the
New Age movement. However, the Wisdom is also intended to be an au-
thentic spiritual path and to give the power to live a life of service. Critics
of the New Age movement are often sadly near the truth in saying that orthodox religion is more spiritual, and orthodox science more rational and
effective, than the comfortable beliefs of the New Age. As Francis Bacon
said in his *Advancement of Learning*:

'So as in this part of knowledge, touching divine philosophy, I am so
far from noting any deficience, as I rather note an excess; whereunto I
have digressed because of the extreme prejudice which both religion
and philosophy hath received and may receive by being commixed together; as that which undoubtedly will make an heretical religion, and
an imaginary and fabulous philosophy.'

PART I: BACON'S NEGLECTED VISION
OF A HERMETIC SCIENCE

Baconian Science: the Reformation of Renaissance
Hermeticism or its Replacement?

We have spoken of the Wisdom. Its most systematic form in the West
can be called Hermeticism, which may be defined initially as the fusion
of religion and science. Although religion may seem in our human social
world to consist of rules, beliefs and practices, it springs from the aspira-

tion to another, higher reality that the heart 'knows' instinctively and immediately, but at first completely non-rationally.

Beyond scientific truths derived from observation and reason, there are other truths, which come to humanity through Divine Inspiration. There is also an inner 'soul knowledge', which comes from assimilating deeper lessons of life. The quote from *The Advancement of Learning* with which this article opened, characterizes knowledge from God and Nature as that of the priest and philosopher respectively. Speaking Hermetically, the third factor, integral to the power and fortune that Bacon attributes to kings, is wisdom.

What is wisdom? In deep accord with the Wisdom, Bacon distinguished between what would now be called science, imaginative intuition or wisdom, and pure inspiration from God. He called these Learning, Sapience and Revelation. He had much to say about Learning and Revelation. Using the religious language of Genesis, he compared nature to the lower waters, and the divine to the upper waters; these in turn are illuminated by the light of nature and the divine light, as Paracelsus had earlier taught. Thus, we have two main sources of information – the Bible and Nature – which Bacon called the Book of God's Word and the Book of God's Works.

As Bacon hints, the philosophy of Hermes Trismegistus is one that regards Learning, Sapience and Revelation as equally important. The spiritual path (which is essentially experiential) can also be seen as threefold. It can be purely mystical, the craving for reunion with the source of our being; it can be visionary, aspiring to discern the spiritual reality behind manifest life, and the relationships and affinities of the inner reality; it can even aspire to the power to bring spirit into the natural world, acting as a true magician or healer to overcome all beings' alienation from their Source.

For a Hermeticist, Sapience has a particularly strong connection with the power of imagination, which connects the 'world' of religious inspiration with that of reason. Hermetically, the Divine Light could be compared to the sun, and the Natural Light to the moon; and between them lies the realm of the soul, where there is potentially the conjunction of sun and moon, a kind of 'third light'.

Bacon mentions this aspect of imagination in *The Advancement of Learning*, but overall he emphasizes the power that Wisdom can give, rather than the role of imagination in producing it, thus tending to suggest that humanity must now use science *instead* of Wisdom to know nature.

Thus, Wisdom constitutes an important gap in Bacon's writings. It seems he believed that whereas the ancients had gained their knowledge of nature through Sapience, or innate, intuitive knowledge, this ability had been lost in the course of history.

If Bacon's work was totally contrary to the spirit of the Hermetic tradition, why have some authors as well as members of esoteric 'brotherhoods' venerated him so highly, regarding him as not only as sympathetic to possibility of the Wisdom, but one of its leaders, even the Imperator of the Rosicrucian Order? This veneration (sometimes bordering on idolatry) is ironic in view of the fact that his reputation as a philosopher largely rests on having refuted such supposedly speculative systems.

The academic consensus would traditionally have been that an 'occult' view of Bacon was ludicrous: his commitment to conventional religion and empirical science and his opposition to mixtures are evident in his main works. However in the last fifty years, various scholars have shown the general Hermetic influences in Bacon and other early modern scientists like Boyle and Newton.

Supplementing the academic picture with the information on Rosicrucianism that is now available, it is evident that Bacon was immersed in the Hermetic tradition, that he knew it inside out, and that its language was ever at hand as he formulated his science, with the qualification that the Bible was even more important, and that Bacon seems to have viewed the Bible as a Hermetic book, much like a Jewish kabbalist.

The present author has given a number of lectures demonstrating that Bacon developed a unique Biblical Hermetic science, weaving four chief categories of symbolism into his scientific writings in elaborate and precise detail:

1.   The Six Parts of the Great Instauration – modelled on the Six Days of Creation. The term 'Instauration' is a clever manifold symbol, relating to the *stauros* or crucifixion pole and to the brazen serpent of Moses.

2.   The three-tiered Pyramid of Knowledge, modelled on the Tetractys and the Tree of Life, deliberately missing its fourth part – the capstone – to represent the mind's humility before Divine Wisdom, and requiring ladders for philosophers to ascend and descend it, like Angels.

3.   The Book of Nature and the Alphabet of Nature, modelled on the rosicrucian–kabbalistic philosophy of writers like Lull, Paracelsus and Bruno which Bacon seemingly rejected.

4. Biblical numerology, connecting St John's Gospel to the Jewish Prophets and the Egyptian Mysteries and revealing the relationship of science and religion.

Nevertheless the common New Age view of Bacon as a typical Rosicrucian is inadequate. Bacon's attacks on the basic intentions behind the occult sciences are too systematic and passionate to be incidental. It is perfectly possible for a modern Hermeticist to say 'scientifically I ignore the doctrine of the four elements, but spiritually I hold to it and one day I expect science will make its own connection with the Wisdom', but there is little evidence that Bacon took that view. Indeed, it may be that Bacon's Hermetic kabbalistic reading of the Bible and Nature is deeper than what passes for much contemporary esotericism.

There were many texts of alchemy, magic and philosophy which appeared to describe ancient knowledge uniting religion and science. The problem, even for people who sincerely wanted to believe these texts, was that many of their claims about nature were demonstrably untrue or not provable. What is more, some processes were religiously and morally suspect, especially those involving ritual magic.

For Bacon, the structure of Hermetic thought – a many-levelled world of Archangels, Angels, planetary forces, visible and invisible matter, all linked by analogy to basic facts of God's nature, and expressed in the Bible – had to be right. But the actual information in Renaissance occult texts regarding nature was probably mostly inaccurate, and the faculty of intuitive knowledge of nature was apparently lost.

Since there was no hope of obtaining reliable scientific information from the old texts (irrespective of the spiritual truths they might contain), the only way to retrieve the scientific part of the Wisdom was to start again, returning to basic empirical science and rebuilding the Temple of Wisdom from the stones lying in ruins all around.

Ultimately, Bacon's inductive method was intended as a scientific way of retrieving the ancient knowledge and power of Egypt and Atlantis, by a process analogous to cryptography.

Bacon's view of the need for an Instauration, a re-erection of the Temple of Wisdom, may be true for science – including the lost magical science of Atlantis – but it is fundamental to the Wisdom to claim that there is an unbroken, valid esoteric tradition focused on reintegration with the Divine and the healing of Nature.

Bacon was religious; there is even documented evidence that he was a visionary and received revelations and visions. The first English biography of Bacon, written by his chaplain Dr. Rawley, contains these lines:

'I have been induced to think, that if there were a beam of knowledge derived from God upon any man in these modern times, it was upon him. For though he was a great reader of books, yet he had not his knowledge from books, but from some grounds and notions from within himself; which, notwithstanding, he vented with great caution and circumspection'.

One does not have to believe in the Wisdom to have a dual commitment to religion and science: Bacon called for research into the connections between the Angelic Hierarchy and nature. He devoted his major scientific research to investigating 'spiritus', the traditional term for astral or etheric matter. What is more he described it in such concrete terms that the reader is reminded of the clairvoyant descriptions of later Theosophists like C. W. Leadbeater. In these respects he was utterly unlike the scientists with whom he is normally grouped.

But there is no evidence in his writings that he was sympathetic to an intuitive, speculative, or imaginative approach to nature, or to the grand occult theories of the ritual magic traditions. And if these elements are removed from the Hermetic texts, precious little may remain of the occult sciences, which were outgrowths of the Wisdom. Bacon emphasized and taught separation; he alluded to synthesis, but did not teach it. And it is not easy to see how he could ever have built a bridge to it, if the arguments in his works *The Advancement of Learning* and *Novum Organum* are taken seriously and are definitive. He was a powerful enemy of false Hermeticism, yet his science may ultimately require the imagination and inspiration of the Wisdom.

Science's Misunderstanding of Bacon's Induction and Theory of Forms

Almost everything that is thought about Bacon's role in the history of science – by friend or foe – is wrong. Bacon has somehow become a cultural stereotype, so that people are under the illusion of having understood him, frequently without having read him. Bacon contributed to this by his habit of secrecy, ambiguously using old language in new senses, referring liberally to Hermetic and classical philosophies that were already going out of fashion, and writing his great works in Latin just when it ceased to be a universal language.

For example, he has traditionally been called the inventor of the misunderstood 'inductive method', supposedly involving countless unbiased experiments until the correct theory emerges. But the greatest figures in science such as Galileo, Newton, and Einstein, did not operate in this way at all. An empty mind is neither possible nor useful in modern science; the caricature of Baconian induction is not how science develops and never has been. On this basis, a typical twentieth century scientist would have seen Bacon as a dreamer with little practical experience of science … except that Baconian induction is something quite different.

Scientists normally make use of models, as John Waterman notes in the article contained elsewhere in this collection (pp. 149–57). Waterman's remarks accurately describe science as it is generally practised, but they have little to do with science as described by Bacon in his Novum Organum. Likewise, Waterman says that Bacon has been generally understood, unlike Steiner, whereas actually Bacon has been almost completely misunderstood, and cruder ideas of science than his own have been attributed to him.

Scientists generally apply a hypothetico-deductive approach of devising then verifying or falsifying theses focused on one part of the laws of cause and effect, the part called efficient causality – i.e. 'if a is done to a certain kind of thing, then b will result'. Likewise the roots of modern physics lie more in applying approaches that grew out of astronomy to the whole of nature, making systematic use of mathematics.

By contrast Bacon was not at all interested in models, excessive reliance on abstract mathematics and speculative astronomy, nor in laborious repeated experiments on the level of efficient cause. For this reason, Bacon is often regarded as having misunderstood the direction of modern science and thus unimportant compared to Galileo or Newton. Yet his unique and misunderstood method of induction was particularly focused on moving up the Pyramid of Knowledge to reach the Formal Cause, or Form. It is likely that twenty-first century science will vindicate his approach and show – to the surprise of scientists – that the conventional hypothetico-deductive method is only a subset of the greater method that Bacon defined better than any scientist before the age of the computer.

In philosophy the term Realism refers to the belief that ideas, essences or abstractions represented by single words like 'green' or 'oak' are real entities, and 'Nominalism' to the belief that 'green' does not refer to a separate reality, but is merely a name representing all the many things we call 'green'. Most modern science is implicitly Nominalist, (despite challenges from some deeper-thinking mathematicians, physicists and philosophers); but Bacon was a Realist, although in an unusual sense.

The Platonists called these essences Forms or Ideas. Bacon retained the traditional doctrine that true philosophy or metaphysics concerns Forms. The easiest way to understand Bacon's idea of science is to consider different answers to the question 'what is greenness'?

For Platonists – it is an Idea, a profoundly real part of a separate 'World of Ideas'. These ideas form a hierarchy, and knowledge is a spiritual ascent to mental contemplation of moral ideas such as justice, truth, beauty and the supreme Idea, The Good, which is similar to the religious idea of God put into philosophical terms.

For Aristotelians – there is no separate 'world of ideas', but everything has a Form, through which it is what it is. If I have a ball of clay, it has the form of a clay-ball; if I remould it into a figurine, the matter persists, but it now has the form of the figurine, and this form is its defining reality.

Bacon's genius was to define greenness (or any other essence) as simply that material configuration which all green bodies share, and to see that such a form must be real, which implies a Mind behind nature. The reason Bacon advocates multiple experiments without theory is not a crude view of scientific experimentation as blind repetition: it is that we must move from analysing the nature of many green things to greenness itself, which requires a suitable data bank as a basis to infer the fundamental physical structures or motions. In the age of database technology it is finally possible to implement Bacon's method, as soon as science realizes that the Form must actually exist.

Bacon says that what is unique about his method of induction is this process of ascending and descending the 'ladder' on the pyramid of knowledge. A Baconian science would make much more use of general, apparently abstract questions about material things, such as 'what is density' or 'what is malleability'. Not only would this be extremely useful in practice, as Bacon said; it would begin to make possible the decryption of the Alphabet in which the words in the Book of Nature are written.

This method allowed Bacon to conclude that heat was essentially motion, around two hundred and fifty years before mainstream science finally agreed. This brilliant insight was neglected, perhaps because most scientists thought like mathematicians, calculating motions in bodies they could see, or thinking in shadowy imaginations about invisible things like atoms while assuming that they behave much like things they could see, like billiard balls. Bacon, however, thought like a linguist or cryptographer. In the age of the computer and the Internet, he may finally find recognition.

The point is that Bacon's view of nature was God-centred. If there is a creative mind behind nature, nature must be linguistic: as Genesis describes creation, God conceived of all the kinds of beings that we know by different names and brought them into existence, with all the qualities and variations of colour, size, strength, inclination that beings possess. That is why, where Genesis describes the various things God 'said' in creation (such as 'Let there be Light'), John's Gospel simply says that all things were made through the Word, the Logos.

Looked at the other way, if nature proves to be linguistically structured, as implied by the Baconian science of the Alphabet of Nature and of Forms, this would be strong evidence for the Mind of God in nature. As Bacon said in his Essay of Atheisme: 'I had rather believe all the fables in the Legend and the Talmud and the Koran than that this universal frame is without a mind'.

Computer science, studies of language and the brain, parapsychology and allied fields of complexity and information theory may bring humanity by a slow, dangerous route to the same view that Bacon developed by pure philosophical intelligence. At that time, scientists who previously denigrated the Wisdom may then claim its insights as their own triumphs! Hopefully, they will have learned religious devotion by then, or it would have been better for humanity if science had never been invented.

Yet Bacon's doctrine of Forms was not merely materialistic: he believed in a many-levelled world of nature, man and God. He stated that he would only demonstrate his inductive method with respect to nature, but that it should be applied to the whole universe.

It is important to realize that from the scientific viewpoint Bacon was right to attack lingering Platonic or Aristotelian doctrines which were diversions from investigating the Mind in nature (which may or may not be the God of Religion...).

However Plato and Aristotle's theories are not just academic philosophy, but act as bridges to other, higher modes of thought and consciousness. Plato's doctrine of Ideas aimed to explain the relationship of nature to a spiritual-ethical world, and Aristotle's thought really springs from an interest in the world of formative forces. Bacon's theory answers a different question, and rejects their questions. Losing these, we lose our connection to the Wisdom.

It seems Bacon was aware of the Mystery background to Plato's teaching regarding Ideas, for he said, in language meaningful to students of the Wisdom:

> But it is manifest that Plato, in his opinion of ideas, as one that had a wit of elevation situate as upon a cliff, did descry that forms were the true object of knowledge; but lost the real fruit of his opinion, by considering of forms as absolutely abstracted from matter, and not confined and determined by matter; and so turning his opinion upon theology, wherewith all his natural philosophy is infected.
>
> [*The Advancement of Learning*]

The Wisdom in the Age of Science

Many followers of the Wisdom take a similar view to those religious believers that say that material science describes the mechanism of nature, and religion the deeper purpose and basic causes of life beyond the machine. They happily admit that concepts of 'four elements' or a '*primum mobile*' and systems of alchemy and astrology are not scientifically valid in literal form, but they recognize these concepts as powerful symbolism aiding the path to transmutation of nature and self-realization through meditation and prayer. Furthermore, they welcome science's part in breaking down literalist rather than mystical religion.

Yet what we call modern science involves an unprecedented challenge and opportunity not just for our civilization, but the Wisdom itself. Deep thinkers cannot rest content with a 'double truth' in which the science they accept underpins their medicine and the technology that lights and heats their homes, while the spiritual path, and any religious and moral views they may accept, speak different languages.

It is intellectually dishonest to portray Bacon as a typical Hermeticist or rosicrucian. In denying the Hermetic synthesis, Bacon's work demands what it does not deliver. It appears to attack what it cannot exist without. It formed part of the movement that cut off the branch on which it sat.

This is a mystery that may not be solved by the rational mind, but may lead us beyond the mind to intuition.

PART II: THROUGH THE PILLARS OF HERCULES

Bacon, Shakespeare and King James

'Perhaps at this length of time I may be forgiven if I break the Oath of the Mysteries that bind to secrecy concerning the names of initiates and suggest that the key to the Bacon–Shakespeare controversy may lie in the fact that Bacon and Shakespeare were members of the same Order?'
[Psychic Self-Defence, Dion Fortune]

The present author is strongly of the opinion that 'Bacon did not write Shakespeare' although the issue is much more complex than Stratfordian scholars yet accept, and it is highly likely that Bacon had some part both in the planning and the execution of some of the Shakespeare plays. However, the best research of the Francis Bacon Society has presented strong evidence that, amongst other things:

• Bacon was the victim of a political coup which resulted in his being 'set up' for a political fall resulting in his disgrace and banishment, and was essentially innocent of the charge of being a corrupt judge.

• Bacon was a witty and good-hearted man, a brilliantly creative thinker, speaker and writer and by no means a dry intellectual; a lover of poetry, patron of poets and recognized as a concealed poet himself by his contemporaries.

• He was identified as the author of two Shakespeare Poems before any plays were ever published with the name Shakespeare on them, rightly or wrongly.

• The Elizabethan an age was rife with anonymous, pseudonymous and collective authorship; the most plausible explanation for the various anomalies thrown up by the 'Authorship Question' is that a group of writers and students of the mysteries engaged in a joint educative project to enrich English language and literature.

Bacon, Shakespeare and King James were three pillars of British spiritual life with unique missions in science, art and religion. I propose that the threefold literary blossoming of Elizabethan and Jacobean culture is unlikely to have occurred by chance but was designed by a circle of advanced students of Hermetic philosophy, in line with Dion Fortune's claim.

Despite the strong circumstantial evidence for Bacon's involvement in the Plays, one feels not only the presence of group work, but also a single inspiring genius, which is not Bacon but another. Religion and Science are public, visible 'pillars'; Wisdom in its earthly reflection as creative imagination is hidden and esoteric; it is entirely appropriate that there is a mystery around William Shakespeare.

Bacon's role was actually central to the entire project. As executive in the realm of intelligent creativity, his was the great mind behind Learning, the worldly, 'natural' aspects of religion, science and art. Science as we know it belongs to our plane; art and religion are projections from higher realities. Bacon thus was the Master Builder of the modern age, the seminal figure for human civilization. This required him to be, not a saint, but fully human able of knowing the light and the dark.

Like Hiram the Master Builder, Bacon's destiny was to suffer the marks, the retribution of Cain without having personally deserved it, and in many respects this came through his relationship with King James, who played the part of Solomon . Bacon was often hated, slandered, had money troubles, was accused of corruption and greed and made a scapegoat. The view of later, unbiased historians increasingly suggests he was 'more sinned against than sinning'. He knew that he was destined to be misunderstood and that he would be vindicated and his work completed only in a distant future.

He played the dangerous and unpleasant role of evoking, in a Faustian way, natural science and subjecting it to the spirit, in the expectation that human goodness and tolerant religion would evolve society to a point where the venom of knowledge was utterly drawn, where, we might say, the Prince of This World is not only defeated spiritually, but throughout nature; then will the New Jerusalem be upon us and God's will done in Earth as in Heaven.

Yet now that Bacon's world is upon us, it is all the more imperative that we remember Bacon's call for 'charity', love in action, or we shall enter a New Atlantis that is worse than the Old.

From the perspective of the Wisdom, Bacon's mission to erect the Dark Pillar of matter and constriction, and his opposition to all that seemed to oppose his mission made him a destructive force in some ways. His science in a sense is a koan or riddle, even a great, useful delusion. There are great Hermetic intentions behind this.

Francis Bacon and Rudolf Steiner

If the Romantic movement had not come to restore the claims of art and imagination, and then parts of the Wisdom been made public in the nineteenth century, even the adoption of Bacon's vision would have remained the shell that makes his *New Atlantis* in some ways a cold and disturbing vision of the future.

Using only a little imagination, a Hermeticist could foresee this kind of scenario:

> a religious-scientific society arises; its leaders develop a bridging eso-teric science denied to the masses who become slaves to the religious-scientific machine of the dark New Atlantis. The elite 'brothers' are sincerely devout, but their spirituality is constantly sucked into increasingly 'magical' machinery, not finding an outlet in study and teaching of the Wisdom. The Angels and ancient gods are 'recognized' as natural forces that function in technology and could be accessed through neural implants.
>
> Bacon's teaching that nature is coded, a reflection of the Logos, is exploited dangerously as science develops into a modern black magic. Artificial Intelligence and genetics are studied together as mind and forces of nature converge in the organic realm; weird plant-machines are grown which have electrical spirits associated with them. Beauty and goodness are regarded as having nothing to do with nature, and plants and animals as we know them cease to exist. Neo-Egyptian ex-periments in genetic engineering lead to a totally unfree society cen-tred on privileged 'blood lines' of those with propensities to extreme longevity and unusual psychic powers.

Perhaps intuition of these possibilities gave Rudolf Steiner inspiration to develop the artistic, qualitative science of Goethe as an antidote to modern science. Goethe was both a great poet and a visionary scientist; he kept his heart and mind together just as consistently as religion, science and art were separate in Bacon's true but incomplete teachings.

Bacon was born in 1561 and Steiner in 1861. Thus Waterman's article was written on the hundredth anniversary of Steiner's birth, and also the four hundredth of Bacon's. Intuitively, he addresses a connection that is deeper than he may have realized. We cannot do this fascinating subject justice here, but comparison of their biographies shows strong similarities in the pattern of their lives.

Some very brief examples: both men were essentially alone with their thoughts, and engaged in careers seemingly unworthy of their obvious abilities until the turn of their respective centuries; they then became influential figures who worked ceaselessly to lay foundations for a new philosophy. Around the age of 60, both men suffered tragic strokes of destiny, which threatened to destroy their life's work, but each recovered to give out more writings and fresh insights reaching a culmination around the twenty-third year of the century, but died before they could see the results of their work. In each case, their followers' work was interrupted by a major war.

From the Hermetic point of view, the relationship between these great philosophers goes very deep and very far back in history. One sees two lines of influence, stretching back through Greece and Europe on the one hand, and the East on the other, going back to ancient Zoroastrian times when the Wisdom began to split.

Science is a direct challenge to the Wisdom, and Francis Bacon and Rudolf Steiner are the only two great philosophers who have addressed the situation and offered radical solutions.

Bacon separated religion and science. His advocacy of the rosicrucian approach to religion and culture was uniquely eloquent, though shared by others. But he also put equal energy into describing and inspiring material science. There is nothing in his system that intrinsically forbids a path to the Wisdom. But his attack on Plato and Aristotle undercut the traditional props on that path, leaving only the path through religion, which was not followed by the Churches. It may be that Bacon actually held to the traditional view of Hermeticism as occult, even to the extent of pretending to be opposed to it in public while practising it in private. But he regarded his philosophy as a new 'Birth of Time' symbolized historically by the discovery of America

For a larger reproduction, see p. 57

and the Reformation, which heralded the retrieval of the old Wisdom of Atlantis.

The ancient way to the Atlantic – associated with Atlantis – was through the Straits of Gibraltar, or Pillars of Hercules. Our modern enlightenment is a spark caused by the friction of Bacon's two poles – or Pillars – of science and religion. It may not matter that Bacon challenges earlier descriptions of what lies beyond: by bringing us to the Pillars, we will be blown through by the winds of destiny, come what may.

But what his system does seem to disallow completely is a fusion of alchemy and material science in the physical world. And this is the crux for our moment in time.

The Wisdom path of the soul has existed for aeons. It generated the occult sciences of alchemy, astrology and magic. But these only work in the unfallen parts of nature where there is a clear channel for Grace; they do not rule in and cannot substitute for the inorganic where cold, severe rules reign. There is a place for faith healing, and a place for materialistic medical science. We may not live by bread alone, but we still need bread.

We still await a holistic vision that recognizes science yet shows how it is linked with alchemy and how it can serve the good as part of One World.

Bacon's neo-Hermetic science, Steiner's Goethean science and the Wisdom of alchemy will all play their part in building a culture that will not disintegrate in the battle between material and spiritual values. Bacon's work alone cannot do this.

Concluding Thoughts

Revelation and Learning were strong in Bacon, but Sapience was masked.

Steiner's mission was in Sapience, yet fired by Learning, which is why he called his work spiritual science. Sapience and to a lesser degree Learning were strong in Steiner, but Revelation was obscured.

Spiritually, we see a triangle, which must be completed by a third figure whose prime mission was in the realm of Revelation, yet fired by

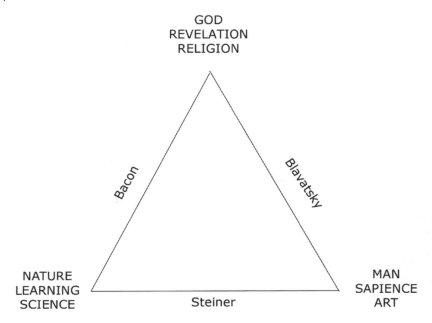

Wisdom. I suggest this person was Helena Petrovna Blavatsky, founder of the Theosophical Society. Where Steiner taught a scientific way to Wisdom, Blavatsky assumed the Wisdom and put it at the service of the Masters in fulfilling the Divine Will.

Revelation and Sapience were strong in Theosophy; Learning was masked.

Bacon's science can be seen as the final seed of a dying, ancient Intelligence.

Steiner's path relied on the connection between the true Christ and human culture.

The force of the future is hard to conceive fully. As Bacon brought Intelligence into nature, the Will must be raised from being an elemental power connected with our instincts, through morality and conscience, to spiritual at-one-ment. This way of Power implies the harmony of all religions, and the unity of East and West. I can envizage this unity being mediated on the one hand by Rosicrucianism and the other by Sufism.

This triangle explains Theosophy's instinctive regard for Bacon and why Steiner's work is problematic for both.

Bacon fulfilled the requirements of Learning for accuracy and effectiveness, and Blavatsky for unquestioning surrender to the Highest.

Steiner had perhaps the hardest mission, in that he represented the Wisdom itself in human terms. His work's survival depends much more on such human qualities as fellowship and beautiful living among his followers than that of Bacon or Blavatsky.

Bacon, like Prometheus, gave humanity knowledge and independence, including freedom from elites of secret wisdom. There is no other author who will provide a better training in kabbalistic thinking then Bacon, purely from reading his thoughts on science and religion. A person could easily be led from reading Bacon's scientific works to reading the Bible with Johannine philosophical awakening and thus to Rosicrucianism...which would sit in fierce, ironic tension with the direction of Bacon's science.

Once Bacon is understood, Steiner's work will become particularly relevant. This will involve the development of a universal Christianity, which will not contradict any other faith, but form the capstone of all religions.

Once this happens, Blavatsky's true impulse will become particularly relevant.

The gifts and trials caused by such 'titanic' interventions are affairs of the gods. Whether Bacon, as a personality, was friend or foe of the evolving Hermetic tradition must remain a holy mystery. When he attacks ways of thinking that may lead to bad science, such as talk of four elements or astrological correspondences, we may say 'it was right for science that he said this, yet I follow the spiritual tradition'.

Bacon, Steiner and Blavatsky were true to their genius. That their teachings in the outer world seem to disagree is less important than that those drawn to Mystery Wisdom should prioritize making peace with all whose life's work springs from the same sources. It is only specious philosophy that tries to make the words of spiritual teachings agree intellectually – that is unnecessary, and as impossible as squaring the circle. Wisdom is found within the soul.

Only grounded in the Wisdom can we do justice to Bacon's Great Instauration and Steiner's Anthroposophy, which must not be separated from Theosophy. The gods inspire humans to shape earthly life in the unfolding cycles of time. That may lead to apparent disagreements between the followers of their representatives; but that is the affair of the gods.

The return path to Beauty, Truth and Goodness leads to the Wisdom and beyond the appearances, to oneness with the Mind, Heart and Will of God.

THE LIVES OF FRANCIS BACON:
AN ESOTERIC PERSPECTIVE

Phillip Lindsay

Francis Bacon, the Enlightenment and Esoteric Astrology

Studying the life of Francis Bacon brings illumination upon some of the greatest events the world has witnessed in the past five hundred years. Bacon was more than a philosopher and statesman – he wore many hats and fostered numerous ideas; he was an Initiate and a great guiding hand over modern civilization. Hence understanding Bacon not only derives from an examination of his life, but also other lives or identities before and after that incarnation - all steps upon the way to spiritual liberation; these lives will be considered further in the text.

Esoteric Astrology is inextricably entwined with the science of the seven rays, those streams of force that pour into this solar system, conditioning life on all planets and in all kingdoms. Everyone incarnate has certain ray attributes pertaining to the quality of the soul, personality, mental body etc. The rays are 'great lives' that manifest in very specific cycles and

Phillip Lindsay has been teaching Astrology and the Ageless Wisdom, working internationally as an astrological counsellor, for over twenty-five years. His recently published books include, *The Shamballa Impacts, Masters of the Seven Rays, The Initiations of Krishnamurti, Soul Cycles of the Seven Rays, The Destiny of the Races and Nations, The Hidden History of Humanity* and *Songs to Varuna*.

His website, www.esotericastrologer.org, is dedicated to showcasing the leading thinkers in the world today on Esoteric Astrology and the Seven Rays. Phillip can be reached at phillip@esotericastrologer.org for personal astrological consultations. His current project is related to subsequent volumes of *The Hidden History of Humanity*: see www.hiddenhistoryhumanity.com.

sub-cycles – as a complementary pattern that overlays the vast cycles of the zodiacal ages. The rays condition the unfoldment and development of consciousness in humanity and its civilizations.

The year 1425 AD witnessed the beginning of a cycle of the Third Ray of Active Intelligence. The Renaissance in Europe was the major result of this influence – along with the addition of a sub-ray cycle of the fourth ray – the ray of art and beauty.

Francis Bacon (1561–1626) was born and lived his life very close to the span of the third sub-cycle of the third ray (1553–1618), intensifying the expression of this ray's themes. These two cycles of '3' recall the fact that the cipher of 33 in the name 'bacon' and also the word 'free', which 'Francis' means. The 33rd degree is also a major degree in the Freemasonry that Bacon regenerated. Codes, ciphers and a labyrinthine mind are all symbols of this third ray of active intelligence.

Ray Cycles Prominent During the Life of Francis Bacon

Bacon was born in the sign of Aquarius, heralding the approaching Aquarian astronomical cycle and his future role as the Mahachohan or Lord of Civilization. This department is one belonging to a trinity, shared with those exalted Beings who hold the offices of the Manu and the Christ. Thus can be seen the conditioning of the third ray over many lives (perhaps as the soul ray), eventually finding its apotheosis in the third part of the triangle of Will (1), Love (2) and Intelligence (3) – the latter being the Mahachohan.

One of the expressions of the Third Ray of Creative Intelligence is that of the philosopher, and it has a close association with the fifth ray of science, a major ray associated with Aquarius. Great souls come into incarnation taking advantage of rays that they are well developed upon:

It was Francis Bacon who was much impressed by the materialist theories and the resultant discoveries of both Copernicus and Galileo, who delineated the principles of the inductive scientific method, and argued that the only knowledge of importance to man was empirically rooted in the natural world. The age had finally arrived whereby it was believed by a clear system of scientific inquiry, a new approach, that man might exercise mastery over the world. It is with such thinkers as did

Ray	Effects	Subray	Effects
3 Active-Intelligence 1425	Rapid intellectual development. European Renaissance.		
		3 (5) Active-Intelligence 1553-1618	Elizabethan Age. Most of Bacon's life.
		4 Art, beauty. 1618-1681	European Renaissance, fourteenth to seventeenth centuries
		5 (3) Science. 1681-1745	Intellectual questioning. Invention, industry.
2 Love-Wisdom 1575	Great compassion. Developing democracy.		
5 Science. Knowledge. 1775	Intellectual questioning. Industrial Revolution.		
6 Devotion, Idealism Waning from 1625.	Religious devotion. The Inquisition. Mysticism.		
7 Order or Magic 1675	Reorganisation in many fields of endeavour.		

Ray Cycles Prominent during the Life of Francis Bacon

follow Bacon – Voltaire, Rousseau, Montesquieu, Paine, and Jefferson – that this scientific approach was applied to political and social issues; and so arose the liberal, the humanitarian, and the belief in a sense of human progress and the belief that the state could be a rational instrument in bringing peace to the whole of society.

Many of the qualities described above pertain to the Fifth Ray of Science. If the sub-cycles of the Third Ray are counted more esoterically, i.e. backward, starting with the seventh sub-cycle in 1425, then Bacon and his generation were born in a fifth ray sub-cycle (1553–1618).

Bacon was a triple Aquarian (Sun, Mercury, Ascendant in Aquarius), with a pioneering Aries Moon. The Seventh Ray of Ceremonial Order or Magic was strong in him and its colour is purple or violet; at his wedding, 'he was clad from top to toe in purple'. The seventh ray is not unlike the third ray, in that it is a materialising and organising ray, bringing spirit into matter.

Merlin the Magician is one of its archetypes, indeed, occult rumour has it that this was a previous incarnation of Bacon. A play written by Bacon in 1583 called 'The Birth of Merlin' may even contain clues to this mystery.

Bacon was followed by several philosophers of this era, such as Hobbes, Locke, Hume, Mill and Paine – who organized and disseminated the great confluence of thought that characterized the Age of Enlightenment (1687–1789); they all helped create the philosophical foundations that developed later into the Age of Reason in the eighteenth century.

The Age of Enlightenment was an intellectual movement begun in England, spreading over Europe and the rest of the world; it was rooted in an intellectual scepticism to traditional beliefs and dogmas, and by contrast was 'illumined' or 'enlightened', compared to the superstition and dark ignorance of the Middle Ages. The Enlightenment focused on the power and goodness of human rationality, esoterically the lower concrete mind. It paved the way for the other 'rays of mind' (7 & 5) and their respective cycles in the next few hundred years.

An example of rays seven and three working together, was the English Bill of Rights (1688) which occurred just after the Seventh Ray cycle began (1675), marking the end of the King's claims to absolute rule by 'divine right' and imposing upon him a measure of accountability to Parliament.

This process had really commenced during the rule of King James I, for whom Bacon served as Chancellor of the Exchequer. The English Bill of Rights was one of the primary philosophical stones in the foundation of the French and American revolutions, and was born of its own 'Glorious Revolution' of 1688. Here we can see the revolutionary qualities of Uranus (ruler of the Seventh Ray) and the genesis of the Seventh Ray cycle in 1675. Therefore the Age of Enlightenment was profoundly influenced by the Seventh Ray: 'an intellectual scepticism to traditional beliefs and dogmas' – quite Aquarian for its time.

The cycle of Ray Three finished its fourth sub-cycle in 1681, just after 1675, the start of the Ray Seven cycle. This fourth sub-cycle relates to the Fourth Ray, closely connected to 'pure reason' or *buddhi*.

However the 'reason' of this age was not the *pure reason, buddhi*, or intuition of the occultist, but an intellectual questioning that challenged the mysticism and superstition of the age. The Sixth Ray of Devotion and Idealism was the influence that gave rise to mysticism and its shadow, superstition; it began to withdraw in 1625 but is still very strong today because it was in 'incarnation' for such a long period.

The influence of the Seventh Ray brings order out of some of the chaotic effects of the zealous and somewhat inquisitional Sixth Ray; it was an incredibly liberating time for independent thinkers to be less influenced by the Church. (This underlay the optimism of the Puritans who travelled to America in the early 1620s.) For some thinkers, there would have been some alignment between the lower intellectual reason and the higher intuitive reason.

The fifth sub-cycle of Ray Three (1681–1745) covered a large part of the Age of Enlightenment, emphasizing this intellectual questioning and preceding the cycle of the fifth ray of science that started in 1775. The '5' cycle also corresponds to Britain as the birthplace of the Bill of Rights and a leading nation of the Fifth Rootrace, London as a fifth ray soul and the inventions at the beginning of the industrial age – to name a few.

The cycle of the rays Three, Five and Seven brought on the Industrial Age and technology revolutions. Science has brought great benefits to humanity, but environmental degradation and the corporatization of technological products has over-shadowed these accomplishments. The manipulation of technology by the few at the expense of the many (e.g. pharmaceuticals, big oil) has resulted in a temporary monopoly and holding the world to ransom.

This current predicament is related to two factors: one is the separative nature of the Fifth Ray of Science, that can be coldly calculating, creating separation between man and environment, between man and fellow man.

The other reason pertain to the shadow expression of the seventh ray and Aquarius – group co-operation and organizational processes selfishly utilised to benefit the corporate entity, not the people. In a way this is to be expected, as at no other time in history have human beings worked as internationally and corporately as they do today. During this cuspal period between Pisces and Aquarius, there is much confusion and resistance to change, hence the old ways of doing business are still deeply entrenched. The more altruistic attitudes of large groups will emerge as the forces of Aquarius wax in strength and the opportunistic habits of the current players will eventually wane.

The Lives of Francis Bacon and the Path of Initiation

The Master Who concerns Himself especially with the future development of racial affairs in Europe, and with the mental outgrowth in America and Australia, is the Master Rákóczi. He is a Hungarian, and has a home in the Carpathian mountains, and was at one time a well-known figure at the Hungarian Court.

Reference to Him can be found in old historical books, and He was particularly before the public eye when he was the Comte de St. Germain, and earlier still when he was both Roger Bacon and later, Francis Bacon.

It is interesting to note that as the Master R takes hold, on the inner planes, of affairs in Europe [written 1919], His name as Francis Bacon is coming before the public eye in the Bacon–Shakespeare controversy.

...The Master R. is upon the seventh Ray, that of Ceremonial Magic or Order, and He works largely through esoteric ritual and ceremonial, being vitally interested in the effects, hitherto unrecognized, of the ceremonial of the Freemasons, of the various fraternities and of the Churches everywhere.

The lives mentioned above are most likely ones where this identity took a major initiation. Initiations are rarely taken in the long journey of the soul and represent signposts of spiritual achievement. Initiation is conferred upon someone through their own self-initiated efforts in some lifetime or other, that reaps its reward further down the road.

The personalities mentioned here and in order of their proposed initiations are:

Identity	Date	Initiation	Plane
Saint Alban	death 209 AD	2nd Baptism	Astral
Roger Bacon	1213 – 1294	3rd Transfiguration	Mental
Francis Bacon	1561 – 1626	4th Crucifixion	Buddhic
Francis Rákóczi	1676 – 1735	5th Adeptship, Master	Atmic
Count St Germain	1735 – 1784	6th Chohan, Custodian	Monadic
Lord of Civilisation	1925	7th ?	

The Lives of Francis Bacon

St Alban. Although not mentioned in the above quotation, St Alban has been included here as a possibility and fulfils some of the criteria for the second degree – where the control of the astral body is demonstrated. He is widely regarded in esoteric circles as being a previous incarnation of Bacon. A Roman soldier who converted to Christianity, he became Britain's first martyr when beheaded by the Romans. The town of Saint Albans (previously Verulam) near London was named after the saint. Within the walls of Verulam, which he took for the name of his barony (Viscount St Albans), Francis Bacon built a refined small house that was described by the seventeenth-century diarist John Aubrey.

Roger Bacon. Alchemist, scientist, inventor, English Franciscan philosopher and educational reformer who was a major medieval proponent of experimental science. Bacon studied mathematics, astronomy, astrology, optics, alchemy, and languages. He was the first European to describe in detail the process of making gunpowder, and he proposed flying machines and motorized ships and carriages. Bacon (as he himself complacently remarked) displayed a prodigious energy and zeal in the pursuit of experimental science; indeed, his studies were talked about everywhere and eventually won him a place in popular literature as a kind of wonder worker. Bacon therefore represents an historically precocious expression of the empirical spirit of experimental science, even though his actual practice of it seems to have been exaggerated.

Note also that Roger Bacon incarnated in 1213, a date very close to the signing of the Magna Carta in 1215. The subsequent lives of Bacon are all deeply connected to the themes of liberty, freedom and the development of democracy. It is most noteworthy that he spent his lives associated with the 2nd, 3rd and 4th degrees within the entity known as Britain, a mature soul in its own right that is relatively advanced upon 'the path'.

Bacon also appears as first scientist in 'The Black Rose', set in the Middle Ages. His personal presence in the narrative is brief, but includes a demonstration of gunpowder and a few sentences outlining a philosophy of science which might as easily be attributed to Francis Bacon centuries later.

If Roger Bacon had taken the third degree initiation in that lifetime, he fulfils the criteria quite easily. The term 'rich young man' is typically a reference to a third degree initiate because of the richness of the range of awareness and the quality of the personality vehicles. 'Rich in his aspiration and in his recognition; he was rich as the result of age-long experience and evolutionary development.'

The third degree is where the 'transfiguration' takes place, where the candidate has demonstrated the wide control and subsequent illumination of the mental body. The theme of experimentation continues through other lives and speculated identities, as will be touched upon later.

Within a relatively short space of two thousand years, this soul became an adept. There is no hard and fast type of rule for this kind of situation; it all depends upon individual karma and cyclic or astrological opportunity for initiation. But once the second and third degrees are achieved, evolution to perfection is relatively rapid.

Notwithstanding however, other relatively advanced beings may have to wait thousands of years between initiations. The reasons are varied, one of which is that the individual, even at a relatively advanced stage, may choose to walk the 'dark path' for a series of lives, before coming to their senses. High initiates have and do 'fall'; their climb back up the mountain may be delayed by a long period of time.

Francis Bacon. Lawyer, statesman, philosopher, and master of the English tongue, is remembered in literary terms for the sharp worldly wisdom of a few dozen essays; by students of constitutional history for his power as a speaker in Parliament and in some famous trials and as James I's Lord Chancellor; and intellectually as a man who claimed all knowledge as his province and, after a magisterial survey, urgently advocated new ways by which men might establish a legitimate command over nature for the relief of man's estate.

But Bacon was far more than this. It has been demonstrated by several writers that he was the author of the Shakespearean plays, working through the actor Shakespeare – either through the process of automatic writing or using him as an amanuensis (likewise it is speculated through Christopher Marlowe and others); that his works are still so popular may hint at the influence of the Bard through the waxing strength of the Seventh Ray and the Aquarian Age coming into manifestation. On the theme of Shakespeare:

> After Jesus Christ no other individual has done so much to develop and expand the human sense of an interior life. If Jesus Christ planted the seed of interior life, Shakespeare helped it grow.... No single writer has populated our imagination with as many archetypes ... Falstaff, Hamlet, Ophelia, Lear, Prospero, Caliban, Othello, Iago, Macbeth, Romeo, Juliet.... The characters inhabit the collective imagination, they help form our attitudes to life.

It has been further speculated that Bacon was responsible for the translation of the King James Bible. He was closely associated with (and probably led) some sects of the Freemasons and Rosicrucians, orders dedicated to the preservation of the Mysteries and the welfare of humanity. As such it is said that he wrote secret ciphers relating to these traditions into the Holy Bible and the Shakespearean plays. In many ways Bacon influenced Western ideas very deeply through his widely disseminated writings, and his influence in the court of James I of England.

This period in English history saw the establishment of true democracy and the beginning of the end of the monarchy. Bacon 'called all the wits together' of his age, instigating the conscious renaissance of the key aspects of human civilization. He was well equipped for such a task, as an Aquarian reformer helping to inaugurate the Aquarian Age. It is further believed that Francis Bacon feigned his own death in 1626 and made a transition to Eastern Europe in preparation for his next identity as Count Rákóczi.

One of the names for the fourth initiation is the 'great renunciation'; it occurs when the vehicle called the causal body, that has served the soul for untold aeons, is destroyed and there is direct contact with the monad or spirit. Buddhic (as in Buddha) awareness now supervenes. The intuition (buddhi) becomes the uniting principle that synthesizes all the lower bodies and the new adept now creates at will.

Francis Rákóczi. In his next incarnation as Francis Rákóczi, he became Master of the Seventh Ray ashram, probably around 1676, right at the start of the Ray Seven cycle in 1675.

There is a very plausible argument for Francis Bacon having been 're-born' or, more accurately, 're-emerging' around 1676 as Francis Rákóczi, of the royal house of Transylvania. It is interesting to note that this 'birth' or emergence in1676 coincides almost exactly with the start of the Ray Seven cycle in 1675. This would have been closely connected with the fact that Master R was the master of the Ray Seven ashram—and was incarnating at the start of the cycle of the ray that he embodied.

Later Rákóczi's death in 1735 was also said to have been feigned, as was that of St. Germain in 1784. Behind all these personalities was the one Adept, ingeniously covering his tracks all around Europe. The importance of the Rákóczi life may be reflected in reference to him as Master R. His co–workers—the other Masters—call him 'The Count', in reference to his following 'incarnation' as Count St-Germain. Rákóczi's 'death' in 1735 would have allowed him to make the transition to this new identity.

Presumably it was this lifetime that Rákóczi became a fully-fledged adept, a Master of Wisdom, 'a rare efflorescence of a generation of enquirers.' As a Master has mastery over the lower three worlds, he can build and discard a body at will, for purposes of service; it is called a 'mayavirupa', a body of illusion. He now joins that small band of adepts who constitute the inner government of the Earth, who watch over and guide human evolution, always inspiring but never interfering with human free will.

Count Saint-Germain.
'It was in 1743; the rumour spread that a stranger, enormously rich to judge by the magnificence of his jewellery, had just arrived at Versailles. Whence did he come? That is what no one has ever been able to learn. His countenance, haughty, intellectual, acute, struck one at first

sight. He had a pliant, graceful figure, delicate hands, a small foot, an elegant leg which set off a well-fitting silk stocking.

'The small clothes, very tight, also suggested a rare perfection of form; his smile showed the most beautiful teeth in the world, a pretty dimple adorned his chin, his hair was black, and his eyes were soft and penetrating. Oh! what eyes! I have nowhere seen their equal. He appeared about forty to forty-five years old. He was met again within the smaller apartments, where he had free admission, at the beginning of 1768.'

The Comte de St-Germain was certainly the greatest Oriental Adept Europe has seen during the last centuries. He was recognized as a brilliant scholar and linguist, and his skills ranged from chemistry, poetry and music to history. In relation to the latter, he had the ability to recall all the major occurrences of the past two thousand years.

This surely must be a confirmation of his future role as Mahachohan, Lord of Civilization. St-Germain was also a skilled artist and able to create luminous effects in his paintings, particularly of jewellery, by mixing mother of pearl with his colours.

The presence of Ray Three was quite marked in St-Germain's ability to speak virtually any language fluently. Ray Three of course has a direct relation to that third 'department'—the Mahachohan's, which he would take over later in the twentieth century.

His knowledge of chemistry was also so astute (reflecting his past knowledge as Roger Bacon) that he was able to remove flaws from precious stones; which skill he demonstrated to Louis XV. He spent much of his time involved with alchemical experiments, as attested in the memoirs of the Italian adventurer Casanova.

St-Germain has also been credited with assisting the Freemasonry revival (as had Francis Bacon) and working with Cagliostro the Kaballist and magician, a previous incarnation of H.P. Blavatsky. He was also associated with the semi–mythical figure of Christian Rosencreutz (1378–1484), who was a personification of the Rosicrucian philosophy and the mysticism of the Rosy Cross.

The Mahachohan: Lord of Civilization. After his appearance as Count St-Germain, Master R went on to eventually take the exalted post of the Mahachohan, Lord of Civilization. The Mahachohan holds this office for long periods that can span several races. This third department corresponds to the Third Ray of Active Intelligence, and of this quality the Mahachohan is the greatest expression. Thus can be seen the predominance of this ray in the earlier life of Bacon.

The Mahachohan's responsibility is to ensure that inner spiritual purpose finds its expression and materializes upon the physical plane. The third aspect or Ray is the 'Mother' Ray that gives birth to all forms—bodies, ideas, culture, civilization—through which spirit can find expression.

The Mahachohan manipulates the electrical forces hidden in Mother Nature. Hence he works very closely with the devic or angelic kingdom whose responsibility it is to build all the forms in nature, be it a blade of grass, a tree or a flower or a human being.

> 'We now come to a consideration of the vast Ashram controlled by the Master R. He is the Lord of Civilization and His is the task of bringing in the new civilization for which all men wait. It is a third ray Ashram, and therefore enfolds within its ring-pass-not all the Ashrams to be found upon the third Ray of Active Intelligence, upon the fifth Ray of Concrete Science and upon the seventh Ray of Ceremonial Order. All these Ashrams are working under the general direction of the Master R. He works primarily through the Masters of these three types of ray energy. He Himself at this time is occupied with seventh ray energy, which is the order-producing energy upon our planet.'

An momentous historical occult event occurred around 1925 when Master R, who was previously the custodian or Chohan of the Seventh Ray, assumed the post of the Mahachohan—the major department of the Third Ray:

> 'When ... the Master R. assumed the task of Mahachohan or Lord of Civilization, His Ashram was shifted from the seventh Ray of Ceremonial Order to the third Ray of Active Intelligence.... It is this influence [of Aquarius] also which has enabled the Master R. to assume the mantle of the Mahachohan and become the Lord of Civilization—a civilization which will be conditioned by the rhythm of the seventh ray.'

Benjamin Franklin's Great Similarity to Francis Bacon

Benjamin Franklin was a printer, author, diplomat, philosopher and scientist. His achievements were numerous and extraordinary, uncannily similar to the two Bacon lives and exemplary as a Capricorn initiate.

His well-known inventive ability stemmed from his Aquarian mind, reflected by Mercury placed in that sign (same as Francis Bacon). It gave him a 'lightning-like' intuition, and as Aquarius is related to electricity, the symbolism of his famous kite experiment to prove that lightning is electricity, reflects his intuitive approach A large part of his life saw his progressed Sun, Mars and mid-heaven in Aquarius.

In 1747, when he was engaged in electricity experiments, transiting Uranus (lightning) was conjunct his progressed midheaven (career). Later in 1752–1753, he was recognized for his achievements such as the invention of the lightning rod – his progressed midheaven was conjunct his natal Mercury in Aquarius at the time. As Mercury is related to the number five, and as the Fifth Ray pours through Aquarius, it would have provided a good expression for a Fifth-Ray mind, which Franklin probably possessed.

But Franklin, like Bacon, was a philosopher, reformer, founding father, scientist, Freemason and Rosicrucian. There is much evidence to suggest that he was involved in many behind-the-scenes activities both in America and Europe. He was a contemporary of Count St-Germain and was close to all the political machinations of the day.

Franklin pioneered his republican ideologies as American minister to France from 1778 to 1785, but in a universal and unprovincial way. Liberty, equality, fraternity! As a philosopher and statesman he had much influence upon Europe and France in particular, helping to prepare the way for the French Revolution. As leader of the American Philosophical Society, he was able to influence the thinking of many French intellectuals and philosophers.

Franklin managed to obtain from Louis XVI, money, soldiers and ships to fight the American Revolution. Ironically, and perhaps purposely on his part, the revolutionary ideas network – built up during that time – helped to topple Louis ten years later.

France aided the Americans to exact revenge against the British for France's recent defeat in the Seven Years War, and to garner America as a trading partner. France also looked to America ideologically, as the new Utopia (or, as Francis Bacon put it, the 'New Atlantis'), recently risen across the Atlantic.

Some of France's more enlightened assisted in the American Revolution, using it as an outpost of French revolutionary ideals, perhaps hoping for some reciprocity somewhere in the future. Marquis de Layfayette, Vicomte de Mirabeau, the Brissot de Warville, were some of these individuals, who had much help from Jefferson and Franklin.

Franklin was very much the social leader of Paris, impressing all with his wit and simple dress, in the mould of the pious Quaker. His writings were translated into French; he encouraged the idea that the French could be noble republicans. He even managed to heal cleavages between the followers of Rousseau and Voltaire, some of the main players in the French Revolution.

The Role of Masonry

Francis Bacon, the 'Father of Modern Science' and one who had done much groundwork for Masonry in the Elizabethan era, was a Mason and member of the company that founded Virginia and the Carolinas. He was associated with fraternities throughout Europe, having taken initiations in many lodges. Freemasonry provided a non-partisan spiritual framework through which the 'magic' (manifesting of spiritual principles) could work in the New World:

'Bacon worked through carefully chosen representatives in America and through the Masonic lodges to help prepare the ground in the early years for a new government in America. From behind the scenes he initiated and guided the plan for America to be the testing ground for these spiritual principles of government - for America to be the 'new order of the ages', Novus Ordo Seclorum, on our Great Seal.

Bacon referred to America as 'The New Atlantis' in his book by that name, and envisioned an ideal society that he hoped would develop in America. For America was a new nation being born, a fertile ground for these ideals, without the prejudices and crystallized patterns of Europe. It was a nation where the Divine principles of freedom and equality would be officially proclaimed for the first time anywhere in the world, and where 'life, liberty and the pursuit of happiness' for all people would be anchored on earth.... Bacon was honoured in 1910 by

Newfoundland on their tri-centennial commemorative stamp as The
Guiding Spirit in colonization schemes."

The continent upon which the United States of America was founded,
was also the 'old Atlantis':
'Ray 7 — Order and Magic, via Uranus. This influence is inherited
from the Atlantean world, which still rules the territorial aspect of the
States, which is a remnant of old Atlantis. It is this that produces the many
magical, spiritualistic and occult groups which flourish today in the States.'
Modern Masonry has its roots in England on June 24th, 1717. The date
falls within the First Ray sub-cycle (fifty years) period of the outgoing 1675
Seventh-Ray cycle (Ceremonial Order or Magic). Masonry is a teaching
along the First Ray line, while politics and statesmen are also influenced by
it, which may be the reason many leaders are attracted to Masonry.

The horoscope for modern Masonry has the Sun in Cancer conjunct
Jupiter and Venus, giving a great depth of expression of the Second-Ray
energies of Love–Wisdom. The horoscope is very similar to the Magna
Carta, one of the first blows for freedom in the Western world. The Cancer Sun in the Magna Carta represents the family of Humanity, and in
Freemasonry, the 'brotherhood' is the family who nurture and sustain certain spiritual principles. The Templars provided the same function at the
time of the Magna Carta as the Masons later did in the eighteenth century.

The emphasis in this chart is upon the Law, with Saturn-ruled Capricorn rising and Moon both opposing Jupiter, T-squaring Saturn in Libra.
Saturn is a degree away from Saturn in the U.S.A. horoscope; the timing
of that latter chart was very much influenced by astrological and masonic
principles.

Like the influences of the Templars behind the scenes of the Magna
Carta, many masons helped bring the Declaration into being, the most
famous being Benjamin Franklin, Grand Master of Pennsylvania. Franklin
and Thomas Jefferson were two of the major contributors of the committee of five appointed to draft the declaration. Washington was a Mason
and General of the Army at the time.

Benjamin Franklin was Provincial Grand Master of the Philadelphia
Masonic Lodge, and assisted in the initiation of Voltaire into the Lodge of
the Nine Sisters in Paris, the lodge in which Jefferson was said to be initiated.

'... in the eighteenth century, Masonry was very powerful, both spiritually and politically, and most of the best minds of Europe and America were Masons. It was dedicated to developing the perfected human, and promoting the virtues of good citizenry, philanthropy, liberty, and brotherhood. It also supported the concept of a government built on consciousness, wisdom and knowledge harmonized with law. It was long a cherished dream of the initiates of the secret societies of Europe, and of the Enlightenment thinkers of the eighteenth century.

'These spiritual principles of government were brought to America by the European brotherhoods of Freemasons, who established a network of lodges in the new colonies, and catalyzed the founding of America as a new nation. According to historian Bernard Fay, 'Masonry alone undertook to lay the foundation for national unity in America.' The Masons were the only group in America highly organized enough to plan a revolution. By the oath of secrecy in the lodges, a brotherhood dedicated to the principles of liberty, equality, and fraternity developed. Paul Revere began his famous ride after he left an adjourned meeting of a Masonic lodge.'

Conclusion

Thus the remarkable journey of one soul is envizaged. The occult perspective according to the seven rays and esoteric astrology afford a glimpse into a deeper world of energy and forces that shape civilization over massive periods of time. They give us a bird's eye view and help us understand where we fit in as individuals and groups – in the greater scheme of things. Indeed:

'There are more things in heaven and earth, Horatio,
than are dreamt of in your philosophy.'

THE MASTER 'R'

Grace Cooke

IT IS WITH some reluctance and diffidence that we attempt to write about the great initiate known as the Master R. By whose authority do we write of him? It is by his love and guidance, and his association with us in the formation and work of an inner brotherhood, that we shall endeavour to convey a picture of this illustrious one; who labours unceasingly through the opposing earth conditions for the upliftment and betterment of all humanity, irrespective of race, caste or creed.

Throughout the centuries—nay, through many ages—the White Brotherhood, banded together under different names and guises, has continued its work of drawing men together into groups and brotherhoods, to labour for the moral and spiritual advancement of humanity. Many of its leaders are still unknown to men, but there are exceptions, as in the case of one who in certain circles is referred to as the Master R, because it was thought by some people that in one incarnation he was the son of Prince Rákóczi of Transylvania. We ourselves believe this is open to question, and that the initial 'R' refers to a mystical name by which he is known in an inner group.

Through the years, at different periods of history, he is to be found

Grace Cooke (1892–1979) was the medium for the spirit guide White Eagle and the founder, with her husband Ivan, of the White Eagle Lodge. She wrote this article for the first volume of the Lodge's magazine *Stella Polaris* in 1951 and it is reprinted here because it is in many respects definitive of the esoteric tradition surrounding the Master R/Francis Bacon. Note the references on pp. 126–7 to the Polaire Brotherhood, which links the present volume with its predecessor, THE VIEW (2009). The White Eagle Lodge work continues: see www.whiteagle.org. A couple of errors have been silently corrected and the article is reprinted by kind permission of the White Eagle Publishing Trust.

endeavouring to guide mankind into the path of light. In England he was known in a former incarnation as Roger Bacon, and three centuries later as Sir Francis Bacon. This soul in both incarnations did much for the advancement of science, English law, literature, horticulture, natural history and philosophy. His work in the formation of secret occult brotherhoods and societies is known to many students of occultism, and an interesting book describing his work is *Francis Bacon and His Secret Societies* by Mrs Henry Pott.

A study of the akashic records reveals the existence of these brotherhoods of the inner light, schools of the ancient wisdom and temples of the mysteries, as they are sometimes called, in past ages, as in Atlantis (the lost continent beneath the Atlantic Ocean). Previous to its submergence the knowledge given in these inner brotherhoods or mystery schools was taken by 'The Brothers' to the Andes and the Himalayas, where it has been preserved right to the present day. The brotherhood was also established in Egypt, Greece, and later in the French Pyrenees, as well as other parts of France and Britain.

The remains of vast stone temples of this ancient brotherhood of the White Light—of the Inner and Spiritual Sun—are to be found in Britain, at Avebury and Stonehenge in Wiltshire, in the Hebrides, on the Cotswolds, in Cornwall, and across the Channel at Carnac in Brittany. The mystery of their origin still remains unsolved by archaeology. These are actually relics of the Sun-temples built by the inner brotherhoods of ancient races. Since then other brotherhoods have been formed to carry on their tradition and heritage.

Manly P. Hall, in his *Encyclopedia of Hermetic, Masonic, Rosicrucian, Symbolical Philosophy*, writes:

Many times the question has been asked, was Francis Bacon's vision of the New Atlantis a prophetic dream of a great civilization which was so soon to rise upon the soil of the new world ? It cannot be doubted that the secret societies of Europe conspired to establish upon the American continent 'a new nation, conceived in liberty and dedicated to the proposition that all men are created equal'. Two incidents in the early history of the United States evidence the influence of that silent body which has so long guided the destinies of peoples and religions. By them nations are created as vehicles for the promulgation of ideals, and while nations are true to these ideals, they survive; when they vary from them they vanish like the Atlantis of old which had ceased to know the gods.

In his admirable little treatise, *Our Flag*, Robert Allen Campbell revives the details of an obscure, but most important, episode of American history—the designing of the colonial flag of 1775. The account involves a mysterious man concerning whom no information is available other than that he was on familiar terms with both General George Washington and Dr Benjamin Franklin. Little seems to have been known concerning this old gentleman; and in the materials from which this account is compiled his name is not even once mentioned, for he is uniformly spoken of or referred to as 'The Professor'. He was evidently far beyond his three score and ten years; and he often referred to historical events of more than a century previous, just as if he had been a living witness of their occurrence; still he was erect, vigorous and active— hale, hearty, and clear-minded—as strong and energetic every way as in the prime of his life. He was tall, a fine figure, perfectly easy and very dignified in his manners; being at once courteous, gracious and commanding. He was, for those times and considering the customs of the colonists, very peculiar in his method of living; for he ate no flesh, fowl or fish; he never used for food any 'green thing', any roots or anything unripe; he drank no liquor, wine or ale; but confined his diet to cereals and their products, fruits that were ripened on the stem in the sun, nuts, mild tea and the sweets of honey, sugar or molasses.

He was well educated, highly cultivated, of extensive as well as varied information and very studious. He spent considerable of his time in the patient and persistent conning of a number of very rare old books and ancient manuscripts which he seemed to be deciphering, translating or re-writing.... He was a quiet, though a very genial and very interesting member of the family, and he was seemingly at home on any and every topic coming up in conversation. He was in short one whom every one would notice and respect, whom few would feel well acquainted with, and whom no one would presume to question concerning himself—as to whence he came, why he tarried, or whither he journeyed....

By something more than a mere coincidence the committee appointed by the Colonial Congress to design the flag accepted an invitation to be the guests, while in Cambridge, of the same family with which the Professor was staying. It was here that General Washington joined them for the purpose of deciding upon a fitting emblem. By the signs which passed between them it was evident that both General Washington and Doctor Franklin recognized the Professor, and by unanimous approval he was invited to become an active member of the committee. During the proceedings which followed, the Professor was treated with the most profound respect and all of his suggestions immediately acted upon. He submitted a pattern which he considered symbolically appropriate for the new flag, and this was unhesitatingly accepted by the other six members of the committee, who voted that the arrangement suggested by the Professor be forthwith adopted. After the episode of the flag the Professor quietly vanished and nothing further is known concerning him.

It was during the evening of July 4th 1776, that the second of these mysterious episodes occurred. In the old state house in Philadelphia a group of men were gathered for the momentous task of severing the last tie between the old country and the new. It was a grave moment and not a few of those present feared that their lives would be forfeit for their audacity. In the midst of the debate a fierce voice rang out…. The debaters stopped and turned to look upon the stranger. Who was this man who had suddenly appeared in their midst and transfixed them with his oratory? They had never seen him before, none knew when he had entered, but his tall form and pale face filled them with awe. His voice ringing with a holy zeal, the stranger stirred them to their very souls. His closing words rang through the building, 'God has given America to be free.' As the stranger sank into a chair exhausted, a wild enthusiasm burst forth. Name after name was placed upon the parchment; the Declaration of Independence was signed. But—where was the man who had precipitated the accomplishment of this immortal task? … who had lifted for a moment the veil from the eyes of the assemblage and revealed to them a part at least of the great purpose for which the new nation was conceived? He had disappeared, nor was he ever seen again or his identity established. This episode parallels others of a similar kind recorded by ancient historians attendant upon the founding of every new nation. Are they coincidences, or do they demonstrate that the divine wisdom of the ancient Mysteries still is present in the world, serving mankind as it did of old?'

These two incidents will perhaps indicate the nature of the activities of the Master R. Some years ago we ourselves received clear and precise instructions as to the making of a symbol to be used in the work of an inner occult group, which we were told was to be formed in the near future. This symbol, although unknown to us at the time by earthly means, was subsequently found to have been a symbol often used by Francis Bacon in his secret societies.

This great soul appears again in eighteenth-century Europe as the Comte de Saint-Germain, leaving the world guessing as to his origin and the source of his immense knowledge. Mrs Cooper Oakley in her book *The Comte de St-Germain* (Theosophical Publishing House) gives the history of the life of this remarkable man which extended well over a century, during which history records his appearance in most of the courts of the countries of Europe including London, Paris, The Hague, Vienna, Brussels, St Petersburg, Venice, Leipzig and others. Many letters from eminent people are quoted in this book testifying to the high character and influence of this illustrious master in European politics. He was known to have appeared and reappeared throughout at least two hundred years after his supposed death. He himself stated that he was going to India, after which there appears to have been a period of silence.

It was from the White Brotherhood in the fastnesses of the Himalayas that we received the first direct message from the Master R. It came by a special occult means of transmission to the Polaire Fraternity in Paris. Our first actual meeting took place on the 27th January 1931, soon after the passing of Sir Arthur Conan Doyle, when we were invited to meet a messenger from the Polaire Fraternity. This Brotherhood had received precise instructions through their occult means of communication to seek out a certain medium in London through whom 'They '(the initiates) wished to work for a particular purpose; and through whom they wished at a later date to form a Brotherhood in Britain which would work to help humanity through the coming 'Years of Fire' (those of the Second World War). This meeting with the messenger from Paris took place in the famous library of the late Mr W. T. Stead's home in Smith Square, Westminster. When the Polaire brother entered the room, after a sweeping glance at the assembled company, he walked straight across the room to the writer of this article, as though he knew her well; and spoke to her of work she had done in the past in an earlier incarnation for the brotherhood in Egypt; and also of the special mission which had been entrusted to her in her present life. He gave this message in a few precise words and almost immediately the company then adjourned to the séance room. A remarkable occurrence followed. Within a short space of time the presence of the Master R, or as he was known to the Polaire Fraternity, the 'Chevalier Sage', appeared; a figure clear to see in the astral light, with clear cut features and dark, luminous eyes from which divine love and the wisdom of the ages seemed to shine. He held in his hand a certain symbol of the Brotherhood, unknown to the writer at the time, but well-known to the messenger from Paris. He then influenced her to say certain words (words which had been pre-arranged between the Brotherhood in the Himalayas and the Paris Brotherhood), which would be proof to the Polaire Brotherhood that it was the Master speaking. He gave a sign which had also been prearranged as an additional proof that it was he, the Chevalier Sage (or the Wise Knight) who was communicating.

The Polaire Brotherhood had already received, through their special magical means of communication, information from the secret Brotherhood in the Himalayas to the effect that he who was known to them as the Chevalier Sage had been previously known in Paris as the famous Comte de St-Germain.

To sum up: 'By their fruits ye shall know them', said Jesus; and by this, as well as by the secret signs given to their pupils, are all the Illumined Ones recognized. 'They' mostly work unseen and usually their real mission is unknown to ordinary mortals, with whom they sometimes mingle in daily life, although such incidents as those we have quoted are rare. They cause their agents to be used for the formation of societies and brotherhoods pledged to labour continually and selflessly for the advancement of knowledge, the arts, science and all those things concerned with the betterment of man's life on earth. From time to time they appear amongst men to inspire them with divine wisdom and love, and to guide the destinies of nations towards world unity and universal brotherhood.

Those who know humbly and gratefully acknowledge their unswerving love and patience, which has been the strength behind their endeavours to love and serve their fellow men.

THE HOROSCOPE OF FRANCIS BACON

Simon Bentley

MOST IF not all readers of this book will already be aware of the history of Bacon's time, and how very difficult, very dangerous and at times very 'muddy' life was in those days. He was born into a world in which there was much religious conflict. These and other matters are illustrated very clearly by the great, and even to the untutored eye obvious, emphasis on the twelfth house in his horoscope. In his day, the twelfth was direly referred to as 'the house of self-undoing', but more positively and from a spiritual viewpoint it can be regarded as the house through whose experiences one has the greatest opportunity to go inward and upward, hence the connection with religion. This can mean inward in one's own self, what we 'do' inside ourselves spiritually, mentally, dealing with those problems and difficulties that we all face. A strong twelfth can also mean dealing with inward and spiritual things for or with others, and of course what we know of Bacon's history suggests that he did much of that too.

But how much of that would we have seen on the surface? The ascendant, the rising degree, is in Pisces, a sign traditionally regarded as spiritual and often religious, but very difficult to grasp; it is often hard to see what really lies behind its outward manifestation. With both Pisces and the twelfth house, things are seldom what they seem. Sometimes people who have these influences strong deliberately pretend not to be what they are,

This is a lightly-edited version of a talk Simon Bentley gave in the Temple of the White Eagle Lodge on Sunday January 25th, 2009. Simon evinced an interest in astrology long before he went to Cambridge University and studied, among other things, the history of science. He trained in horticulture before taking up astrology full time. A student of Joan Hodgson, founder of the White Eagle School of Astrology, he became its Principal after her death in 1995. His book, *Homes in the Heavens,* came out in 2009.

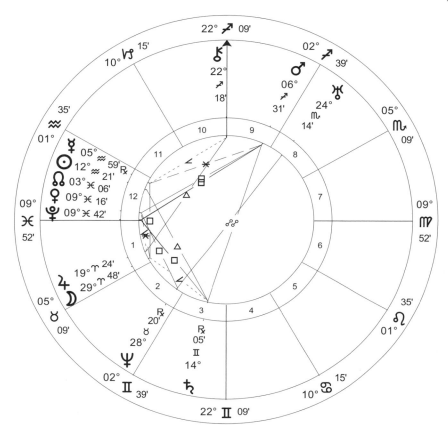

Birth Chart of Sir Francis Bacon. Bacon was born on 22nd January 1560/1 Old Style, which is 1st February 1561 New Style. The exact time of birth is not known. William Lilly calculated his horoscope for a time of 7.30 am; it is not known on what basis he used that time. Attempts to rectify the chart have been made by various astrologers; the one used here is set for a time of 8.41 am local mean time and seems to me to fit the known facts best.

or pretend to be what they aren't; sometimes circumstances force dissemblance upon them, sometimes it is a matter of other people's impressions being mistaken, however hard they may try to project a truthful image of themselves. Many of the greatest actors and actresses have much Pisces and twelfth house influence in their horoscopes. Indeed, drama is said to be a twelfth-house profession; my own experience of horoscopes confirms this.

In the horoscope of a mature soul, a strong twelfth house often signifies a life in which one is prepared to sacrifice almost anything for the sake of an ideal, a particular destiny, even if in the end it means literally laying down one's life. It seldom works out quite that drastically, but the twelfth is a house that somehow seems to reflect the kind of inspiration and idealism that lays ego completely aside. In some ways, Bacon's life as it was known by the people of his time would have belied this. He was known for being very widely knowledgeable and having his fingers in an enormous number of pies. He was also a brilliant man in every sense of that word. Exceptionally, also, he was someone who seemed to be capable of going really deeply into the hidden secrets of almost anything in life, another typically twelfth-house trait. In his political life, his life as a statesman and as an important figure at court, he was of course privy to all sorts of secrets, some of which would have made him extremely uncomfortable. There are other areas of life too where his ability to investigate became almost legendary, as we shall remember later. However, behind all those different fields in which he was interested was a single-minded effort to promote truth, knowledge, understanding and justice, all qualities we can readily associate with his Sun–sign, Aquarius.

Bacon was born on February 1st, 1561 NS, putting the Sun firmly in Aquarius, in which sign Mercury is also placed; both are in the twelfth house. Aquarius is one of the three signs associated with the air element. Air is symbolic of the mental plane, the ability to think, and those with important planets in air signs learn to recognize the power of thought, and the powers of the spoken and written word that go with it. Life tends to be lived at the mental level and particularly in this case with both Sun and Mercury, which is itself the planet of thought and communication, in air. Here is someone who is rational, objective and always has a strict regard for the truth, very characteristic Aquarian qualities. They do not have time for hypocrisy or affectation. Sometimes they devote their whole lives to searching for the truth or, as the symbol of the man carrying the watering pot shows, pouring out truth for the benefit of others. I think one would say in Bacon's case that he did both.

Another important feature of Bacon's life was his great interest in science. He invented 'scientific method' as we would understand that expression today. In his time very few people were involved in any systematic scientific work, but he conducted all sorts of experiments in many fields, particularly with plants. (The latter point reminds one that this was the man who said that 'gardening is the purest of pleasures'.) He was very disturbed by the lack of a scientific approach to understanding the world in which he lived. It is very typical for Aquarians to be involved in science. They are frequently drawn to scientific professions and also to situations where they share their knowledge with others. Air mixes with all the other elements easily, so that air people tend to be sociable, although Bacon, with the sensitive and reticent Pisces rising, would have found that side of life more difficult than many Aquarians. The air signs are said to be the signs that teach the human soul the lesson of brotherhood, so they are each linked with 'getting on' with other people in some way. For Gemini, it is about getting on with one's brothers and sisters, one's cousins, siblings, peer group—the people you have to live with whether you like it or not. For Libra it is partnership, marriage, rivalry, all one-to-one situations; for Aquarius, friends, associates, groups of people and the wider world.

The Moon's north node in Bacon's chart is also relevant to this work of brotherhood. In any horoscope, the north node has much to do with the 'direction of travel' in the life. (The south node, the opposite point, symbolizes what one is used to, where one comes from, things one has already developed, talents one already has.) The north node is the challenge of the present and the future—that which inspires effort to reach a goal. So when reading a horoscope an astrologer will tend to have one eye on the north node while thinking about the Sun, as the Sun is the heart of the horoscope, pointing to the deep purpose behind the life. But the north node also has a lot to do with what the soul is trying to achieve. Bacon had the north node in Pisces, clearly showing the attempt to overcome barriers between people and peoples, particularly as it is in the twelfth house, while the south node, opposite to it in Virgo, shows his abilities to analyse, to be scientific, to be ordered, and the legal mind that can deal with details.

While people remember that Bacon was much travelled in his mind and spirit, they tend to forget that he also travelled physically, especially when young. He was sent to Europe for three years when he was still in his teens. Astrologers will quickly note Mars in Sagittarius in the ninth house, which is concerned with foreign countries and customs, as well as travelling in the mind. Mars is also linked harmoniously with Mercury, further indication of a life involving travel. The ninth house, and indeed the twelfth because they are both linked in different ways with the planet Jupiter, are chiefly concerned with those experiences which bring about expansion of consciousness, the twelfth house more specifically spiritual things, the ninth house academic matters, travel, foreign countries and customs, any kind of experience that broadens one's horizons. Where one has Mars placed is where one puts most of one's energy, so clearly for Bacon much energy went into that side of life. So Mars in the ninth strengthens still further the investigative side of his character.

Many people are familiar with Bacon in two very different guises. There is Bacon the statesman, the scientist, the person who led the life that other people saw, but there is also the 'hidden' Bacon, the Brother, the spiritual leader, the man who could decode ciphers, the man who could hide spiritual truth in literature, the man who ultimately had a hand in inspiring much spiritual work that is taking place today. I would be doing him a great disservice if I didn't write about both these sides.

With regard to the former, on reading his biography I was very struck by his scientific achievements, touched on above. He was also a brilliant lawyer; one of his biggest personal problems, it seems, was that his skill in both the law and politics showed up the lack of ability in many of those around him. He seems to have tried hard not to show others up, but even so became a target for all sorts of unpleasantness. There were of course various reasons for this, most of which we shall probably never know, but this kind of difficulty not infrequently goes with a strong twelfth house, because in being prepared to give up anything and everything for what one really believes in and what one knows one has to do, one often finds oneself doing just that. There were, too, so many instances in his life in which he couldn't take the credit for something he had done, or had to 'take the rap' for something somebody else had done, the latter culminating, of course, in his 'fall from grace' precipitated by James I. Not for nothing was the biography of Bacon by Alfred Dodd entitled *The Martyrdom of Francis Bacon*.

Chiron, a relatively recently discovered 'planetoid', cannot be ignored in Bacon's chart and often has an important influence in life; it has the symbolic name 'the wounded healer'. Where Chiron is, there are apt to be 'woundings' but also opportunities for healing. In this horoscope, Chiron is right on the midheaven, the very top of the chart, extraordinarily appropriate for Bacon when one considers first of all that there have always been doubts about his parentage – one's parentage, socially speaking, comes under the tenth house whose cusp is the midheaven – and also the way in which he was forced to destroy his own reputation. All through his professional life, too, he never obtained the promotions to which he was entitled at the right time, or sometimes at all. He was constantly impeded, despite his extraordinary abilities. It is perhaps as well for him that he had the Moon in Aries (albeit right at the end of the sign) with Jupiter, showing plenty of enthusiasm and energy as well as his pioneering work in various fields.

Bacon's 'hidden' life, though, actually *required* others not recognizing him for what he was, another typically twelfth-house or Piscean situation. He needed to do his 'real' work under cover, but it caused problems and much heartache for him; 'not being recognised for what he was' began soon after birth with the doubts about his parentage mentioned above. In her splendid *Sir Francis Bacon, a Biography*, Jean Overton Fuller relates how she consulted a top geneticist concerning this matter, without mentioning Bacon by name, and was told that there was a less than one in five thousand chance that he was actually the son of the couple who brought him up. Appropriately the horoscope does confirm doubts about parentage. For information about this, one looks particularly at the tenth house and the fourth. Sagittarius is on the tenth cusp, usually regarded as signifying the father, Gemini on the fourth, usually signifying the mother, although sometimes the two are reversed. Both Gemini and Sagittarius are 'dual' signs – Gemini the twins, Sagittarius the centaur, half man and half horse. While hindsight is always a wonderful thing, it does nevertheless seem very likely from the horoscope that he was not the Bacons' son. Astrologers will also notice that the ruler of Gemini and therefore of the fourth house, the house of home and family, Mercury, is in the twelfth house and retrograde, strongly suggesting 'a skeleton in the cupboard'.

By definition, there is much we do not know about Bacon's 'hidden' life. One of the things that strikes me most in Jean Overton Fuller's book, despite all her research, is not what she says but what she does not say. However, many will be aware from their own involvement in spiritual matters, of Francis Bacon's inner work. Some would say he led a 'double life', but he would never have achieved what he did without it being hidden, hence again the emphasis on the twelfth house. Indeed, one hardly dares imagine, in the religious and political climate of his time, what would have happened if people at large had known what he was up to. This secrecy had many positive effects, also giving rise to his much-remembered injunction to his 'brethren' to seek every opportunity to do good by stealth. How very twelfth house, hidden, secret! How very 'Pisces rising' too: it looks like one thing on the surface, another underneath. And how much today's world needs people to 'do good by stealth'!

There is another very potent indicator in the horoscope of someone who had to do much in secret, and that is Pluto rising; indeed it is almost exactly on the ascendant. Venus is there too. Notwithstanding the decision to 'downgrade' Pluto a few years ago, as far as astrologers are concerned nothing has changed. Pluto remains a very important planet and experience has taught astrologers that it is strongly linked with the sign of Scorpio, which many will recognize as the sign through which we deal with some of the most hidden and often difficult parts of the human personality, particularly emotionally speaking. Pluto, as god of the underworld, is about hidden depths. It is also about power, but it normally works below the surface for a long, long time, and only occasionally is it seen coming through to the surface, rather like volcanoes which slumber away quietly for years until they erupt. When Pluto does emerge, great events and great change occur. Bacon's rising Pluto also suggests that he wielded a great deal of influence in his outer life, as indeed he did. People paid close attention to what he said and he was consulted on all sorts of important matters of state and international relations. However difficult other people tried to make his path, he was one of the most influential figures of his day and well known not just in this country but all over Europe and further afield. An individual with strong Pluto, if in the right place at the right time, can bring about major change. Bacon's invention of modern scientific method has already been mentioned, as has his legal work. He achieved a great deal else, of course, but despite all this his influence is still in many ways not fully acknowledged. That goes with Pluto as well, because of its association with what is hidden.

I sometimes wonder how the ordinary people of the time would have felt had they actually met him. They would have been aware of his reputation; they would have realized that he was at court and a very senior figure, and they would have realized his legal capabilities. What would they have made of him as a person? Would they have sensed any of the things that lay behind? I actually doubt it, except to a very limited extent. Of all the horoscopes I have ever talked or written about, I think this is one of the most hidden, one of the most difficult to interpret. Interestingly enough it reminds me of the horoscope of another individual who has strong relevance to spiritual work – Sir Arthur Conan Doyle. In terms of the signs of the zodiac Doyle's chart is very different, but in terms of house positions it is very similar. Doyle too had a heavily tenanted twelfth house; for many years he kept his interest in spiritual matters secret; he was also much given to investigation, interested in what was hidden. In his case his twelfth-house planets were in Taurus and Gemini, but he still had the same penetrating vision and application.

Pluto can keep working at something, rather like a strong Saturn (which Bacon also had), ferreting out information, looking for answers to things long after everybody else has given up. In Bacon's chart Saturn is harmoniously linked with the Sun in Aquarius, the 'fixed' air sign, indicating that the ability to concentrate was very great, but as if having Pisces rising wasn't enough in 'veiling the real person', Saturn in Gemini in the third house is not easy from that point of view either, because on the surface of things it will have rendered communication very difficult at times (the third is the house of communication). Saturn in Gemini is a position that often leads to shyness, for example. Put it in the third house and it tends to be even more so. It must have been hard sometimes – he would have been very aware he had to choose his words carefully; if he was writing something, every word would have been weighed. Yet, with Aquarius strong, interacting with others would have been very important. What he was really trying to do, with Sun in Aquarius in the twelfth (among other things), was no less than to promote worldwide brotherhood. When a well-known spiritual teacher talked in recent times about 'brotherhood wide as the world' he meant it very seriously, as a realistic goal and something that one day all will reach and understand. But that goal was recognized by some in Bacon's day: that is what he was trying to do. The Sun in Aquarius shows the urge to brotherhood. The twelfth house ultimately overcomes barriers, reaching inward to the source of life, the unity of all life. It may throw up difficulties, but it is in overcoming those that one gains that ultimate freedom to be one with everyone and everything else. For me, without doubt, the concept of worldwide brotherhood was the basic motivation behind everything that Bacon did.

Why is Bacon so important for us now? It is because he has set a standard, as well as a methodology, by which the kind of work that many are now called to do spiritually can be successfully achieved. It is evident from his horoscope that it is an extremely difficult task, but one would not expect it to be otherwise.

In Bacon's chart Venus is exalted in Pisces, rendering it very strong; it is also rising and exactly conjunct Pluto. Pluto tends to magnify the influence of another planet it touches. Venus is all about divine love, not an emotion, but the love of the Creator for the creation, the kind of love that is implied in Jesus' saying 'Not a sparrow falls to the ground without your Father'. Venus conjunct Pluto in Pisces implies potentially that degree of consciousness. Pluto is ultimately at home anywhere or everywhere. Dealing as it also does with mass consciousness and very large groups of people, it is about brotherhood beyond just the world, brotherhood over the whole universe indeed. At the spiritual level of life, the two planets Venus and Pluto therefore go together very well, although it is a much more problematical combination at the earthly level. Venus is concerned with the expression of divine love, while universal brotherhood goes with Pluto. Bacon was a citizen of London, a citizen of England, a citizen of Europe, a citizen of the world, but not just those things. He was, far, far more, a citizen of the solar system, a citizen of the galaxy, a citizen of the universe. He was (is) a soul whose real work knew no bounds, knows no bounds, and never will know any bounds, and who has set humanity a shining example. Humanity, both individually and collectively, can learn from his life much that it needs to know in order to pursue the path of true brotherhood and the life of the spirit.

In conclusion, there is so much about Bacon and his life for which there are no words. I know that he wrote these particular words at the end of a tragedy, but I would still like to say, from a positive viewpoint, 'the rest is silence'. In silence, indeed, is to be found the heart of God.

FRANCIS BACON, THE SEVENTH RAY AND MUSIC

Frank Perry

The Theosophical Society and other spiritual streams (apart from Rudolf Steiner) recognize the incarnation of Sir Francis Bacon as being one of a certain Master known as the Master R. A few of his other such incarnations were Roger Bacon (1214–94) and the Comte de St-Germain (1710–84). Madame Blavatsky (founder of the Theosophical Society in 1875) stated that she worked with certain Masters, namely the Masters Morya and Koot Humi and also the Master R (in the case of the latter with her two volumes of *Isis Unveiled*). Within this trans-Himalayan occult hierarchy referred to by HPB (which she also referred to as the White Lodge, the Great White Brotherhood, etc.), the Master R is known as the Head of the Seventh Ray of Ritual and Ceremonial Magic, and it is further stated that this is the Ray that will govern humanity for the next few thousand years. It is understood that there are Seven Rays. There is also another period of time, derived from the Great Year of Plato – also referred to as the precession of the equinoxes – where the coming Age is known as the Aquarian Age and the keynote of this age is Brotherhood. It is also stated that this Master holds the destinies of Europe and the USA in his care.

Frank Perry has been a follower of the spiritual path in this lifetime since leaving school at the age of 16 in 1964, and has studied numerous writers, especially Manly Palmer Hall & Dane Rudhyar. He is a practising spiritual astrologer, sound healer, writer, artist, and a recording artist with over 100 album releases on 33 labels: Chicago Blues, Avant Garde, Jazz and a pioneer of New Age and Tibetan Singing Bowl music in the UK. He was a trance medium at the age of 16 and has done psychic portraits of the spirit guides at that time. Later he became deeply involved with the White Eagle Lodge. He is an honorary member of both the British Harry Partch Society and the Sound Research Group.

Sir Francis Bacon, during his lifetime and in his subsequent lifetime as the Comte de St-Germain, was known to have been associated with the Freemasons and the Rosicrucians, while Bacon also had his own group known as the 'Knights of the Helmet' (see Alfred Dodd: *The Martyrdom of Francis Bacon*), drawing their inspiration from Pallas Athena. So in the lives of this Master we find a strong connection with groups of an altruistic, philanthropic, and philosophical bent – that is, group work devoted to assisting humanity and embodying the principles of the ideal of brotherhood. The Rosicrucians and Freemasons both find roots in the ancient initiation schools and can be considered as constituting an unbroken line from those ancient days. The word *theosophia*, being derived from two Greek words meaning divine wisdom, was coined by the Neoplatonists in the second century A.D. and was intended to connote the truths revealed to humankind from the remote ages past, sometimes and more recently referred to as the perennial wisdom.

The adept, the Comte de St-Germain, played violin and composed music as an amateur so that we find an immediate link between this Master and working with sound. In Bacon's own time several of the Rosicrucian apologists included music in their speculative philosophy relying heavily upon the findings of Pythagoras – most particularly Robert Fludd. The Comte de St-Germain once admitted that he had assisted John Dee in the production of his book, *A True Relation of What Passed Between Dr. John Dee and Some Spirits*. There is evidence that Francis Bacon met John Dee, who was involved with magic, astrology, alchemy, spiritism, and the esoteric arts and was frequently consulted by Queen Elizabeth 1. John Dee also worked with Edward Kelley in contacting angels and spirits and published his book upon their findings. So we can see that certain persons in Europe were exploring these regions, and esoteric branches of ancient thought were in something of a revival during the lifetime of Bacon. The creatures of the invisible world find themselves portrayed in the works of Shakespeare – *A Midsummer Night's Dream* and *The Tempest* immediately spring to mind. Magic involves cooperating with angels and other denizens of the invisible realms while (in white magic) also demanding that we purify ourselves and raise our vision in order to attract beings from the higher regions for the benefit of humankind.

Mantra is linked to this Seventh Ray in the book *The Masters and the Path* (1925) by Charles W. Leadbeater, and prior to that by Ernest Wood in

Raja Yoga: The Occult Training of the Hindus – so that sound, and likewise the effect of sound upon consciousness and the being, is understandably enjoying ever-increasing attention. Ever since the 1960s, when the Beatles had joined Maharishi Mahesh Yogi and his school of Transcendental Meditation, and they each being given their own mantra, this aspect of sound has been brought ever more into the public gaze. Since around that time it has become quite normal to find a rather prophetic quote from *The New Atlantis*, the unfinished work written by Sir Francis Bacon in 1623 upon a wall in recording studios, namely the following:

> We have also sound-houses, where we practise and demonstrate all sounds, and their generation. We have harmonies which you have not, of quarter-sounds, and lesser slides of sounds. Divers instruments of music likewise to you unknown, some sweeter than any you have, together with bells and rings that are dainty and sweet. We represent small sounds as great and deep; likewise great sounds extenuate and sharp; we make divers tremblings and warblings of sounds, which in their original are entire. We represent and imitate all articulate sounds and letters, and the voices and notes of beasts and birds. We have certain helps which set to the ear do further the hearing greatly. We have also divers strange and artificial echoes, reflecting the voice many times, and as it were tossing it: and some that give back the voice louder than it came, some shriller, and some deeper; yea, some rendering the voice differing in the letters or articulate sound from that they receive. We have also means to convey sounds in trunks and pipes, in strange lines and distances.

During the twentieth century, certain composers extended their vocabulary by moving into quarter tones and even lesser tones, to the extent that some worked with 72 or even 96 tones to the octave (our common scale has 12 tones to the octave). The 'lesser slides of tones' mentioned in our Bacon quotation finds its embodiment in what are termed microtones. They are sometimes also referred to as 'the notes between the notes'. The classical music of Northern India always used quarter tones, and also embodies microtonal slides. Certain composers also explored microtonality in their music.

Yet another phrase taken from another old book finds ever-increasing recurrence today! I refer to the opening words of St John's Gospel, 'In the Beginning was the Word and the Word was with God and the Word was God.' Maybe we can now understand this better. In the sacred traditions of India there is the path of *Nada Yoga* – the path of achieving divine union with God through working with sound. We find therein the fourfold process of sound with three of these residing upon non-physical planes and ending with the spoken word. Certain schools of music in India practise this yogic technique, such as the Dhrupad form of singing (also known as temple singing), and while this tradition is rather ignored in modern India, it is finding an ever-widening public in the West. The main feature of *Nada Yoga* lies in the *anahata* sound and the *ahata* sound. The term *anahata* means 'unstruck sound' or sound not made by the striking together of two objects. In other words, it is an inaudible sound or a sound heard within oneself, not stemming from any outer source and sometimes referred to as 'the Voice of the Silence.'

During the last century, certain musicians from India were invited over to the West to teach their form of singing, particularly in North America. One such was Pandit Pran Nath (1918–96) who was a *nada yogi* and he taught several composers – in particular those responsible for forming what became known as the Minimalist school – namely, La Monte Young and Terry Riley. These two were both disciples of Pran Nath, and La Monte Young in particular went on to compose pieces that can be seen to bear close similarity to the sacred Word of India – namely OM. The minimalist movement is characterized by comparative simplicity sometimes with drone-like pieces (similar to Indian music – the tambura with voices over, and sometimes instruments over it). In the instance of other minimalist composers we can find repetitive rhythmic and melodic patterns similar to mantras – particularly in the works of Philip Glass and Steve Reich. Uday Shankar (1900–77), brother of Ravi Shankar, toured the West with his Indian dance troupe in the 1930s but a far deeper impact developed when Pran Nath first entered New York in 1970.

Again we find the gradual influence of this sacred Name entering into a variety of musics, and most especially in the Harmonic singing developed in the West by American David Hykes (b. 1953). This is a form of singing that emphasizes the several tones living within the one tone, through vocal techniques that have been developed in a number of countries but most especially in Mongolia, Tuva and the Altai regions. A brotherhood of tones is sounding beyond the fundamental, and melodies are drawn from these – providing an otherworldly effect where one can hear the voice within the voice and along with it a sensation suggestive of being able to actually live and breathe within the space created by these vocal tones. The voice is expanded through this vocal technique and our listening experience like-wise expands into the awareness of this parallel universe of accompanying tones. The listener becomes ever more alive to what is living within the spaces of the intervals that obey the laws of nature, first introduced to our western world by the sage of Samos (Pythagoras, a previous incarnation of the Master Koot Humi) over 2,500 years ago.

Music is not solely a collection of tones produced by instruments. Music already exists in humans as a harmony between their three vehicles of thinking, feeling and willing. Whenever there is harmonious agreement between our thoughts, feelings and actions, this produces a kind of music. The ideal of a disciple in the spiritual tradition is to achieve this harmony within themselves in order to harmonize with all the beings on earth and throughout this entire universe. Being true to that spiritual fire, or light, or voice, within corresponds to sounding our very own note in true harmony within the universal Being. Within the Seventh-Ray ideal of universal brotherhood, harmony can be seen to be the very basis of the work – beginning with inner harmony and then extending to harmony with everything that exists.

The Seventh Ray being linked with ritual, we also notice the significance of Stravinsky's 'Rite of Spring', which was dedicated to the Russian artist Nicholas Roerich (1874–1947). Roerich was a slavophile and expert on ancient pagan peoples of Russia. The raw and vibrant fiery energy of this work stirred violent reactions in the audience at its premiere in 1913 in Paris. At the beginning of the twentieth century, hundreds of artists were adhering to the teachings of Theosophy in their art, andseveral composers too were attracted to these selfsame teachings, or spiritual stream, seeking ways to apply these teachings to their composing. They included Dane Rudhyar (1895–1985) and fellow 'American Ultramodernists' Henry Cowell and Carl Ruggles. The British composer Cyril Scott (1879–1970) was an avowed Theosophist who also claimed (via a spirit medium) to be in contact with the Master Koot Hoomi who advised him on his music. Others included the Danish composer Ruud Langgaard (1893–1952), and more famously the Russian Alexander Scriabin (1872–1915). This spiritual 'new wine' required 'new bottles' to give vent to the spiritual energies reaching the earth, and it led to these composers experimenting with new forms of music making, oftentimes questioning the very foundations of the inherited traditions of Western music, and both seeking and unfolding viable alternatives. World music began early last century, in the 1930s with Henry Cowell (1897–1965) and Alan Hovhaness (1911–2000) in the 1940s, whilst various improvizing jazz musicians moved into musical forms and embraced several disciplines in the early 1970s. They thereby simulated a synthesis and blending of musics that could be seen as a manifestation of the principle of sharing – or what we might prefer to call brotherhood.

The rising popularity of shamanism today can also be seen to relate to this ray of ritual – alongside of a manner of music-making that has nothing to do with technical ability. It stems from a very different level of brainwave activity. Our daily thinking is known as Beta brainwave activity, whereas altered states of consciousness, experienced by the likes of Zen Buddhist or Tibetan Buddhist monks, resonate at a slower speed and relate to brainwave states such as Alpha, Theta, and Delta. These are the ones we enter while in meditative states of consciousness or even when giving spiritual healing or entering into trance states.

Another sonic area that allows the listener to enter into these subtle realms is found in the ritual instruments of Tibet, China, Japan, and India, namely singing bowls, bells, and gongs. They were developed thousands of years ago to assist with meditation and other ritual practises including tantra, that aspect of the spiritual path where several disciplines are sewn together, as it were. These too can be very rich in harmonics or overtones, so that we find colour, sound, words, and movement working together upon our consciousness. Synthesis is a characteristic of this Seventh Ray, according to the Tibetan Master Djwhal Khul (who is known as the Master most knowledgeable on this subject of the Rays). For example, while tantric Tibetan Buddhist monks are filing the colours into building, and creating the form of the sand mandala, they are also chanting appropriate mantras for that mandala. In relation to the term Master perhaps it is useful to clarify that we mean master over themselves and not master over others! And when we refer to the trans-Himalayan occult hierarchy perhaps it would be better to invent a new term such a holarchy, rather than hierarchy, as the term hierarchy could be misleading.

Composers such as the Italian Giacinto Scelsi (1905–88) developed compositions where that which is found to live in the single note is explored and forms the basis of entire pieces of music, or otherwise informs his creative works. Of course, with Western orchestral instruments we seldom have a single tone when a note is played, but rather a main tone with a combination of several subtler overtones, less dominant in the sounding note, that provides us with the special timbre of each instrument and enables us to identify the instrument on which the note is played. That is to say, the same note played upon a violin, oboe, clarinet, trombone, vibraphone, etc., sounds different because of the unique selection of the other tones which make up the overall sound that is found within each family of instruments. A very good overtone singer, such as American expert David Hykes, can reach the sixteenth harmonic (in Mongolia, etc., the singers more commonly go no higher than the twelfth harmonic) so that while all of these sounds exist within the voice, through a variety of techniques, it becomes possible to focus upon each of these constituent harmonics at will – so that, in effect, the singer will produce two or more notes simultaneously, alongside melodies rooted in nature.

Listening to the sound of an ocean wave breaking upon the shore it is possible to hear many sounds within what we perhaps speak of as one sound. An infinite series of overtones lives within that one natural sound of the ocean. Linked to this Seventh Ray is also the world of the angels, and the angels of nature come to mind too. We find certain composers, or musicians, working with the sounds of these elements, fire, water, wind and rocks. With 'The Tamburas of Pran Nath' (a 1999 CD by La Monte Young), it is possible to hear twenty-four separate tones within what most of us would hear as one sound – a drone.

In a purely materialistic paradigm, music can be found to be the organization of sound. For instance, compositions can reflect a mere playing with organizing these sounds – or, again, the expression of particular emotions, or attempts to represent nature (Claude Debussy, Arnold Bax, Frank Bridge, Frederick Delius, etc.) – or even the application of certain philosophies (as found in the works of Dane Rudhyar). More recently, we find the overtly religious music of the Estonian, Arvo Part, and Englishman, John Tavener (Russian and Greek Orthodox respectively). However, with the increasing Seventh-Ray influence, a more magical element can be seen to be returning in our working with sound. Dane Rudhyar was at pains to speak about the magical aspects of the tones with which he composed. The Italian composer, Giacinto Scelsi, corresponded with Rud-hyar and was likewise concerned with the spiritual and magical aspects of sound and tone. The composer, music theorist, inventor, and musical instrument maker Harry Partch also approached his work with sound in ways embracing magic. Many rock or pop musicians have connections to magic, or witchcraft, or wicca, etc. (either black, grey, or white) whilst pagans use sound and/or music in their rituals. Most religions work with sound, and especially bells.

The ancient science of working with sound in this magical way is found in mantra. The ancient Vedic mantras are sound formulas evolved to at-tract the various devas (gods, goddesses, or angels or inner world beings of light) to assist us along our spiritual path, as distinct from the language of daily parlance. There are four methods of working with mantra. The first is *shabda yoga*, where the use of the sacred sounds is derived from the Vedic tradition. Then we have *shakti yoga*, where the sonic aspect of the tantric tradition comes into play. Next is *bhava yoga*, wherein we find the devotional chanting of the bhakti tradition, and finally *nada yoga* which, although involved with sound and music as we have seen, doesn't truly specialize in mantra but rather concerns itself with the musical intervals that are also employed during mantra recitation.

Today we can see manifestations of the Seventh Ray in many forms, even if unsuspected ones. Ritual and ceremonial largely relate to groups of people – so that, for instance, we can even see the Seventh Ray in TV, where millions of people can join together at a given time and share the watch-ing of a programme – together although not together physically. We see it in organized crime, where gangs of people work together, and in large supermarket chains, where a few people own a large number of shops ca-tering for a wide range of articles – thus taking a larger share of the wider market. There are rituals (even if participation is largely unconscious) that bind large numbers of people together, such as those witnessed at football matches and at rock music concerts. Any activity that has for its purpose the bringing together of individuals involves ritual to varying degrees.

We can also see evidence of the activity of this Seventh Ray in the fields of science with ESP, psychosomatic medicine, and where scientists tap and use the hidden forces of nature, as in nuclear fission. In America we now have 'psychic cops', who have modern equipment designed to communi-cate with ghosts, or the spirits of the dead, and it is usual for them to have a psychic medium present too, oftentimes with the equipment confirming the perceptions of the medium.

Roger Bacon (whom we identified as an incarnation of this Master) is credited with introducing the lens into our Western world, leading to the development of microscopes and telescopes that have revolutionized our understanding of nature. Microscopes have led to the awareness that this material world is composed of precious little actual material substance, while the telescope has led to the discovery that we live in a galaxy of 110 billion stars – and that this galaxy is but one in a universe of over 200 billion galaxies. Many scientists accept that with so much life surrounding us it is unlikely that we are alone, that we are the only form of intelligent life in this vast universe. Thus, again, we find ourselves expanding our sense of sharing life to incorporate many levels of beings. UFOs do exist, inasmuch as science is unable to provide accounts for every single phenomenon in this area and hundreds of cases are truly unexplainable. Einstein's famous theorem $E=mc2$ has proved sufficient for many scientists, but there are others who insist that intelligence, consciousness, or awareness must also play its part in the formula.

Since the Master R is concerned with group work and the promotion of the principle of brotherhood, it is encouraging to see an increase in charitable works and the self-sacrifice involved in giving money to help those less fortunate – be that via Band Aid, Live Aid, or Save the Children – alongside those appeals that emerge whenever tragedy hits the people of one or more parts of our planet.

A far more challenging task lies in the bringing together of disparate individuals, such as in the United Nations, where we must perforce follow a line of dissonant harmony. That is, a group of separate beings with little in common must forge a way forward and find a new way of relating together. In this instance, consonant harmony would relate more to the family unit – where a return to the source of the family recreates, or reconnects to, an initial harmony. This is a turning back to a harmony that existed previously, whilst dissonant harmony in the social context is moving toward a new manifestation of harmony. Similarly, in the life of the individual, when disharmony has arisen there is a choice of re-establishing the previous harmony ('back to normal') or moving forward into a new rhythm that incorporates changes that have taken place within the inner life of the individual so that a return to the past is no longer a viable option.

In my own work I am using sound in an occult manner. That is to say, I study the effect upon the various levels of consciousness of my instruments (most particularly the sacred ones found to be most potent in these areas) and improvize with these extra-dimensional aspects as additional determinants. For example, when composing pieces for the seven main chakras I turned to certain sacred instruments from Tibet that exert a strong effect upon these chakras. In this way I am consciously aligning with the the inner-plane potential that resides within the instruments and bringing my vibrations into sympathetic resonance with these higher realities. Thus I seek to actualize these energies upon the earthly plane through a form of at-one-ment between intention and result. This manner of working can be seen to have links with the Seventh Ray too.

There are four planets that have an affinity with the Seventh Ray, and these are Saturn, Jupiter, Uranus, and the Moon. Each of these has its own way of working with the ray. For instance, Saturn would be concerned with strict observance of the ritual and a certain punctiliousness, whilst precise timing would be emphasized alongside self-discipline and an impersonal or dispassionate performance of one's duties. Jupiter, being associated with the Higher Mind, would have more to do with the symbolism involved and what we might regard as the more religious aspects of ritual.

Just as certain everyday activities can become imbued with deeper meaning and significance within a ritual context (for instance, drinking from a cup and Holy Communion), so ritual provides the sanctification of such activities and eventually leads to a deeper understanding of the significance of every action along our spiritual path. From this ritual context, the act of music-making or any other creative act takes on an altered significance. When successfully applied, those qualified to appreciate such qualities will identify with them through the artwork, and so on. We find a reflection of this within the realm of rock or pop music, whereby both the musician and the audience may be under the influence of the same drugs – often with the music designed to complement the aims of taking that particular drug. The only drawback is that it is but a temporary break from the habit-patterns (*samskaras*), so that these quickly return once the effects of taking the drug has worn off. Only spiritual effort can bring about the final overcoming of these dispositional factors and grant true freedom.

The ancients linked the Air element to the human mind or thought. Therefore, as we move further into this Aquarian Age, we should not be surprised to find the question of thought becoming more important. A certain painting by Nicholas Roerich entitled 'The Arrows of Heaven, The Spears of The Earth' (painted in 1915) comes to mind. The sky is orange with red forms like arrows (symbolizing the negative thoughts of the two warring factions) that have finally led to actualization via the spears of men that we see in the lower part of the painting, in the form of the warring armies. The artist is showing how the prior period of negative thinking, which has swayed the masses involved, has finally led to the outcome of hostilities. We may also bring to mind that phrase in the Bible, 'For as a man thinketh, so he becomes' (Proverbs 23 : 7). Roerich, with his wife, met his Master in London in 1921 – namely the Mahatma Morya, Lord of the First Ray.

This air element brings us to ponder upon the breath. One technique for slowing down our restless mind lies in deep breathing. Through the act of breathing we share life with all living beings – our fellow humans and the animals and insects. The ultimate ideal for this element resides in the truth of brotherhood, and we find a manifestation of this in the Bodhisattva ideal of the Mahayana Buddhists. The highly-advanced being relinquishes the attainment of *nirvana* and sacrifices this in order to assist all beings into that state, thus showing great compassion.

In the four great initiations of the ancients that of air is concerned with learning to discriminate between the lower mind and higher mind. According to the teacher White Eagle, of great assistance in the passing of this air initiation is sound, breath, and the throat chakra. In the life of Jesus the Christ we find the Sermon on the Mount to be associated with this initiation and therein stated in the beatitudes are the necessary soul-qualities for passing this test, namely humility, meekness, purity, and peace.

Humanity passes through this period under the influence of the astrological Air Sign of Aquarius, but it is understood that the initiates in any one such period always work with the opposite sign of the zodiac. During the Age of Aries, Moses gave the Ten Commandments or Laws, when the opposite Sign of Libra rules over laws, and during the Age of Pisces the Master Jesus was said to have been born of a Virgin (Virgo the opposite sign to Pisces). Similarly, in this Aquarian Age the initiates will work with the energies of Leo. Leo is a Fire Sign ruled over by the Sun and thus associated with light, life, and warmth. Interestingly, Uranus (one of the rulers of Aquarius) is considered to be an octave of the Sun and, more particularly, is related to the inner Sun or individualized Fire of the divine spirit immanent within humanity. The opposite to light is darkness, although it is more helpful to think of these two as principles working together – rather as we must oppose the movement of both hands in order to open a jam jar. From this perspective of the higher mind, we see evil as representative of an unevolved condition and, applying the philosophy of non-dual thinking, God cannot be two but rather must also embrace the negative or less-evolved manifestations of life in a total whole. Within the fairy kingdom, it would be unkind to expect a fairy on their first day of work to create a rose. Such a majestic flower would take them some years into their evolution before they were capable of such work. Perhaps we may consider that weeds are their first creations and yet valued equally by the creator – or their angelic charges.

Linked with synthesis and beauty, the Seventh Ray brings more the sense of being part of one huge family of created beings spread throughout the entire universe and with being(s) upon many levels of existence (including that of the so-called dead and even extra-terrestrials). This expanded awareness of sharing life with all of creation extends to the animal kingdom, bringing greater care for both the animals and the earth which sustains us leading to movements such as the campaign for compassion in farming and organic farming.

There are very many cycles – the Platonic Great Year, Manly P. Hall's 600-year cycle (which he named the Phoenix Cycle), the various planetary cycles (for instance, the Jupiter – Neptune cycle of about 166 years) – to name a few. There is also a cycle of the elements, and in that cycle we find that each of the major periods in the history of the earth has been marked by the predominance of one of the four elements, earth, water, air, and fire. In this cycle, our present era is to be dominated by fire, so that by linking ourselves to the sun, which is true fire, and by contemplating the spiritual sun we can gradually change the vibration of our being until we feel that we become at one with the sun. In this fiery purification the dross of our lower nature is transfigured so that the Rose of the Solar Logos (universal Christ consciousness) blooms upon our Cross of matter.

Although the ancients made the element of Air correspond with thought and the mind, they related the element of Fire to divine love. Therefore, during this coming age the initiates will learn to work with the white magic of divine love.

BACON, RUDOLF STEINER AND MODERN SCIENCE

John Waterman

THE CENTENARY of Rudolf Steiner's birth ... helped to make his name and work better known. Nevertheless, the body of teaching that he called Spiritual Science is still very far from being widely accepted or understood.

This makes a curious contrast to another 1961 occasion – the four hundredth anniversary of the birth of Francis Bacon. Although Bacon lived three centuries before Steiner, his work makes a direct appeal to the present age. Centenary articles and lectures about Bacon have all emphasized his astonishing *modernity*.

How is it that Bacon can speak across four centuries in a way even today, which meets with instant comprehension, while many people find Steiner, who died as recently as in 1925, strange and difficult?

The answer is connected with the evolution of human consciousness, about which Steiner spoke so often and with such emphasis. In a lecture given in 1920 Steiner described Bacon as the 'inaugurator' of the modern

John Waterman was the 'nom de plume' of John Davy, onetime Science Correspondent to the Sunday *Observer*. In an article published in *Baconiana* in 1968 (volume LI no. 168, here slightly abridged) but evidently written before, he refers to both the four hundredth anniversary of the birth of Sir Francis Bacon and the centenary of Dr Rudolf Steiner's birth in 1961 by investigating the varying influences which both men had on the development of science in modern times as the direct result of a possible evolution in human consciousness. John Davy was for a time also General Secretary of the Anthroposophical Society in Great Britain, which is part of the General Anthroposophical Society founded by Dr Rudolf Steiner in 1912. The publishers are grateful to the editor of *Baconiana* and to the Francis Bacon Society, for permission to reprint the article, which remains © The Francis Bacon Society, founded in 1886.

age. There is an obvious sense in which this is true, since Bacon was one of the earliest advocates of science, and it is the ever-spreading power and influence of science, above all, that distinguishes our age from earlier ones.

It is almost uncanny to find in Bacon passages which sound like leading articles in today's technical and scientific journals. We find him urging that there should be more scientifically qualified people in Government, expressing anxieties about the shortage of scientific manpower, and emphasizing that applied science is the key to prosperity.

Bacon's central achievement, though, was to define and describe the modern scientific method – and, above all, to emphasize the importance of impartial observation and experiment. Much of what he says seems commonplace now, but in his day it struck an entirely new note – so much so, that only a few of Bacon's contemporaries were really stirred by his idea. Nevertheless, thirty-six years after his death, his *Novum Organum* inspired the founders of the Royal Society, and today the seed that Bacon planted has sprouted into luxurious growth.

But when Steiner called Bacon the inaugurator of the modern age, he was referring not only to the age of science, but to the age of the Consciousness Soul. Modern science has arisen because of a change in human consciousness. During Greek and Roman times the form of consciousness which Steiner called the Intellectual Soul was developed. Greek science remained essentially an intellectual activity, in which physical experiment never played an important part.

A new stage in the evolution of consciousness began in the fifteenth century, the beginning of the age of the Consciousness Soul. Bacon was one of the first individuals in whom the new outlook began to express itself strongly.

A characteristic feature of the Consciousness Soul (or Spiritual Soul, as Steiner also called it) is that each individual feels himself to be an island. All traces of the instinctive clairvoyance of earlier times, with its experience of participation in a world of spiritual beings, has gone. Awareness has withdrawn into the fortress of the skull, where the ghosts of the older perceptions flit through the consciousness in the form of thoughts. At the same time, awareness of the world revealed by the senses has increased enormously in importance. Eyes and ears have become windows communicating between 'inner' and 'outer' worlds which in earlier times were not that sharply distinguished from each other.

In this way, man's original unitary has fallen apart into two halves. Modern man no longer feels himself to be a participant in nature or in a spiritual world; he has become an onlooker.

How is this change reflected in modern science? The early development of science was still much influenced by an outlook characteristic of an earlier age; still imbued with many attitudes and habits which really belong to Greek and Roman times, to the Intellectual Soul. Even today, this is still true to some extent. One example of this is the dichotomy between 'pure' and 'applied' science.

The ideal of 'pure' science is knowledge for its own sake. The purpose of experiment is to aid the understanding, to throw light on a puzzle presented by nature. It is designed to enrich man's inner life. Applied science, on the other hand, is concerned with the external world, with doing rather than thinking, with increasing material rather than spiritual wealth. The emphasis is on controlling rather than understanding nature, on power rather than knowledge.

The pure scientist, though he may be a creative thinker, is in one sense a consumer, while the applied scientist is a producer. The pure scientist consumes sense impressions and digests them in his mind. The applied scientist uses the concepts that result to produce effects in the world of nature. Pure science is specially connected with the senses and the head, while applied science is an activity which finds expression through the will.

Obviously, there is no such thing as a purely pure scientist, any more than there could be a wholly applied one. Any form of scientific observation involves some activity of the will – particularly when an experiment is set up – while no applied scientist could start work unless he were first able to form concepts about what he proposed to do.

This indicates, I think, how 'pure' science is still coloured by the outlook of the Intellectual Soul. It is expressed, too, in the use of Latin and Greek for scientific terminology and even, until comparatively recently, for scientific theses.

This was just what Bacon wished to overcome. He lamented the overpowering authority of Aristotle, the constant looking back to the past, that characterized the learning of his day. He wanted the slate to be scrubbed clean of tradition, and scientists to start to fill it in anew, basing everything on careful observation and experiment. But the most characteristic thing about him is that he was not really interested in knowledge 'for its own sake', but only in what could be done with it. 'The real and legitimate goal of the sciences,' he wrote, 'is the endowment of human life with new inventions and riches' (*Novum Organum*, Bk. 1). Thus Bacon was not only the first scientist, but the first applied scientist, in a quite modern sense.

It is really only in this century that a deliberate effort has begun to apply science to industry and agriculture. The 'industrial revolution' made very little use of science in the strict sense. Most of the new machines were designed and built empirically, by inventors rather than by scientists. Little or no theory was used.

With the discovery of electricity, the situation changed rapidly. It is possible to handle steam power, and to put it to work, with the help of a few rules of thumb derived from experience. But the use of electricity calls upon scientific theory at every step.

Since then, scientific theories have been put to work on a steadily expanding scale. Chemicals, plastics, electronics and radio, atomic energy and aeronautics are now completely dependent on highly evolved concepts.

There is a sense, then, in which science has only just become truly Baconian. From Bacon's time right up to the end of the nineteenth century, the Consciousness Soul was still not fully developed. A powerful legacy from the Intellectual Soul age tended to keep science in the universities, making it a contemplative, almost monastic activity. Applied science had far less status. Of course, many scientists realized the potential power of science. But the traditions of learning for its own sake were still very strong, and it is only in the last few decades that the 'scientific revolution' has really got going.

But Bacon's outlook is maturing today in a deeper sense than is often realized. For the basic attitudes which inspire applied science are gradually colouring pure science as well. The concept of knowledge for its own sake is gradually losing its meaning, since it is becoming increasingly difficult to define the word 'knowledge'.

Bacon's conception of knowledge is characteristic: 'We... rear a holy temple in (man's) mind, on the model of the universe, which model therefore we imitate' (*Novum Organum*, Bk. 1). The human mind is for Bacon a kind of building site on which 'models' of the outside world are erected through the activity of the individual. The word 'model' is significant, because it is in constant use by physicists today.

For a nineteenth-century scientist, a theory was rather more than a model. It was a picture of the real world existing outside the observer. Thus atomic theory pictured minute billiard balls as the ultimate constituents of matter, and it was taken for granted that if the theory were correct, such balls actually existed.

Since then, the situation has become far more complicated. A whole series of 'models' is now used by science to deal with matter. Thus an atomic 'particle' may be treated as a kind of billiard ball, but also as a kind of wave, and as a kind of electrical cloud. One 'model' for the nucleus of the atom is a series of concentric shells; another is a kind of 'liquid drop'.

Some of the 'models' being used, especially in physics, cannot be 'visualized' in any direct way at all, but only defined mathematically. They no longer have any content which can be related to sense experience. They may still be 'models' – but they are no longer 'pictures'.

It is clear, therefore, that atomic billiard balls cannot 'really exist' in the simple sense. You cannot dissect matter down to tiny indivisible material objects. In fact, when you get into these realms of the very small, the whole concept of 'matter' becomes difficult to define. The atomic physicist no longer deals with 'things' but with 'forces' and 'events'.

All this has compelled philosophers of science to take a close look at what is meant by words such as 'theory' and 'model'. But I do not want to go into the philosophy of science in detail – partly because the majority of modern scientists are not philosophically inclined. I am more concerned to describe what scientists today actually do – even if they make philosophical mistakes.

The most characteristic feature of the outlook of modern scientists is its pragmatism. A theory is not used because it is 'true', but because it is 'useful'. The main test of the truth of a theory is whether it works. As experiment has come to dominate science, theories are coming to be treated more and more as mere tools, as provisional working models. They are no longer revelations of what 'nature' is 'really like', but implements for conducting experiments and uncovering further effects.

In this way, 'pure science' is gradually becoming, in effect, a kind of applied science. 'Knowledge' is less a matter of understanding the world of nature than of learning how to produce various effects. The actual phenomena in which science deals are now largely man-made. New theories are built up on the basis of phenomena which reveal themselves only under the most elaborate experimental conditions – which themselves embody elaborate theories. Numerically, far more scientists are now involved in experimental work than in theorizing.

If one now stands back and looks at this progress from Greek times to the present day, the transformation from the Intellectual to the Consciousness Soul age emerges clearly. Particularly striking is the gradual withdrawal of human consciousness from its dependence, first on revelations from the spiritual world, then from the authority of the past and finally from the authority of 'nature' as perceived by the senses. The scientist is no longer a 'knower' – he has become almost entirely a 'doer'.

The world we live in today we have shaped for ourselves. Not only the things but many of the ideas we use are the outcome of our own activity, and owe little to tradition. We feel free to think what we like, to experiment almost without limit, and science is being used to transform the world. The ideals of Francis Bacon seem to be coming to realization in the most thorough way.

It is also clear, though, that this process of withdrawal is in danger of going too far. In everyday life, people still contrive to keep their feet on the ground, so to speak, and to relate their thoughts to the world revealed by their senses. But science is becoming increasingly esoteric, dealing in forces and entities which are not accessible to the senses, and in concepts which are inaccessible to all but a few who have gone through the necessary mathematical discipline.

At the same time, this very esoteric activity is having the most drastic exoteric effect. New inventions and discoveries pour in upon the world, and society can barely digest the effects of one scientific discovery before it is faced with another. Why is this?

It should be clear by now that the power of science derives from its 'models' – from the concepts which are then embodied in material form, as electronic computers, atomic reactors or supersonic aircraft. The question is: where do these models come from? They cannot be derived entirely from the sense world, since they are often, so to speak, non-sensical: they contradict normal sense experience in all kinds of ways.

There are several cases on record where new 'models' have flashed into a scientist's mind as a kind of inspiration. One of the best known is the experience of Kerkulé, who was riding on a London bus when he suddenly saw, dancing before his mind's eye, the now familiar benzene ring, six carbon atoms holding hands in a circle, with hydrogen atoms attached. This model proved to be the key to a vast section of organic chemistry and showed the way to making all kinds of new synthetic substances.

Not all scientific inspirations are as dramatic or well-defined as Kerkulé's. Yet I believe that a very large proportion of scientific advances, if traced back carefully to their origins, would be seen to derive from similar moments of sudden insight.

Steiner was born just as Baconianism was beginning to mature. He lived to see many of the early fruits of the scientific revolution – electricity, wireless, aircraft. And his life's work is related to Bacon's in a twofold way. He was concerned to turn men's attention once again to the world of spirit, but without losing the consciousness of self which would not have developed without Bacon's impulse.

In the realm of science – which is what this article is mainly about – Steiner pointed repeatedly to Goethe as the inaugurator of a new impulse, and he saw his own work as continuing Goethe's and taking it further.

In Goethe's approach to nature, there is the same interest in the world revealed by the senses as we find in Bacon, and the same emphasis on the importance of avoiding prejudice and preconceived ideas. But there is something more – Goethe emphasized that the scientist must never lose sight of the *phenomena that nature reveals to him*. He must not build mere *imitations* of nature in his mind, models which at best embody only part of the truth. Instead, he must form his thoughts in such a way that the spiritual realities which are behind the impressions of the senses can flow also into his mind. The outer expression of a plant, encountered through the senses, and the inner expression admitted through thinking, then meet in the soul and reveal the true being – the primary Phenomena behind the plant.

The 'models' of modern science are a kind of caricature of the primary Phenomena with which the natural science of the future must be concerned. And as long as science is preoccupied almost entirely with producing effects and performing experiments, it will give men more power, but not the wisdom to use it properly.

What is needed is a reawakening of 'pure' science in a new sense, making full use of the powers of consciousness won since Greek times. In such a science, progress would depend more on acquiring new faculties than on performing new experiments. This does not mean that there should be no experiments. But the starting-point would need to be a clear apprehension of the real phenomenon with which the experiment was concerned. This cannot happen as long as concepts are treated merely as serviceable tools, constructed in the human mind for a strictly practical purpose.

Modern science has brought us to the point where the sheer power of human thinking has been amply demonstrated. But because there is still no awareness that thinking has any connection with spiritual worlds of spiritual beings – either benign or malign – there is no feeling of *responsibility* towards thoughts; only towards deeds.

Steiner has said: 'In the years to come, for many millennia, it will be essential that we acquire a sense of responsibility for a thought we take hold of'. He goes on to say that critical point comes when the thought is imparted to others, written down or spoken out. Then it has been let loose in the world, so to speak.

Today, there is a tremendous pressure in science to rush hastily into print in order to forestall rivals in the same field. New ideas, ad new experiments, are not allowed to mature in the mind, but are thrust out immediately into the world. It may seem an offensive analogy, but it is really as though science were afflicted with a kind of spiritual diarrhoea.

The question of responsibility was raised in an acute form by one of the most extraordinary achievements of science – the atomic bomb – which turned an abstruse conception into a fearful weapon after a few years of hectic work. This gave many scientists a considerable shock. The apparently disinterested activities of the laboratory could suddenly uncover a tremendous new force – and once uncovered, there was a kind of helpless feeling among scientists that nothing could prevent it from being put into practice (although some attempts were made). For a time, there was much discussion about the responsibilities of science towards the world, and whether scientists should try to keep potentially dangerous discoveries secret.

It was concluded, quite rightly, that this couldn't and shouldn't be done. But scientists are continually aware that some apparently academic paper in *Nature* may have revolutionary implications for the whole world.

It was never suggested, however, that scientists should feel responsible for what they *think*. But once scientific thinking can come alive, can begin to reach to the spiritual realities behind the world of nature, the need for responsibility will become more apparent. And it is Steiner who pointed the way to such a new kind of thinking, dealing in living thoughts instead of ghost-like models.

When Bacon published the *Novum Organum*, he inaugurated a kind of thinking that has gradually and effectively eliminated the remnants of the past that clung to human consciousness. This method has reached maturity today, and threatens to fall gradually into decay unless it is given new life. The Consciousness Soul must now take the next step: to re-establish a connection with the spiritual realities of the world. The 'Novum Organum' for this step was brought into the world by Rudolf Steiner, in works such as *Knowledge of Higher Worlds* and *The Philosophy of Spiritual Activity*.

It is thus highly appropriate that Steiner and Bacon should be remembered together, and at the same time – and not surprising that Bacon should be easily comprehended while Steiner is still difficult. Since Bacon's day, his new way of thinking has still to be acquired – and it will be a strenuous, arduous task.

FRANCIS BACON, RUDOLF STEINER AND THE DEVELOPMENT OF HUMAN CONSCIOUSNESS

Expanding on the Article by John Waterman for
Baconia (Vol LI, no. 168), which precedes it in the present volume

Sylvia Francke

RUDOLF Steiner, the Austrian thinker and educationalist, who lived between 1861 and 1925, has described how Sir Francis Bacon was a key figure in the development of consciousness when his new perspectives on science at the beginning of the seventeenth century transformed the ancient concept of nature – a concept that began in the Mystery Centres of antiquity – into a form of science that is still accepted in the modern age.

In his article, John Waterman asks: 'How is it that Bacon can speak across four centuries in a way even today, which meets with instant comprehension, while many people find Steiner, who died as recently as 1925, strange and difficult?'[1]

Steiner demonstrated how a metamorphosis of the acquisition of knowledge has taken place as a result of humanity's development within this evolution of consciousness. When we study this it becomes clear that Steiner, like Bacon, marks the beginning of a yet another new relationship we have to the created world. In the late nineteenth and the twentieth century Rudolf Steiner had prepared the foundations for a new form of

Sylvia Francke studied for the stage and for the teaching of Drama at the Rose Bruford College in Kent. She is an Anthroposophist, being a student of the spiritual scientific research of Dr Rudolf Steiner. Sylvia has used this background of knowledge as an aid to solving the mystery of Rennes-le-Château in her book, *The Tree of Life and the Holy Grail*. In this article, she expands on John Waterman's 1968 article and attempts to show how Francis Bacon's legacy resonates with Rudolf Steiner's descriptions of 'an evolution in human consciousness.'

thought and a further science of nature, revisiting our understanding of the earlier form of Mystery knowledge, and making it once more accessible for twentieth- and twenty-first-century humankind. Steiner's idea of an evolution of consciousness is not only applied to a review of history but also shows how the development of the young child runs parallel to the development of humankind as a whole. It is this concept which lies behind the ethos of his education systems. In his autobiography, *The Story of My Life*, Steiner outlines how we have now reached a point in evolution where each individual human being can once more investigate the secrets of creation and his own origin within it.

While man is evolving from birth onwards he stands consciously facing the world. He attains first to physical perception. But this is at first an outpost of knowledge. In this perception there is not at once revealed all that is in the world. The world is real but man does not at first attain to this reality. It remains at first closed to him. While he has not yet set his own being against the world, he fashions himself perception which is void of being. This conception of the world is really an illusion. In sense perception man faces a world of illusion. But when from within sense-free thought comes to meet the sense-perception, then illusion is permeated with reality and ceases to be illusion. Then the human spirit, living its own life within, meets the spirit of the world which is now no longer concealed from man behind the sense world but weaves and breathes behind the sense world.[2]

Rudolf Steiner's spiritual research develops from this sense-free thought and it is from knowledge gained in this way that all of the practical activities stem which branch from the Anthroposophical movement that he founded. This research has affirmed that all of creation has come into being from a spiritual source, the Cosmic Intelligence, with which humanity was once connected.

The acquisition of human freedom and independent thought was achieved by man's gradual estrangement from the Spiritual World. Steiner describes how the story of Adam and Eve eating of the Tree of Knowledge, the Fall and the loss of Paradise depict real events in world evolution. He demonstrates how, as a result of the Fall, man increasingly descends into matter and increases the power of individualized thinking to the same extent that he loses contact with his true origin. The Tree of Knowledge is replicated in the branching structure of the central nervous system, the

Tree of Life, banished to East of Eden, represents the secret of Life itself that we may not have access to until we can reverse the effects of the Fall. The Tree of Life has also been described as The Holy Grail, Paradise as The Grail Castle. True knowledge of these events and their secrets has been guarded by the hidden brotherhoods throughout history.

The view that human consciousness is in a constant state of change and that humanity has developed between a world of Spirit and a world of matter must of necessity go hand in hand with an understanding of reincarnation, without which it would be impossible for a human individual to traverse a great vista of developing consciousness taking place over the span of many thousands of years. In this vista, definite changes take place in the relationship human beings have to the spiritual world on one side and to physical existence on the other. As we look back we see how consciousness of our spiritual origin has diminished, while experience of physical creation has come increasingly into focus. What is it that is active in this changing orientation between the human being and these two poles of experience?

Rudolf Steiner describes how it is the human *soul* which is active in this capacity.

> Through the body we belong to the physical world. With our spirit, we live in a higher world. Our soul binds the two worlds together during our lifetime.... Between the Body and the Spirit the Soul lives a life of its own. It is served by its likes and dislikes, its wishes and desires, and places thinking in its service.[3]

Steiner indicates definite times in history when each change in this orientation intervened in evolution. He describes the successive stages in human consciousness as 'soul-epochs'. The human individual goes through many incarnations in the course of this evolution, experiencing each new soul epoch in turn. At the same time it could be said that in world religion there is a gradual transition from pantheism to monotheism. This was once brilliantly described by a lecturer in the example of a photograph where only the background or foreground could be in focus, where definition can only be experienced in either the foreground or background at one time. The multitude of the Pagan Pantheon blurs into a single God as human beings begin to wake up as individuals and focus on the myriad of forms emerging in physical creation.

The last vestiges of knowledge from earlier times were given in Plato's philosophy. Rudolf Steiner describes how a connection was made from the earliest form of consciousness, the Sentient Soul Age, to the subsequent Intellectual Soul Age, by a collaboration between Plato and Aristotle.

Plato had been able to communicate the essence of the Mysteries in wonderful pictures to men, to write authentically of Initiation, but he was not capable of evolving a Logic of thought, nor could he, as the outcome of sense-perception, present the natural science of Eleusis in the form of logical thoughts. Aristotle had inevitably to take over this task, because he … was to make preparation for the descent of the Cosmic Intelligence.... Man was not merely to receive the Cosmic Intelligence through revelation but to evolve Intelligence out of his own inner forces. Preparation for this was made by Aristotelianism - that remarkable philosophy which arose in the twilight period of Greek culture and was the impulse underlying the campaigns of Alexander the Great in Asia and Africa. By means of Aristotelianism, earthly Intelligence emerged as though from the shell of Cosmic Intelligence. And from what later was called Aristotelian Logic there arose the intellectual framework on which the human intelligence of all subsequent centuries was based.... The earthly-human intelligence was established, while, as a result of the campaigns of Alexander, the culture of Greece was imprinted upon those peoples who at that time were ready to receive the cosmopolitan impulse.[4]

Steiner has spoken from his spiritual research of how a meeting had taken place between Plato and Aristotle when Plato was an old man and realized that his teachings would no longer be suitable for mankind. He foresaw that understanding would become abstract and more clearly allied to earthly things. Plato knew that in future the language used in the communication of knowledge would have to stimulate the undertaking of independent investigation. In the centuries that followed, this Aristotelian knowledge was turned into the early development of science 'which was still much influenced by an outlook characteristic of an earlier age; still imbued with many attitudes and habits which really belong to Greek and Roman times, to the intellectual soul.'[5] It was in his opposition to this attitude of the Intellectual Soul Age that Francis Bacon aided yet another transformation into the next Soul Age.

Just as Plato had sealed the ending of the Sentient Soul Age by handing the reins of evolution to Aristotle, so Bacon helped to cause the gradual termination of the Intellectual Soul Age by rejecting Aristotle's influence in the future course of science.

In the first third of the fifteenth century, the next stage in the evolution of consciousness began: the Consciousness Soul Age, which we are still experiencing today. Christian Rosenkreutz (1378–1484), the founder of the Rosicrucian Brotherhood, was thirty-five years of age when this age began. His mission, and that of his fellow Rosicrucians, was to bring about a metamorphosis of the original mystery wisdom, to foster the development of the human being in the physical world without losing the spiritual substance from which it had proceeded – eventually leading through to the discovery of spirit through the senses. The first Rosicrucian writings were printed in 1614, 1615, and 1616. Francis Bacon was very much involved in the work of the Rosicrucians, being one of the first individuals in whom the new outlook began to express itself strongly. He was striving towards the liberation of thought and judgment which would be necessary for the future Soul Age. Until the dawn of the Consciousness Soul Age, thinking was guided by the doctrines of the great Philosophers of antiquity and Church authority. Ideas which were not based on these authorities were condemned, sometimes punishable by death. Because of this 'in Bacon's time science had to develop separately from Initiation Wisdom which remained esoteric, or veiled in imagery and Hermetic symbol, like much of Bacon's more occult writing; Steiner was one of those who had the mission to bring the wisdom into the open and into a language that all can understand.'[6]

Rudolf Steiner has described Francis Bacon as the inaugurator of the modern age, and by the time Steiner was born and during his formative years this was well on its way. Steiner has also spoken of how the time had to come for the free and personal use of Intelligence, and the freedom of the human Will. For today's consciousness the original instinctive vision that penetrated to the spiritual world had to disappear. Enforcing this was Francis Bacon's mission at the dawn of the Consciousness Soul Age. Nearly four hundred years later Rudolf Steiner indicated that, with the close of the nineteenth century, the age that had opened up the use of human intelligence and free will had run its course. He spoke of how we are now entering upon an age when humanity would regain access to the spiritual world by transforming those very thought-processes which had been opened up through our emancipation from the old, fading belief-systems.

The following statement made by Selma Lagerlof, a twentieth-century Nobel Prizewinner, carries the impulse begun by Francis Bacon and developed by Rudolf Steiner to a higher level:

> It is not for our age to offer a religion which is full of unsubstantiated miracles; rather should religion be a science susceptible of proof, it is no longer a question of believing but of knowing. A further doctrine is that it is possible to attain knowledge of the spiritual world by firm, conscious, systematic thought. A man should not sit like a mystic wrapped in dreams but should exert his intellectual powers to the full in an endeavour to see the world that is hidden from us.

Footnotes

[1] John Waterman *Baconiana* (Journal of the Francis Bacon Society. Founded 1886. Vol LI.No. 168)

[2] Rudolf Steiner. *The Story of My Life*, Chapter 10. Page 115.

[3] Rudolf Steiner. *Theosophy*. Page 83. Anthroposophic Press NY 1994

[4] Margarete and Erich Kirchner-Bockholt. *Rudolf Steiner's Mission and Ita Wegman*. p. 61. Rudolf Steiner Press, London 1977.

[5] John Waterman, *Baconiana* (Vol LI.No. 168)

[6] James North. Council Member of the Francis Bacon Society. In correspondence

[7] Selma Lagerlof, 'Endorsements for Spiritual Science as an Approach to Bible Studies', http://spiritualsciencebiblestudies.org/endorsements.html

THE CYCLE OF RE-SYNTHESIS

Tim Wyatt

EXAMINING Sir Francis Bacon's life and works, we clearly see the genius of a far-sighted polymath yet from a twenty-first century perspective we are also confronted with something of a paradox. On the one hand we have an individual profoundly influenced by medieval magic and cabala[1] and a committed exponent of alchemy (though deeply critical of some alchemists and their methods). On the other, we have an arch-pioneer of empirical rationalism, who, basing his conclusions on the observation of external things, founded and popularized deductive scientific methodology[2] and thereby laid the bedrock of the scientific revolution which was to follow.

We have in Bacon a visionary and a conduit between the Middle Ages and the Seventeenth Century, whose radical synthesis shaped and dominated scientific inquiry for subsequent centuries. We see a man inhabiting two separate worlds.

Dubbed the Father of Empiricism, Bacon enjoyed a prominent, influential and diversified career as a parliamentarian (serving as MP, Attorney

Tim Wyatt is an occult investigator who has spent decades researching esoteric subjects as well as alternative streams of thought in science, history, religion and philosophy. He has a particular interest in alchemy, the noetic sciences and symbolism. The author of many articles and books, he is a writer, playwright, broadcaster, journalist and award-winning documentary-maker with forty years' experience in all sections of the media.

He has worked as a communications consultant with government agencies, the public sector, private businesses and other organizations. A regular lecturer and speaker to a variety of groups throughout the UK, he continues to produce films with spiritual themes. He is the co-founder and editor-in-chief of the occult publishing house Nosegay Books, a member of the Theosophical Society and occasional actor.

General and Lord Chancellor) jurist and author but was plunged into disgrace when prosecuted as a major league debtor. A patron of democracy and an editor of the King James Bible, he is also widely credited as the author of William Shakespeare's plays, the pivotal influence behind secret societies and a man who faked his own death in order to carry on his work from the shadows.

Bacon's big project, the Great Instauration of Science, was 'directed towards a return to the state of Adam before the Fall, a state of pure and sinless contact with nature and knowledge of her powers'[3]. And Frances Yates, a prominent Renaissance scholar, also makes the crucial point here that 'Bacon's science is still, in part occult science', encompassing magic, astrology and alchemy.

This grand plan was conceived as a 'step-by-step restoration of paradise upon earth, but coupled with the illuminations of mankind'[4]. This attempt to understand the universe was based on the great truth and law of love and would increase cycle by cycle.

> ...the Great Instauration concerns the acquisition of *all* knowledge (Bacon's stated goal), for entirely philanthropic or charitable purposes, and therefore includes knowledge of the human psyche and human ethics as well as knowledge of the nature and operations of divinity within all manifest life, physical and metaphysical. All too often Bacon is called materialistic and utilitarian (in the materialistic sense), which is a travesty of the truth...[5]

From the modern perspective Bacon's role is somewhat ambiguous and remains cluttered with elements of controversy. The modern Rosicrucian movement AMORC (Ancient & Mystical Order *Rosae Crucis*) openly claims that Bacon revived the order in Germany with the publication between 1614 and 1616 of the three Rosicrucian manifestos, *Fama Fraternitatis*, *Confessio Fraternitatis* and *The Chemical Wedding of Christian Rosenkreutz*.[6] Bacon's posthumously published utopian fantasy *New Atlantis* (1627) is also widely recognized as being a rich repository of Rosicrucian ideas and ideals.

The German Rosicrucian tracts, which precipitated a flap across Europe, are normally attributed to Johann Valentin Andreae, a Lutheran pastor and mystic from Würtemberg. But according to Manly P. Hall and others they were in fact crafted by Bacon. Hall suggests that Andreae may well have permitted his name to be used by Bacon as pseudonym for these tracts.[7] He asserts that not only was Bacon a Rosicrucian but *the* Rosicrucian – and therefore a pivotal and influential figure in the subsequent rise of Freemasonry.[8]

Moreover, Hall is among a large and vocal group which also attributes the authorship of William Shakespeare's plays to Bacon and claims that he incorporated a wide range of Rosicrucian ideas into the texts.

Sir Francis Bacon knew the true secret of Masonic origin and there is reason to suspect that he concealed this knowledge in cipher and cryptogram. Bacon is not to be regarded solely as a man but rather as the focal point between an invisible institution and a world which was never able to distinguish between the messenger and the message which he promulgated.[9]

Sir Francis Bacon was a link in that great chain of minds which has perpetuated the secret doctrine of antiquity from its beginning. This secret doctrine is concealed in his cryptic writings.[10]

Hall subscribes to another persistent rumour about Bacon, namely that he faked his own demise in 1626. Officially Bacon caught pneumonia while scientifically testing whether cold could preserve foodstuffs, by stuffing a chicken with snow. But Hall asserts that Bacon underwent a 'philosophic' rather than physical death. 'He feigned death and passed over into Germany, there to guide the destinies of his philosophic and political fraternity for nearly twenty-five years before his actual demise.'[11]

Hall also believes that Bacon was of the same status as that other death-defying man about town with Rosicrucian and Freemasonic inclinations, the Comte de St-Germain. These two individuals 'are the two greatest emissaries sent into the world by the Secret Brotherhood in the last thousand years.'[12] And he further asserts: 'The cryptic writings of Francis Bacon constitute one of the most powerful tangible elements in the mysteries of transcendentalism and symbolic philosophy.'[13]

Other writers highlight the fact that Bacon's ideas actually pre-date the publication of the Rosicrucian manifestos especially those contained in his seminal *The Advancement of Learning* (1605). Some highlight the paradoxical and perhaps unsavoury aspects of Bacon's character.

To modern eyes, Bacon presents something of a sinister figure. In his public life, he pursued a policy of ruthless opportunism, gaining a number of important posts and rising to the peerage as Lord Verulam and then Viscount St Albans. His fall came when, as Lord Chancellor, he was convicted of taking bribes and was banished from Parliament and the court.[14]

The irony is that despite being the great architect of clandestine cabals with a deep-seated fascination with codes and ciphers, Bacon actually deprecated secrecy in scientific methods. Although interested in many aspect of alchemy, he was especially vitriolic about the 'long tradition of the alchemists of concealing their processes in incomprehensible symbols.'[15]

Equally, Bacon disapproved of 'the pride and presumption of the Renaissance magus' and issued potent warnings particularly against the Luther of Modern Medicine, Paracelsus, who was himself a prophet for the Rosicrucian system.[16]

In Bacon, then, we have a number of intriguing and conflicting influences. We have a cutting-edge thinker and reformer who craved democracy, enlightenment and a return to pristine purity. But we also have a man who created the routines of rationalistic and deterministic science, whose key paradigms and methods have moulded and reinforced the almost exclusively materialistic perspective of reality in the West for more than three centuries. As we shall explore later, it is only in recent decades that a more non-physical perspective has filtered into the laboratory, yet these ideas have only a tenuous hold in much of the wider scientific community.

This still novel non-materialistic approach to explaining the make-up of the universe followed the re-emergence of portions of the ancient wisdom in the last quarter of the nineteenth century. This was under the aegis of the Theosophical Society, formed in 1875 in the United States by Helena Petrovna Blavatsky, Colonel Henry S. Olcott and William Q. Judge. Theosophy's aim was to reconnect humanity to its divine origins in a world hurtling more and more rapidly towards materialism. Scepticism and materialism were its twin enemies. The true relationship between spirit and matter as a unity rather than a duality was at the core of the age-old wisdom elaborated by Blavatsky. In her monumental and often impenetrable magnum opus *The Secret Doctrine* (1888) she leaves us in little doubt that when it comes to materialism Bacon is clearly guilty:

Bacon was one of the first to strike the keynote of materialism, not only by his inductive method (renovated from ill-digested Aristotle), but by the general tenor of his writings.'[17]

Quoting from his essay *Of Truth,* she accuses him of inverting the order of mental evolution when he claims that 'the first creature of God in the works of his days, was the light of the sense; the last, was the light of reason; and his Sabbath work ever since, is the illumination of his Spirit.'

Blavatsky's life is in many ways even more fascinating and convoluted than Bacon's. Like Bacon she was a synthesizer of knowledge. After a lifetime of wandering across four continents, imbibing the lost wisdom from sages and adepts along the way, Blavatsky garnered a treasure-trove of occult knowledge from almost innumerable sources. She not only revived but subsequently globalised the ancient knowledge once the preserve of the Mystery Schools of old. Her resolute opposition to materialism was the unshakeable belief that this was the principal obstacle to mankind's spiritual evolution. For this reason she heaps scorn on most of the scientists and philosophers of her day who embraced purely mechanistic models of the universe.

> Materialism and skepticism are the evils that must remain in the world as long as man has not quitted his present gross form to don the one he had during the first and second races of this Round. Unless scepticism and our present natural ignorance are equilibrated by intuition and a natural spirituality, every being afflicted with such feelings will see in himself no better than a bundle of flesh, bones and muscles, with an empty garret inside him which serves the purpose of storing his sensations and feelings.[18]

Theosophy, derived from the Greek *theo* (divine) and *sophia* (wisdom), was nothing new, although it had largely languished for fifteen centuries since the final pockets of neo-Platonism had been intellectually, politically and spiritually eliminated. Blavatsky argued repeatedly that all religions from Anglicanism to Zoroastrianism, despite their outward garb and inner creeds, had at their esoteric core the same archaic knowledge based on spiritual principles and universal, immutable laws. Sectarianism, doctrinal selectivity and retreats into ritual and ecclesiastical politics had, she believed, caused catastrophic distortions to the original teachings, leaving them largely unrecognizable in their exoteric forms at least.

Strip away the detritus of history and convention, argued Blavatsky, and all religions shared the same key principles based on universal laws now largely eschewed by both science, philosophy and religion. Theosophy's continuing mission has been to oversee a reintegration and re-synthesis of these three now separate disciplines. Theosophy's over-riding truths are that there is no such thing as dead matter or empty space; and that everything is an aspect of the One Life, although the prevailing illusion is that we are separated.

Another theosophical keystone is that evolution proceeds in an orderly fashion through cycles based on a divine plan. These cycles and sub-cycles, based mainly on a septenary (sevenfold) principle, affect humanity and all other departments of nature as they evolve over vast aeons of time. Everything from atoms and galaxies to rocks and human beings proceed through the same inevitable cycle of birth, growth, maturity, decay, death and re-birth. Underpinning, regulating and harmonizing this regular periodicity is the unbreakable principle of cause and effect, underscored by the laws of karma and reincarnation.

If we examine Bacon's place in history and the cycles preceding and succeeding him, we see that his life coincides with not only the wider dissemination of knowledge, but its increasing atomization and alienation via increased specialization. Enthusiasm for *The Advancement of Learning* and the Great Instauration of Science inevitably involved previously entwined modes of thought being separated into an increasing number of distinct and disconnected streams. For the first time religion, science and philosophy were jettisoned into their own unique orbits without any of their previous connectedness or coherence.

Four centuries before Bacon we witness another upsurge in the rescue and dissemination of knowledge, as Islamic and Arab scholars dusted down and revivified the half-forgotten scientific, technological and mathematical traditions emanating from the mighty civilizations of Egypt, Greece and Rome. They spearheaded a renaissance of knowledge - and especially in abstruse areas such as the manipulation of matter under the guise of alchemy. Although involving some areas of specialization, this synthesis was less divisive than the trends appearing in Bacon's time.

New technologies for metal-working, glass-making and chemical operations spread from the Islamic strongholds of Spain. Perhaps the most influential of these Arab technologists, a man who was both a chemist and alchemist, was Jabir Ibn Hayyan, who lived in the eighth century AD. A pupil of the Islamic master Imam Jaffar, he outlined the preparation of acids and other chemical substances unknown to Western science at that time. Unsurprisingly some Western scholars have gone to some lengths to try and prove that his alchemical works especially were forgeries.[19] Also known in the West as Geber, it is from his name that we derive the word jibberish.

Translations of Jabir's work became hugely popular across Europe, where in the centuries before Bacon alchemy developed into an obsession and was practised on an almost industrial scale. Cities like Prague hosted ten thousand bearded practitioners or 'puffers' tending their furnaces for years on end in the usually forlorn hope of creating the Philosopher's Stone to transmute base metals into gold or producing an Elixir of Life to temporarily prolong physical life.

The early medieval period was characterized by other great advancements in metallurgy, warfare and especially architecture. The legendary Knights Templar, founded in 1118, intermingled freely with Islamic scholars and no doubt made significant discoveries of their own as they spent years hacking through the subterranean remains of Solomon's Temple. As their knowledge, finances and influence mounted, the Templars were one of the mainsprings behind a frenzy of cathedral building. Starting in twelfth century France they constructed a hundred gravity-defying structures with their distinctive Arab-inspired ogival (pointed) arches and flying buttresses appeared in a century. These included such spectacular structures as Notre Dame de Chartres, described as 'a crucible for the transformation of humanity'.[20] The architecture of such structures was described by Goethe as 'frozen music'. It was intimately based on sacred geometry in which the use of phi or the golden section (1:1.618) created harmony and proportion.[21]

Four and a half centuries after Bacon's birth, we have witnessed a knowledge 'big bang' unfold and intensify throughout the twentieth century as the telephone, radio, TV, the internet and rapidly emerging digital technologies have interpenetrated all aspects of human activity and now control large swathes of it. This global connectivity has been accompanied by unprecedented mass migrations stimulated by the exponential growth of personal travel on land, sea and air. It is widely seen as the greatest transmission of knowledge in recorded history. Just as the printing press led to a knowledge explosion in the years before Bacon, so did mass communications in the twentieth century.

Information often gets degraded and distorted during its transmission, almost as if it runs out of the very energy required to sustain itself. Look at how history and religions rapidly become disfigured and denuded of truth. Thus the pure and original occult wisdom was the preserve of a few initiates in Mystery Schools. That esoteric wisdom went underground and became downgraded into exoteric knowledge. Over time the knowledge is itself diluted and transformed into mere information. The technologies of the past two decades have tended to further undermine that information and shred it into what you might call digi-trash, diluted to homeopathic levels and concealed in a fizzing miasma of zeros and ones.

There appears to be a mysterious and paradoxical communications paradigm in which the quality of communication is inversely proportional to the hardware available to transmit it. In other words, more usually means less. As the influential commentator Marshall McLuhan declared in the 1960s, the means influence the very communication itself and therefore 'the medium is the message'.[22]

There is no doubt that wisdom lurks in hidden crannies among the ephemeral celebrity gossip and social networking banalia. And despite this headlong plunge into an information smog of trivia, there is a widespread belief that human consciousness is evolving at an accelerated rate.

Over the past century countless commentators from second generation Theosophists to bankable New Age gurus have confidently and consistently predicted this sudden elevation of the human mind. The view that this expansion of consciousness is driven by increasingly embracing spiritual values such as co-operation, service and tolerance has gained traction, along with an acceptance that we are spiritual beings in physical bodies on a human journey and not the reverse.

At present the evidence for this rise of spirit and the accompanying demise of materialism and all its associated baggage of greed, exploitation, inequality, resource depletion, environmental degradation and militant atheism would appear to be extremely flimsy if not non-existent. Financial and economic shake-downs, man-made natural disasters and perma-war show a world in turmoil with itself – heavily alienated by incestuous economics, culture, belief and religion despite all its physical connectivity.

The outward signs are that there is no stirring of a spiritual revolution except amongst tiny, disparate pockets of individuals who are fundamentally ignored by the mainstream.

Religions are increasingly irrelevant to many. The Catholic Church faces its biggest crisis since the Reformation, mired down in doctrinal conservatism and multiple child abuse scandals. Many of those who do choose to remain loyal to religions veer towards sectarianism at best and zealous fundamentalism at worst. Science, too, remains heavily materialistic and deterministic with British biologist Richard Dawkins acting as atheist-in-chief and even Stephen Hawking finally retreating to the view that divinity plays no part in celestial mechanics or explaining the universe's origins.

The trail-blazers of quantum physics such as Niels Bohr and Max Planck strained the materialistic confines of conventional science by redefining the constitution of matter and the workings of the universe. They hypothesized that matter is energy and their successors have gone further in suggesting that energy *is* consciousness.

More recently, other maverick investigators from the scientific community have risked ridicule and professional suicide to extend non-physical explanations of mind and cosmos. The British biologist Rupert Sheldrake's controversial work has centred on the idea of 'morphic fields' of collective information – like the collective unconscious of renowned psychiatrist Carl Jung or the notion of Akashic Records found in the Vedas. These fields have 'morphic resonance' caused by feedback loops from the units in that field, be they human or animal behaviour, cultural and social systems or mental activity.[23]

Earlier Sheldrake proposed the idea of 'formative causation' in which biological phenomena especially become more probable the more often they occur, so that growth and behaviour are patterned by previous events.[24] His ideas caused such outrage in some quarters that he was stabbed during a lecture in the US in 2008.

Scientist Charles Tart, a student of meditation, Gurdjieff and Buddhism, has been at the forefront of psychic research and the extension of the so-called noetic sciences. His primary goal has been to bridge the gap between scientific and spiritual communities along with an integration of Eastern and Western approaches.[25]

David Bohm, widely regarded as one of the best quantum physicists of all time, believed it was necessary to get beyond conventional barriers:

In the enfolded [or implicate] order, space and time are no longer the dominant factors determining the relationships of dependence or independence of different elements. Rather, an entirely different sort of basic connection of elements is possible, from which our ordinary notions of space and time, along with those of separately existent material particles, are abstracted as forms derived from the deeper order. These ordinary notions in fact appear in what is called the 'explicate' or 'unfolded' order, which is a special and distinguished form contained within the general totality of all the implicate orders.[26]

Science has been quick to dismiss the ideas of Bohm and his associates as merely the quack superstitious of pseudo-science but there is increased interest in non-materialistic explanations – especially outside the scientific community itself. And let us not forget that wholesale social, intellectual and political change can happen very quickly indeed, often with little or no prior warning. Who would have predicted that such solid ideological symbols as the Berlin Wall or the Iron Curtain would literally crumble and gurgle towards instant entropy almost overnight? Who is to say that the materialistic model itself is not similarly endangered? There is often no external evidence for a pending catastrophic upheaval until it becomes reality.

We see, then, how prevailing realities and preconceptions can unexpectedly morph out of all recognition. The universal laws of periodicity, polarity and rhythm dictate that this must be the case. The most famous Hermetic axiom 'As above so below, as below so above' tells us that the entire universe is reflected in the most miniscule portion of matter. For this reason most of the world's older religions tell us that if we wish to change the world then we must first change ourselves. Indeed this is the only way of achieving this goal. This is entirely contrary to materialistic thinking because it is based on non-physical, spiritual principles.

Yet what kind of critical mass of individuals do you need to achieve a post-materialist mentality? Surprisingly few, according to devotees of the Transcendental Meditation movement who believe it is the square root of one per cent of the population. In a world of seven billion people this comes down to a little over eight thousand people, the population of a very small town.

Although the Theosophical Society was outwardly created by Blavatsky, Judge and Olcott, it had esoteric origins. Blavatsky consistently claimed it had been formed at the behest of two members of the hidden spiritual hierarchy known as the Great White Brotherhood. The real architects were Masters of Wisdom called Morya (M) and Koot Humi (KH), the latter of whom boldly pronounced: 'Theosophy is the one hope for the future of humanity'.

Despite ongoing squabbles, schisms and splits in the movement, theosophical ideas themselves appear to be undergoing something of a renaissance and enjoying fresh popularity in the twenty-first century, chiming closely as they do with many of the sentiments of the multiplicity of New Age movements which have appeared since the 1960s.

In a recent communication to members, the national president of the English Section of the Theosophical Society Eric McGough highlighted the existence of fresh initiatives to raise the level of spiritual energy in human affairs, a project spearheaded by small but not insignificant groups of individuals. Access to this current was via meditation.

'The Masters have called for this and many other groups have already responded, each in its own unique way. The hierarchy maintain a network of spiritual energy surrounding the globe; like a web of light (with Shambala at its heart). You can imagine this if you close your eyes and think about it. It is made up of threads of mental and spiritual energy, which over time has become joined without a break like a fine mesh. The World Wide Web is a more general version at the physical level, although unlike the hierarchy's web its use is open to corruption.'[27]

For decades since the 1960s there has been febrile anticipation of change via a greater unfolding of spiritual awareness. Predictions of millennial meltdown and fiery Armageddon late last century proved as insubstantial as end-of-the-world fantasies usually do. The ending of the Mayan calendar in 2012 and the painful 150 year transition from the Age of Pisces into the Age of Aquarius – and what these may mean – have percolated into popular culture laced with both optimism and apocalypse.

Given the state of the world, many default to a pessimistic position of pure doom, believing that the end of these cycles will also spell the end of everything. A less entrenched view is that this particular cycle, whatever it is, holds a more positive outcome for humanity: an awakening of spiritual consciousness in greater numbers of people. And as we have seen, it doesn't take many.

Another of Theosophy's chief aspirations is that this awakening will stimulate a synthesis – indeed a re-synthesis – of science, religion and philosophy into a coherent whole in which non-materialistic spiritual science and a wisdom-religion based on the timeless knowledge will be unified in harmonious diversity. It may well be that a more Gnostic approach emerges, in which individuals seek direct knowledge of divine godhead via their awakened higher selves – with no intermediary priest-caste, religious or scientific, involved. Less clear than the aspiration towards a fresh convergence is the time-scale involved. Given the present capacities of human's for spiritual ascent, even optimists say it may be generations – or another cycle indeed – before this is achieved.

However, Theosophy's reviver-in-chief conveyed a strong sense of urgency more than a century ago.

But what has the new cycle in store for humanity? Will it be merely a continuation of the present, only in darker and more terrible colours? Or shall a new day dawn for mankind, a day of pure sunlight, of truth, of charity, of true happiness for all? If Theosophy prevailing in the struggle, its all-embracing philosophy strikes deep root into the minds and hearts of men, of its doctrines of Reincarnation and Karma, in other words, of Hope and Responsibility, find a home in the lives of the new generations – then, indeed, will dawn the day of joy and gladness for all who now suffer and are outcast.

For real Theosophy is ALTRUISM, and we cannot repeat it too often. It is brotherly love, mutual help, unswerving devotion to Truth. If once men do but realize that in these alone can true happiness be found, and never in wealth, possessions, or any selfish gratification, then the dark clouds will roll away, and a new humanity will be born on earth. Then, the GOLDEN AGE will be there, indeed. But if not, then the storm will burst, and our boasted western civilization and enlightenment will sink in such a sea of horror that its parallel History has never yet recorded.[28]

Footnotes

[1] Frances A. Yates, *The Rosicrucian Enlightenment*, London, Routledge Classics, 2002, p. 158.

[2] Manly P. Hall, *The Secret Teachings of All Ages*, New York, Tarcher/Penguin,

2003, p. 32.

[3] Yates, *The Rosicrucian Enlightenment*, p. 158.

[4] Peter Dawkins, 1999, quoted on the Francis Bacon Research Trust website http://www.fbrt.org.uk

[5] *Ibid*.

[6] *Rosicrucian Questions and Answers*, San José, The Rosicrucian Press Ltd, 4th ed., 1947, pp. 120-121.

[7] Hall, *Secret Teachings*, p. 461.

[8] *Ibid*, pp. 240 and 461.

[9] *Ibid*, p. 548.

[10] *Ibid*, p. 549.

[11] Manly P. Hall, *Lectures on Ancient Philosophy,* New York, Tarcher/Penguin, 2005, p. 444.

[12] Hall, *Secret Teachings*, p. 657.

[13] Ibid, p. 558.

[14] Christopher McIntosh, *The Rosicrucians*, San Francisco, Weiser Books, 1997, p.39.

[15] Yates, *The Rosicrucian Enlightenment*, p. 159.

[16] Ibid, p. 158

[17] H. P. Blavatsky, *The Secret Doctrine*, Adyar, The Theosophical Publishing House, 7th. ed., 1979, Vol. I, p.481.

[18] Ibid, p. 480.

[19] Jacques Sadoul, *Alchemists & Gold*, London, Neville Spearman, 1972, pp. 27–28.

[20] M. Louis Charpentier, *Les Mystères de la Cathédrale de Chartres*, Paris, Robert Lafont, 1966.

[21] Scott Olsen, *The Golden Section*, Glastonbury, Wooden Books, 2006, pp. 34–35

[22] Marshall McLuhan, *Understanding Media*, London, Abacus Books, 1973, p. 15.

[23] Rupert Sheldrake, *The Presence of the Past: morphic resonance and the habits of nature*, New York, NY: Times Books, 1988, p. 112.

[24] Rupert Sheldrake, *A New Science of Life: the hypothesis of formative causation*, Los Angeles, CA: J.P. Tarcher, 1981

[25] Charles H. Tart, *The End of Materialism: How Evidence of the Paranormal Is Bringing Science and Spirit Together*, NHP, with the Institute of Noetic Sciences, 2009.

[26] David Bohm, *Wholeness and the Implicate Order*, London, Routledge, 1980, p. xv.

[27] Eric McGough, *Time to Meditate*, communication to members of the Theosophical Society, July 2010.

[28] H. P. Blavatsky, *This Cycle and The Next*, Lucifer magazine, May 1889, Vol. 4, pp. 177–188.

THE OAK ISLAND MYSTERY, SIR FRANCIS BACON AND THE NEW WORLD

Mark Finnan

O AK ISLAND, which lies just off the south-east shore of Nova Scotia, about one hour's drive south of Halifax, was once described by Mendel Peterson, a former Curator of Historic Archaeology at the Smithsonian Institute in Washington, D.C., as being 'one of the most fascinating archaeological sites in the New World dating after the arrival of the Europeans. It could possibly have great historical significance'.

A series of related circumstances and auspicious coincidences led to my living close to Oak Island and to researching the possible connection between the life of Sir Francis Bacon, the esoteric movements and secret societies of his time and what is considered to be North America's greatest unsolved mystery and the longest treasure hunt in history.

In the process it became clear to me that the timeless quest for enlightenment and a more conscious realization of the connection between the spiritual and material worlds had found its way across the Atlantic during

Author, actor and playwright, Mark Finnan has written and lectured about the sacred significance of Masonic and Rosicrucian symbolism and universal themes found in mythology and world religions. His articles have covered such topics as the inner meaning of the quest for the Holy Grail, the purpose of dreams and the transcendental nature of creativity. His work has been presented on A&E and Vision TV in Canada and the U.S. as well as on German television.

A lifelong member of the Association for Research and Enlightenment, he has researched and written about the work of Edgar Cayce, particularly as it relates to personal growth and spiritual development. He was a co-founder of the Shelter Valley Centre, an holistic education and retreat centre in southern Ontario. He lives in Peterborough, Ontario, Canada and is an avid organic gardener and supporter of community-based agriculture. www.markfinnan.com.

the early years of the colonization of North America. There was already evidence that the Hermetic influence that infused the alchemical, cabalist and gnostic mindset found in some quarters during Bacon's time had been transplanted to the New World during the seventeenth and eighteenth centuries by way of secretive fraternities such as Freemasonry. Its inherent idealism and notions regarding the perfectibility of man had helped foster those personal, political and religious freedoms that evolved in North America.

Enthralled by the mystery, I decided to try to discover the origin and purpose of the unusual discoveries made on the island; a manmade deep shaft believed to contain chests and a vault, an extensive and effective water trap system and a cryptic message written on stone found at the ninety-foot level. Several sacred symbols carved onto rocks and a megalithic cross of cone-shaped boulders were also found on the island's surface. It was a task that absorbed most of my time, attention and financial resources for the best part of three years. It resulted in a book *Oak Island Secrets* (Formac Publishing, Halifax N.S., Canada, 2002) and a television documentary. More significantly, for me at least, it took on the nature of a quest that led to some illuminating insights and understandings.

Once, while contemplating the nature and purpose of the Oak Island mystery and Bacon's possible connection to it, I had an insightful visionary experience straight out of his *New Atlantis* allegory. It was suggestive of the marriage of science and Christian mysticism and the interflow of life force from the spiritual to the physical. It seemed that in my focused attention on the Oak Island mystery and its potential significance I had made an attunement to the source of a treasure far more valuable than the pirates' gold some believed lay buried on the small island.

When I arrived in Nova Scotia in the fall of 1992 to spend some time reworking a feature film script I had no prearranged accommodation. After a few nights in a downtown Halifax hotel I started to look for somewhere more suitable, preferably by the ocean. Through a local contact I recalled meeting at an Association for Research and Enlightenment conference in upper New York State some months earlier, I had the good fortune to be able to rent a shoreline cottage in picturesque Mahone Bay. Cresting a hill that gave me my first panoramic view of the area I stopped the car, experiencing an inexplicable but comforting feeling of *déjà vu*. The front porch of my cottage was just a short walk from the water's edge and offered an expansive view of the bay with its many small islands. I was soon to learn that the nearest of these was the privately-owned Oak Island, about which I knew absolutely nothing at that time.

However, during the next two to three years I would get to visit the island several times, observing certain sites, viewing artefacts and conversing with the three individuals still involved in the treasure hunt. I would spend a good deal of time in historical research, focused primarily on the interests and pursuits of Sir Francis Bacon, whose stated purpose had been to 'lay more firmly the foundations and extend more widely the limits of the power and greatness of man'. I would also explore the origins, aims and activities of Freemasonry and the Rosicrucian movement and the influence of both in the colonization of North America. Finally, I would write a book that suggested the possibility of a connection between the alchemical, philosophical and scientific renaissance in Elizabethan and Jacobean England and the underground workings and sacred symbolism found on Oak Island. None of these had been my intention on first arriving in Nova Scotia.

About a month earlier I had spent a week in Norfolk, Virginia, where I had been the guest of American playwright Paula Fitzgerald and her art director husband Edward, both of whom I had known for a long time. My friendship with the Fitzgeralds had begun some twenty-five years earlier in Dublin, Ireland. As an aspiring young actor and playwright with a growing interest in psychology and spirituality I had been exploring aspects of Eastern mysticism such as meditation. The Fitzgeralds meanwhile had come from the U.S. and established the Centre for Living Research. It ran a series of public lectures on a variety of metaphysical topics at the Dublin Shakespeare Society's small theatre and later at the Shelbourne Hotel.

My introduction to the centre was a talk by Edward Fitzgerald on ancient Atlantis and its relevance to us today. The centre encouraged the study of the psychic discourses of the renowned Christian seer Edgar Cayce who, apart from providing what became popularly known as 'health and life readings' had much to say about Atlantis, ancient Egypt, the mystery school tradition and the interaction between the spiritual, mental and physical worlds. He had even commented on the relevance of Masonic principles to the creation of a new order in the Western world. The centre attracted a number of people who like myself were searching for insights and answers not available from mainstream academic or religious sources.

One of the guest presenters had been the New Age visionary Sir George Trevelyan, whose profound perceptions into the unitary nature of life and of the interweaving of its divine and human elements were both informative and inspiring. His elucidation of the whole-world view contained in the Shakespeare plays revealed their underlying philosophical content and deepened my appreciation of them.

The Fitzgeralds had eventually returned to the U.S. and when I later moved to Canada we had reconnected. Paula had previously written several plays about individuals in history whose lives she believed were at times influenced by higher forces. They included *Peace Without Victory* (Woodrow Wilson) and *Nation Under God* (Abraham Lincoln). In early September 1992 she had invited me to take part in a dramatic reading of her latest play *I, Prince Tudor, Wrote Shakespeare* at the library theatre in historic Colonial Williamsburg. The central character in the play was Sir Francis Bacon and, as the play's title suggests, it dealt with the claim that he was both the unacknowledged son of Queen Elizabeth I and the secret author of the Shakespeare plays.

Bacon's role in this historical drama is that of a visionary philosopher toiling in a time of religious and political tensions at home, militant threats from abroad, academic orthodoxy and a country for the most part ignorant of the knowledge required to progress. Bacon is presented as a man not only of much learning but also as an enlightened idealist. He devotes time to writing the plays as a means of serving his fellow man by eloquently and entertainingly depicting life's innate laws at work in human affairs. His hope is that by 'holding the mirror up to nature' in this way, others might become more aware of the knowledge and understanding he considered so necessary for the betterment of humankind. His plays are presented publicly with the willing and well rewarded co-operation of William Shakespeare, actor and manager with the theatre company known as Lord Chamberlain's Men. For certain legitimate reasons at the time the works are intentionally identified as having been written by Shakespeare.

While it is not my intention here to dwell on the topic, the theory that Bacon himself or with others may have written the plays and solicited Shakespeare's help in producing them, has merit. The facts that the plays possess universal and timeless narratives and that they creatively acknowledge the existence of an innate moral law, in addition to in-depth knowledge of a whole range of subjects, make it all the more plausible that they were written by or under the guidance of an individual who was well aware of the multidimensional nature of life, of man's conflicted psyche and his propensity for good or ill depending on his use of free will within the context of a divine creation. The theatre, which was egalitarian in its accessibility and had a history of informing and inspiring going back to ancient times, was an ideal outlet for a man of Bacon's abilities, background and beliefs. In fact he is on record as having viewed the theatre as an effective means of moral education. In *De Augmentis Scientiarum,* an addition to his *Advancement of Learning* and published less than three years before his death in April 1626, he writes

> Dramatic poesy, which has the theatre for its world, would be of excellent use, if well directed. Or the stage is capable of no small influence both of discipline and of corruption. Now of corruption in this kind we have enough; but the discipline has in our times been plainly neglected. And though in modern states play acting is esteemed but as a toy, except when it is too satirical and biting; yet among the ancients it was used as a means of educating men's minds to virtue. Nay, it has been regarded by learned men and great philosophers as a kind of musician's bow by which men's minds might be played upon.

Before leaving the Norfolk home in September 1992, I happened to mention that I was intending to go to Nova Scotia to work on a film script. Fitzgerald immediately recalled having read about an island somewhere off the east coast of Canada that was said to contain a deeply-buried vault which might hold, among other things, the missing original manuscripts of the Shakespeare plays and perhaps other historic documents. Although aware that there had been an attempt to find a similar vault in the grounds of Bruton parish church in Colonial Williamsburg, first by Marie Bauer Hall, later the wife of the remarkable Manly Palmer Hall, and more recently by a group of New Age advocates from New Mexico, I gave the matter no further thought until I discovered, a couple of weeks later, that I was actually living within view and reach of the island Fitzgerald had mentioned. Naturally I was somewhat intrigued by this coincidental turn of events.

After settling in to what was to be my temporary home for a few months and setting to work on my film script, I was introduced to the details of the Oak Island mystery by a few shoreline neighbours who invited me to a coffee morning get-together. On hearing I was a writer they immediately assumed I was there for one reason only and insisted on giving me some articles and a book about Oak Island. That evening, after reading through the various magazine and newspaper articles, my interest was aroused enough for me to pick up the book. The story it told was so amazing that I finished the read in one late night sitting. The many unusual discoveries on the island and the almost two-hundred-year-long treasure hunt made for an intriguing historical mystery. More so, because radio-carbon dating of organic material and artefacts indicated that extensive work had taken place on the island sometime between the mid-sixteenth and mid-seventeenth centuries.

The fact that one theory about the origin and nature of the still elusive treasure involved Francis Bacon, whose alleged secretive life I had just recently helped give dramatic expression to on stage, made the mystery all the more immediate and compelling. I was also more than a little captivated by the publisher's comment on the jacket of the book, the first detailed account of the Oak Island treasure hunt. It suggested that since the author, Reginald Harris, was a past Grand Master of Nova Scotia Masons and intimately connected to the treasure hunt for many years, the whole business might have a Masonic connection. The possible involvement of both Francis Bacon and Freemasonry in a treasure-hiding enterprise that, according to the evidence, required the work of many men for an extensive period of time and which was carried out under a blanket of strict secrecy was too enticing to ignore. In fact, given that I seemed to have been led to it, I felt somewhat compelled to explore the mystery further. I also hoped that I might come across an aspect or clue that would throw some new light on its origin and purpose.

For the benefit of those reading this who know little or nothing about the Oak Island mystery, here is a brief synopsis of the story. In the early summer of 1795 three young men from the mainland rowed out to the nearby island. They began exploring what one of them had earlier discovered, a circular indentation in the ground in a clearing in the oak- tree-covered east end of the island. Their digging opened up a seven-foot-wide perpendicular shaft which had been filled in and covered over just below the surface with a layer of flat stones. After removing ten feet of earthen fill they found a floor of solid oak logs embedded into the side of the shaft.

On removing these, they encountered ten more feet of fill, beneath which was another solid barrier of oak logs. At this stage they abandoned their digging for want of extra hands. They in-filled the shaft and left the island. Assuming they did try to interest others in their discovery, for whatever reason they were unable to get the help needed. However, one of the young men involved in the discovery, John Smith, soon purchased the lot containing the shaft and several other adjoining lots as well.

Historical records relate that it was 1804 before the first organized and concerted effort was made to explore the shaft further. Involving a small group of business associates and brother Masons, it uncovered additional platforms down to the ninety-foot level. One was overlaid with a layer of strangely marked stones. Another was covered with blue, putty-like clay. Still another had charcoal spread on top. Quantities of coconut fibre were also found. Then, on the platform at the ninety-foot level, workmen came across an unusual stone slab containing two lines of cryptic writing, comprised of a series of triangles, circles, rectangles and dots with other lines intersecting and joining at right angles. While the discovery of this cryptic message, which apparently nobody could decipher, must have reassured these early treasure hunters that a valuable treasure lay further below, their hope of locating it was dashed on discovering one morning that water had filled the shaft to thirty feet from the surface. Successive attempts to date, by many others, some utilizing the best drilling and engineering expertise of the day, have also failed to reach the treasure, owing primarily to a highly-effective gravity-fed water trap system that repeatedly channels sea water from the Atlantic Ocean, five hundred feet away, into the shaft. Repeated attempts at pumping the shaft dry and preventing water from entering have been unsuccessful, owing to the fact that there is more than one flood tunnel.

Additional discoveries were made during drilling operations deeper in the waterlogged shaft. Splinters from a large wooden chest or box and three small links of a gold chain, as well as a piece of parchment extracted from what was believed to be a concrete-like vault, fuelled speculation that the treasure was much more than pirates' booty and attracted a succession of determined treasure hunters. One group eventually came across evidence of a manmade tunnel even further down, below the bedrock.

A number of seemingly related discoveries were made at various other locations on the surface of the island. A ten-foot equilateral triangle comprised of large beach stones with a cross incised on its capstone pointed in the direction of the shaft. Geometric markings of a sacred nature and the capital letter G were found cut into large boulders. A man-worked heart-shaped stone was also found. Perhaps the most dramatic discovery was a megalithic stone cross, made up of cone-shaped boulders each weighing about ten tons and spread out over a large area. Finally a small underwater camera sent down some two hundred and thirty feet in a shaft sunk north-east of the original produced images which, although quite grainy, suggested there were additional man-worked tunnels, tools and even another chest-like object in a cavern below the bedrock.

Lack of sufficient funding for what had become a very expensive and extensive operation requiring state of the art equipment caused intermittent halts in the treasure hunt. Protracted differences between two treasure-hunting partners and a drawn-out court case with another had, by the time I arrived on the scene, led to a stalemate in exploration activity. It has only been in quite recent times, after an extended period of inactivity, that professional exploration work has started up again on the island.

Soon after reading about the mystery I had an intriguing dream in which I was shown the location of some treasure on the island. While perhaps nothing more than an unconscious wish-fulfillment, it prompted me to try to get permission to visit and explore the island. Refused, I decided to spend some time in additional reading and historical research. Having worked in the Canadian media but never having read or heard about the Oak Island mystery, my initial impulse was to write a magazine article, emphasizing the possible Bacon connection. A connection not so far-fetched, given that Newfoundland had already issued a Bacon postage stamp commemorating his involvement in establishing the east-coast colony.

Providentially, I learned that the library at Dalhousie University in Halifax contained one of the three largest collections in North America of works by and about Sir Francis Bacon. It became an invaluable source of information about the man, his thought and his work as author, philosopher, statesman and scientist. His belief, as expressed in his work, *The Advancement of Learning,* that man's mental ability could act as 'a mirror or glass capable of the image of the universal world and joyful to receive the impression thereof, as the eye joyeth to receive light' resonated with me. His stated desire to acquaint himself with the knowledge of God's creation through investigation and experimentation in order 'to relieve man's estate, to civilize mankind, to encourage our progress in virtue, to provide the purest and deepest of pleasures and to ensure the only immortality that man can win by his own efforts' had profound and practical implications. Such statements and others in the work seemed to me to be infused with the gnostic and cabalistic concept that humankind was capable of consciously knowing divine order and harmony through our own moral and mental exertions. Along with the contents of *Sylva Sylvarum,* in which he described specific experiments, they certainly were predictive of the many psychological and material developments that have since taken place and the ever-increasing interest in our time in the multidimensional nature of life itself.

On reading Bacon's visionary fable, *The New Atlantis,* with its depiction of a spiritually and scientifically advanced society living in harmony with universal laws, I was pleasantly surprised by its resemblance in some respects to aspects of ancient Atlantis described by the seer Edgar Cayce and the obvious influence of Plato and Rosicrucian ideals in the narrative. I found Bacon's expressed beliefs, his expansive knowledge, his nobility of purpose and his statesmanship to be those of an exceptional individual, not only living in a period in which there were currents of intellectual and spiritual regeneration, but also contributing to it out of his own commitment to humankind's timeless thrust upwards into the light of truth. Given the content of *The New Atlantis,* the influence of Masonic and Rosicrucian thought during the early years of North American settlement as well as many of the progressive developments since then, it was extremely interesting to explore the possible significance of Oak Island in the relationship between Bacon and the New World – the more so because of the obvious involvement of members of an esoteric organization in the sophisticated but highly secretive activity that had taken place on the island some four hundred years ago.

The Nova Scotia Archives proved most valuable in providing me with documentation about the first one hundred and fifty years of the treasure hunt and the people involved. Among the extensive Oak Island collection of papers, newspaper clippings, photos, etc., there was documentation by Reginald Harris, former Grand Master of Nova Scotia Masons and official historian of the treasure hunt up to the late fifties. Several of his notations about Oak Island were written on Masonic letterhead, including confirmation that at least one meeting of the principals involved in the treasure hunt during the nineteen-forties had taken place in the Masonic Grand Lodge on Barrington Street in Halifax. The collection also contained a well-worn copy of a small, privately-published book entitled *The Oak Island Enigma*. Its author, Thomas P. Leary, drawing on the conclusions of Baconian scholar Dr Burrell Ruth of Iowa, suggested that the vault believed to exist deep in the shaft likely contained the missing original manuscripts of the Shakespeare plays. Central to this theory were Bacon's experiments using mercury as a preserving agent for valuable manuscripts. A note by Harris attached to the cover of Leary's book stated that liquid mercury had been noticed on a drill bit extracted from deep in the shaft in 1937. The historical record relating to the early treasure hunt period contained the information that pieces of clay pottery discovered in a discarded pile on the island had also contained traces of mercury. These, along with an old leather shoe found in a small cove on the island's western shoreline, had been confirmed to have been of Elzabethan vintage. My archival research not only added additional material to the theory of Bacon's connection to the mystery but also started me on an investigative trail that pointed to the repeated and prolonged involvement of advanced and prominent members of the Masonic fraternity in the subsequent treasure hunt.

Following a talk I gave about my research into the Oak Island enigma at a conference at a local hotel, a senior American Mason in attendance arranged for me to gain access to the library of the Masonic Grand Lodge of Nova Scotia in Halifax. Walking into the library of the Barrington Street building with its dust-covered bookshelves packed with volumes about the nature and history of the Craft I felt predestined to find whatever information I needed. Later, after striking up a conversation with a BBC TV crew that had been granted permission to film on the island and agreeing to be interviewed by them, I also managed to gain access to it. Once again I felt the universe was conveniently providing me with the means needed to proceed – so much so that I very soon realized I was in a position and had the basis for an up-to-date and in depth book about Oak Island, one that could offer a new perspective on the mystery and an elaboration of the possible Baconian connection.

As I reviewed the various discoveries made on the island and the known history of the treasure search since the opening of the shaft in 1795 and pursued my research on Bacon and Freemasonry, certain factual details, which had either not been noticed, connected or highlighted before, became quite obvious to me. Many of the men connected with the treasure search on the island for one hundred and fifty years or more from 1804 onwards had been high-ranking Freemasons, some of them prominent public figures in politics and business affairs, especially in the U.S. The extensive list included former U.S President, Franklin D. Roosevelt; New York engineer Edwin Hamilton, one time Grand Master of the Grand Lodge of Massachusetts, who had later kept the president informed of his activity on the island; and Gilbert Hedden, wealthy mayor of Chatham, New Jersey, who had corresponded with England's King George VI, a brother Mason, about developments under his watch. The Canadians included Mel Chappell, successful Sydney Nova Scotia businessman, who had served as Grand Master of all Nova Scotia Masons, and Reginald V. Harris, Halifax lawyer and Grand Master of the Grand Lodge of Nova Scotia, head of all Masonic Knights Templar, Grand High Priest in the Royal Arch degree. Harris, who authored the first detailed book about the Oak Island mystery, had also reintroduced the *Societas Rosicruciana* to Canada in the mid-nineteen-thirties. Claiming its origins lay with the seventeenth-century German and English Rosicrucian movements, it had the father of the renowned occultist Manly P. Hall as one of its first Canadian members.

Independent research also uncovered links between some of North America's prominent early Freemasons, including Benjamin Franklin, and Nova Scotia, and by extension with Oak Island. That Masonic principles played a part in the American independence movement and especially in the creation of the U.S. constitution is well known. Naturally I wondered what part, if any, the mystery might have played in these developments.

That most of the leading investors and active participants in the treasure search wereadvanced and knowledgeable Freemasons left little doubt in my mind that some musthave eventually suspected that the island had been used as a depository for something of significance by earlier members of the fraternity. The stone markings and structures discovered were such as would have obvious meaning for anyone familiar with Masonic, Rosicrucian or Christian symbolism. The cryptic writing on the stone slab found at the ninety-foot level in the shaft in 1804, even if indecipherable by those who first came across it, was a prominent clue. Barry Fell, author of *America BC* and *Saga America*, later suggested it likely was written in a code used by Coptic Christians and could read 'if the people forget their god they will perish'. The ten-foot equilateral triangle initially found in 1897 on the south shore of the island and rediscovered in 1937 was even more telling. No other symbol is more widely diffused throughout Freemasonry than the equilateral triangle. Representing the Divine, it denotes the Great First Cause, the creator and container of all things. A circle with a dot in the centre found on a boulder segment and the letter G cut into another boulder are also prominent sacred symbols associated with Freemasonry. Then there is the large megalithic cross found on the north-east end of the island, its expansive construction involving granite boulders each weighing almost ten tons and with an arm expanse of 360 feet on either side of an 867 foot perpendicular. All of which suggested two things to me: first, that activity of an esoteric Christian nature and involving the ritual burying of a treasure of some kind had taken place on the island, and second, that those responsible intended others to know about this at some future time. The sacred symbolism did not end there, however.

The shaft or pit, with its series of barriers, strangely marked stones, layers of charcoal and blue, putty-like clay, the cryptically encoded stone slab, the evidence of chests and a vault, resembled in many ways the core content of the Masonic ritual related to the conferring of the Royal Arch Degree. Like all the other Masonic rituals, it has an initiatory aspect derived from the mystery school tradition and is intended to enlighten the individual morally and spiritually in his progress along the path to perfection. Based on an allegory associated with the rebuilding of King Solomon's Temple in Jerusalem, following the return of the Jewish people from captivity in Babylon, the Royal Arch Degree ritually re-enacts the story of three workmen finding a concealed opening beneath the rubble of the former temple. The opening leads to the discovery of a vault containing a sacred treasure, the Ark of the Covenant and the lost Master Mason's Word.

When the sacred vessel is brought to the surface and opened, it is found to contain the book of holy law, a pot containing the manna or bread God gave the Jews during their wandering in the wilderness, and finally the ever-blooming rod which Moses gave to his brother Aaron. This particular ritual, which one early ordinance suggested should be performed in a sacred space, preferably underground, was taken up by Freemasons in North America many years prior to the discoveries on Oak Island. Assuming that my observations about the ritual nature of the shaft itself were correct and given that the allegory and the parallel process enacted in the degree ceremony represent the rediscovery and reconnection with the divine source within, here was additional evidence that people knowledgeable of the nature of ancient sacred ritual had buried something of value on Oak Island. As convincing and compelling as the accumulated evidence of esoteric activity was, I still had to see how all this might have involved or been related to the life and work of Francis Bacon.

His *New Atlantis* allegory, drawing as it does on the Solomon-Temple mythology so meaningful to Freemasonry and which is resplendent with Rosicrucian concepts and idealism, was also a visionary tract that Bacon no doubt hoped would inspire those who would create a new order in the New World. It is certainly possible, given Bacon's precarious circumstances during the later years of his life and his desire to have his work known to and used by future generations, that he might have arranged to have copies of his accumulated writings and other materials secretly transferred to an appropriately designed, constructed and protected underground hiding place on the east coast of the New World, a region he already had interest in and contact with.

It did not surprise me to discover that there was ample opportunity for such a clandestine enterprise to be successfully carried out. During the reign of King James I, religious and political conflicts in England and Europe, as well as the dangers facing individuals and groups suspected of being involved with the occult or supernatural, had already motivated many individuals to leave for North America. There they hoped to pursue their more liberal and universal religious beliefs free of any persecution. The fact that the interests and pursuits of men such as Cabalist John Dee, Hermeticist Robert Fludd and the philosopher Francis Bacon both contributed to and reflected the aspirations contained in the Rosicrucian manifestos and the emerging Masonic movement of the early seventeenth century and that Dee, Bacon and other associates were involved in promoting and contributing to colonial expansion in the New World, certainly supports the claim that their progressive thought and ideas were carried across the Atlantic to be preserved and to find expression in the maturing years of North American settlement.

That possibility becomes very real on discovering that Bacon's chaplain, devoted secretary and literary executor William Rawley could have arranged to have his master's material shipped across the Atlantic through the offices of an influential figure at the Court of King James I, the man who in 1621 was given the charter, sole access and exploration rights to the newly-named colony he called Nova Scotia. The well-travelled and educated Sir William Alexander, apart from being the King's Secretary for Scotland, was also a philosopher poet and a member of the Masonic fraternity of Bacon's time. Given his learning, his positions at Court and his esoteric interests it is very likely that Alexander and Bacon met and conversed. Alexander, who had gold and silver mining operations in Scotland, would likely have wanted to explore that option in his North American colony. Mining operations at the time were mostly in the hands of a guild or priesthood of pre-industrial mechanics and engineers.

In fact, many of the owners of mines and metalworks belonged to a secret society called the *Order of the Indissolubilisten* which had been established in Germany in 1577. Its members were interested in alchemy and sacred architecture and used the symbol of the compass, similar to Masons. They also referred to God as the supreme architect. One of Alexander's ships reached the coast of Nova Scotia in 1623, three years prior to Bacon's death. From accounts we know it sailed close to Mahone Bay, where Oak Island is located. There is no record of how long the ship remained in the area. It is possible that there was a mining engineer on board, perhaps even Bacon's protégé, the mystically-inclined and talented Thomas Bushell, a man experienced in creating underground works and water flows and who is on record as having been entrusted with Bacon's 'dearest secret'. Bushell was charged with using such treasures as might be gained from the secret entrusted him solely for the purpose of 'the raising, qualifying and endowing of my Solomon's House, modelled in my *New Atlantis* to my proposed ends.' Bacon's Solomon's or Salomon's House, in his utopian island nation of Bensalem, where principles of enlightened Christianity and true public spirit prevailed, was a temple-type research facility in which priest-scientists worked creatively for the benefit and welfare of humankind. It was part of Bacon's vision for the future, based on his insights and aspirations. The question that still remains to be answered conclusively is whether Oak Island, with its four-hundred year old mining and engineering works carried out by members of a secretive spiritual organization and with its still elusive treasure, was intended to serve this idealistic purpose in some way.

Towards the end of my time on the project I got into the habit of meditating on the mystery in the hope that I might intuitively gain an insight into its source and purpose. I was rewarded with a very beautiful vision that suggested to me that a form of creative spiritual energy lay hidden beneath the surface and that this energy, or what it represented, would one day surface again. Intrigued, I later sought the help of respected Nova Scotia parapsychologist Terry Murphy, having known of the use of psychic archaeology on other sites. After spending some time walking over the southern section of the island she told me she had seen 'a solemn procession of costumed individuals arriving on the island and proceeding in a procession towards the pit area'. She sensed that their purpose was to deposit something of sacred significance on the island. While nothing precise could be deduced from either of these experiences, they did tend to reinforce what the symbolism found on the island and other circumstantial evidence suggested, namely that the mystery had more to do with our spiritual nature than anything else.

Regardless of whether or not Oak Island and its secrets were intended to play some part in the creation of a new order in the New World and may yet do so, we know for sure that our lives have been enriched spiritually and materially by Bacon's literary and scientific work, and also by his involvement in establishing settlements in North America. There is no doubt that the mental outlook and profound philosophical perspectives that were enshrined in the American Constitution reflect the ideals and aspirations of such as Francis Bacon and the enlightened brotherhood of his day. Thomas Jefferson, the principal author of the Declaration of Independence, considered Bacon to be one of the leading influences in his life and that of the fledgling nation. While we may well question the use we have made of such knowledge and enterprise to the present, given the economic, social and environmental problems we are now facing, there is no doubt that the esoteric thought-streams of Bacon's time and his illuminating contribution to our perception of ourselves and the world around us have played their part in the evolution of consciousness ever since and to our ongoing interest in the transcendental nature of life.

Bacon's high ideals and aspirations live on. In that regard I can point to the work of the Association for Research and Enlightenment and the Anthroposophical Society, two organizations of many that for years have been contributing by way of conferences, courses and educational programmes to our greater awareness of our true nature and purpose as human beings on this planet. There is an ever-increasing and expanding interest today in genuine spirituality and harmonious transformation, both on a personal and collective level, and the purposeful application of same for the benefit of everyone and the planet. Some leading-edge scientific thinking based on theoretical results in the field of quantum physics is taking us closer to comprehending the mystical marriage of spirit and matter. In-depth, creative psychology is helping us integrate the spiritual, mental/emotional and physical aspects of ourselves as we search for healing and wholeness. More contemporary avenues of awakening into states of higher consciousness have been developed that are enabling us to progress along the path to perfectibility advocated by the Masonic and Rosicrucian movements. The kind of progress suggested in the sacred symbolism found on Oak Island and by which Francis Bacon's vision of a New Atlantis may eventually be realized.

BACON, BURIED TREASURE AND A BURNING DESIRE TO HELP HUMANITY

Dave Patrick and Mark Harris

THE NOTION of buried treasure, hidden away throughout the mists of time, coupled with a utopian vision of a possible future paradise, indicated fertile ground on which to develop a narrative about Sir Francis Bacon, especially if these strands could be pulled through into a contemporary setting.

Such was the start point of this self-professed Baconian novice. Preliminary research threw up two specific areas which appeared ripe for investigation (another case for Sherlock Holmes and Dr Watson, perhaps?). The first question concerned the aforementioned buried treasure, especially in two main North American locations, Bruton Vault in Williamsburg, Virginia, and Oak Island, Nova Scotia. What was the history and nature of this treasure,

---

Mark Harris is an experienced dowser and member of the British Society of Dowsers (BSD). His introduction to dowsing was with the late Hamish Miller, a master dowser and founder of the innovative Parallel Community, which encourages people to live a different kind of life in parallel to the hectic material world in which we currently exist. Other training includes courses and workshops with the current Vice-President of the BSD, Adrian Incledon-Webber, who runs the Dowsing Academy; practical experience includes Dowsing for Health and Dealing with Geopathic, Geopsychic and Electromagnetic Stress.

He has completed the first year of a Diploma in Cellular Energetic Healing based on the work of Barbara Brennan and also incorporates the principles of 'Wheels of Light' by Rosalyn Bruyere in his healing practice. He has undertaken work and training on recognizing the effects of family, ancestral and past life patterns on our energetic body and our presenting behaviours and responses in current lifetimes.

For biographical note of Dave Patrick, see first page of this book

what has been done to find it to date, and what is the Bacon connection?

The second question related to Bacon's fictionalized account of a utopian society, *The New Atlantis*; this synthesized much of his previous work and philosophy into a template widely acknowledged to have formed the basis for the ideals of the Founding Fathers for the United States of America.

These are profound questions in their own right; they become more powerful when associated questions begin to emerge, for example, is there any connection between this buried treasure and the stated utopian ideal, and if *The New Atlantis* really was a vision of a scientific revolution which would benefit the whole of humanity, why do we appear, in the United States and Europe at least, to have what amounts to a scientific dictatorship, operating through a banking and corporate global elite, influencing governments to often push forward policies to the detriment of the wider society?

I discovered that the latter question had been posed by Ursula Seiler in her excellent article 'The Promised Land' (www.ZeitenSchrift.net, 2005). Recognizing that Bacon's treatise lays down a utopian vision for the 'true New Atlantis, namely America', she identifies certain key principles and values Bacon propounded to support his vision, all in the context of a fictitious island named Bensalem.

Here the inhabitants espouse pacifism, live without money as a means of exchange and in their conduct of life follow a moral code. They respect strangers, possess immense knowledge, use a universal language and find out about the outside world by means of systematic explorations. There are class distinctions – these do not depend on wealth, but on wisdom, dignity and age. The first principle of this form of community is respect for life and for the family. And they paid particular homage to science – a true natural science.

This was Seiler's assessment of the current situation, in stark contrast to the above:

Is it not remarkable that the America of today has failed signally in all these domains? Its research massacres life and has become a threat to human dignity. It is characterized by a belligerent attitude to the outside world and toleration of extreme violence within the country, and the slavish pursuit of money, along with its use as an instrument of enslavement. Let us recall that since 1913 not even the dollar has been the property of the American people, but of a number of exclusive Wall

Street bankers who are independent of the political establishment. Moreover, American society shows a debasement of morals which has also brought about the dissolution of families, and the celebration of a capitalism which mocks every form of Christian neighbourly love.

Seiler goes on to say in the same article:

The 'discovery' of America was ... no accident, but was long and carefully planned by initiates. Neither is it an accident that the age of the Renaissance— the rebirth of the old classical knowledge—coincided with the discovery of the New World. The hour had struck, the sacred fire could be carried to the west. The secret orders had given their consent.

Similar sentiments from a business perspective were expressed by knowledge management practitioner Verna Allee, a previous contributor to *The View*, in her seminal 2003 book *The Future of Knowledge* (p. 176), an interesting title given the Baconian context of this book:

Money is not issued by governments, despite the fact that the U.S. Treasury might print the bills. Currency is actually issued by banks. Money can only move into circulation if someone goes into debt to the bank. To pay the debt off, more debt must be created. If you think this sounds suspicious, you are not alone. A growing number of people think this is a very unhealthy state of affairs. It not only makes economic growth dependent on debt; it concentrates power in the hands of those who issue the money – the banks.

Awareness of this problem, or at least the possibility of it arising, is nothing new. Over two hundred years ago, in 1802, third US President Thomas Jefferson issued this chilling warning in a quote attributed to him:

I believe that banking institutions are more dangerous to our liberties than standing armies. If the American people ever allow private banks to control the issue of their currency, first by inflation, then by deflation, the banks and corporations that will grow up around the banks will deprive the people of all property until their children wake up homeless on the continent their fathers conquered. The issuing power should be taken from the banks and restored to the people, to whom it properly belongs.

Whilst driving in my car recently I heard a wonderfully succinct comment on BBC Radio 4's Off the Page: Living Cheap programme (November 4, 2010) where 23 year-old recent graduate Laurie Penny, reflecting on the state of the global economy, and the politicians', bankers' and other corporate influences on it, remarked: 'They lied to us. The game is rigged, and the board is broken'.

Having ascertained that something appears to have gone dreadfully awry regarding the progress towards Bacon's utopian dream, I put any further enquiry in this direction aside until after the other question had been addressed – the search for lost treasure.

'The Game's Afoot!'

Realizing that reliable information on both Bruton Vault and Oak Island appeared relatively scant based on initial research forays on the Internet, one particular event propelled the investigation forward.

In June 2010 I was invited to attend a Francis Bacon Society meeting at Canonbury Tower in London, where the guest speaker was Mark Finnan on 'The Oak Island Mystery'. Also in attendance were Bacon scholar James North and anthroposophist Sylvia Francke, the latter being the person I had contacted a few months earlier following an incredible sequence of synchronistic events (but that story is for the telling at another time). Suffice to say that an integral aspect of the connection was through a book review on Sylvia's book *The Tree of Life and The Holy Grail* I came across on the Internet; it was written by Francis Bacon Society Chairman Peter Welsford, and a pivotal element of the review was a link to Ivan Cooke's book *The Return of Arthur Conan Doyle* (1956), the publication which set me off on my journey of compiling what was to become *The View*.

Mark's presentation provided some useful insights into the nature and history of the Oak Island mystery, an added bonus being his and James' acceptance of my invitation to join Sylvia as contributors to *The View Beyond*.

Some Background on Bruton Vault and Oak Island

Bruton Vault is located in Williamsburg, Virginia, and is said to contain 'the treasure of the Seventh Seal', reputed to consist of a hoard of gold along with priceless documents that, if brought in to the light of day, would challenge our understanding of man's history and reveal the 'secret destiny' of America and our global civilization.

According to the April 2010 edition of *Lost Treasure*, for centuries these documents have been protected by a secret society and their contents have only been viewed by a select few individuals. Bruton Vault is said to have been constructed of brick by members of Sir Francis Bacon's group, and is 10 feet by 10 feet located 20 feet below the altar of the first brick church in Bruton Parish. Using research compiled by metaphysician Manly Palmer Hall (1901–1990), and a group of his students, Maria Bauer (1904–2005), who later became Hall's second wife, in 1938 successfully unearthed the original foundations of the Bruton Parish Church, built around 1676.

Legend claims a number of Bacon's followers travelled to America and secretly transported across the seas the sacred treasures that would be deposited in the Bruton Vault and 144 other hidden Freemasonry vaults located throughout the new American continent (according to the Ascension Research Center, the locations of 121 of these sacred vaults have been identified).

In his article *Lost Secrets of the Bruton Vault* (*Atlantis Rising* magazine, September/October 2010), Steven Sora states:

> If such a valuable treasure exists and is relatively accessible, especially in comparison to Nova Scotia's Oak Island vaults, then why is it still underground? The first reason is that the Rockefeller family owns Williamsburg. They are not only the inheritors of one of the world's greatest fortunes, they are considered by some as the epicenter of the plan for one world government with leadership roles in the Council on Foreign Relations and the Trilaterals. They might simply desire to avoid unnecessary disruption in their park; or, as others believe, they may wish to keep such a treasure to themselves.

Since the 1938 excavation there have been several other attempts to dig for the vault; one that was sanctioned in 1991 found no vault or treasure. Since then Fletcher Richman and his group, 'Sir Francis Bacon's Sages of the Seventh Seal', have been campaigning for another dig to be carried out. Permission for a further excavation has not been forthcoming thus far.

Oak Island is situated off the coast of Nova Scotia in Canada and, like

Bruton Vault, it holds a story shrouded in mystery. A treasure pit was discovered on the island by three young men in 1795, and it is believed that
something of immense vale lies buried more than a hundred feet below
the surface. Excavations over the last two hundred years have revealed an
elaborately-constructed shaft with various underground workings, including a sophisticated set of water traps which has continually foiled treasure
hunters over the years. A 40-foot void at a depth of 140 feet has also been
discovered, and this is presumed to be a natural underground cavern.

Mark Finnan has researched the Oak Island story over the last couple
of decades, and his chapter in this book, *The Oak Island Mystery, Francis Bacon and the New World*, provides detailed background on the history of the
island, and the activities which have been conducted there over many years.

The Dowser Detectives

Because it was not physically possible to visit Bruton Vault in Williamsburg, Virginia, and Oak Island, Nova Scotia, plus the fact that information
relating to these locations was relatively scant, or in several cases vague
or contradictory, I invited my friend Mark Harris, who is an experienced
dowser and who leads a local dowsing group of which I am a member, to
collaborate on using dowsing and related techniques (high sense perception, remote viewing) to help address these questions I had set.

One unanticipated benefit of bringing Mark on board was that not
only is he an accomplished dowser, he also has a deep knowledge of the
Tudor/Elizabethan period of English history and a background in social
science has enabled him to be sensitive to the circumstances prevailing in
Bacon's day (when people could literally lose their heads for speaking out
of turn on certain matters!).

The results were surprising both in terms of content unveiled and the
extent of the way the process developed (especially remote viewing, which
had not been preplanned). The information uncovered, which will be written up in the next part of the chapter, also potentially has major implications
for Bacon's 'scientific method', and its application in the modern world.

To begin this part of the investigation I put my initial questions to Mark,
which were 'What was the history and nature of this treasure?', 'What has
been done to find it to date?', and 'What is the Bacon connection?'

Mark got together a team of three, himself, his wife Elaine (also a pro-
ficient dowser) and a friend Steve Horsfall, a local woodcraftsman Mark

had introduced to dowsing and had trained him in it. A dowsing session was held on Sunday, 26th September 2010 at Mark and Elaine's house in Milton, a small village in Ross-shire, Scotland.

Mark Harris now takes up the story of how the dowsing activities unfolded that day.

It was agreed that the team would use methods outwith the 'scientific method' to verify information, ideas, concepts and beliefs about the birth of Bacon, his death, connections with St-Germain, and connections with suggestions of 'buried treasure' of some form, at Bruton Vault, Williamsburg, and Oak Island, Nova Scotia. However, it was arranged to conduct the investigation with reference to, and in the spirit of, the Baconian model where possible.

With Elaine and Steve having only minimal prior knowledge about Bacon, Bruton Vault and Oak Island, which helped the integrity of the session by avoiding as much mind/opinion as possible becoming involved which could influence the dowsing, the team took a brief background look at website information on Bruton Vault and Oak Island. This was sufficient to create an awareness prior to dowsing, thereby assisting with focus and intent. A quick check of an Internet map was also done to allow the team to focus on the exact geographic location of Oak Island.

The dowsing process was initially agreed to be by pendulum chart set out with responses/quadrants of YES, NO, YES BUT, NO BUT, with pendulums to be used; each dowser chose a pendulum they felt most comfortable with immediately prior to starting.

It was also agreed as being important that we stated the intention to be open to information arriving through other methods which we would label as 'High Sense Perception'(HSP), which some would call 'intuition' or 'sixth sense'. This would include sudden ideas, synchronistic thoughts, pictures/remote viewing. All of this would appear to be possible and occurs due to tuning into the Universal Energy Field (UEF) which is all around us, also known as the Grid, Field, Matrix, Spirit or Akashic records. We also stated the intention to be open to information relating to our investigation arriving at any other time outside of our session.

The sequence of enquiry was agreed as (i) Bacon, (ii) Oak Island,

and (iii) Bruton Vault.

Questions, although agreed beforehand, were left open to amendment or additional questions/clarifications, allowing further dowsing at the time a particular agreed question occurred. Dowsers would all enquire and no one would speak until each person had finished. Answers were recorded in sequence around the table immediately at this point and the group then moved on unless someone had a comment or observation about how they found they had got on with the question. The option to move from group dowsing to individual free dowsing was also stated with the option to change dowsing tool (for example to L rods). Free dowsing within a group is where an individual has a possible insight or feels uncomfortable with a question, the wording, the context and rephrases it in some way that 'feels' right for them. This is where it would be difficult to meet the 'Scientific method' as what we have to do here is accept that *dowsing is a matter of 'opinion' and 'interpretation' and we must trust the information, feelings, pictures, and concepts that we get. It is not measurable.* The context for the questions had to be around 'historical personalities and events as they are recorded and known'. The idea behind three dowsers working as a group was that we would go with the majority answer for a particular question or amendment, as being the most accurate (note - not necessarily the right answer as there is often no such thing; it depends upon perspective and point of view.)

In terms of the process itself, each enquirer asked for permission, protection and guidance, and for information provided to be as accurate as allowed and to meet the highest purpose. Deep breathing, grounding through the legs and base chakra, and visualizing bubbles of golden light were methods used. While this was undertaken I also cleansed the space to be used (smudging, white light and asking permission on behalf of the group to proceed), set up a candle with prayer, and an amethyst stone. Enquirers sat around a wooden table in sunlight facing each other. Questions were agreed immediately prior to the respective stage of the enquiry, 1, 2 or 3. For the dowsing process, information access was semi-blind, in other words questions, although agreed for that stage were then turned upside down, mixed up and shuffled, then collected into a stack. Same size pieces of paper from a pad were used to ensure it was very difficult to anticipate any particular question in advance. Questions were turned over one at a time, were dowsed immediately once read out, and although the topic was known it was not known in what sequence the questions would appear.

It was recorded that at the very start Steve began to feel very cold, which was unusual for him, and I began to feel pressure on my face and feel very hot, signs of tuning into the UEF and it reacting with the enquirers' energy field or aura.

The summaries of the output from each of the three sessions are narrated below. These have been documented as findings from the sessions, but the 'truth' or otherwise of these findings is down to the discernment of the reader, given that dowsing is not an exact science. If nothing else, some of these findings may lead to interesting lines of enquiry in future research investigations.

Session 1 – Sir Francis Bacon

Note: Royston Cave is a man-made cavern in the shape of a beehive, unique in Europe and believed to date from the fourteenth century. It contains an extensive range of wall carvings depicting the Crucifixion, the Holy Family and several saints.

The carvings appear to be of medieval origin and may be linked to the Knights Templar. Other studies suggest that Masonic symbols found in the cave could link it to James I, himself a Freemason and who had a hunting lodge at Royston. It is also probably more than coincidence that it is located at the intersection of two major ley lines, which perhaps reinforces its spiritual significance.

In the context of this narrative, Royston Cave seems to be a copy, duplicate or mirror of Bruton Vault and Oak Island, which themselves are apparently part of a network of places which serve a similar purpose.

An intriguing conclusion from the dowsing session was that Bacon was not the biological son of Elizabeth I but was regarded in a maternal or stepson fashion, although this would appear to have waned as time passed. He was quite possibly the son of Robert Dudley, which would explain the connection with the Queen. Bacon was present in some form at the Founding Fathers' meetings, and was probably an incarnation of the soul/energy known as St-Germain. However his physical body appeared to cease to function and expired at the historical date of 1626.

Bacon did travel to Oak Island but in a previous incarnation as a Knights Templar, on a journey that had specific purpose, to visit the site where the current shaft was to be constructed. The site of the shaft already had importance or significance due to the presence of a natural cavity leading to a cavern. Were there crystals, possibly hidden since Atlantean times, and a vortex at this site and was it already marked in some way? We felt 'yes' to all of this.

Bacon also visited the site of Royston Cave in Hertfordshire in England it would appear, in the 'tourist' sense (not unsurprising as he was a student at the nearby Cambridge University). However, it seems he had already been there in a previous incarnation as a Templar, with a specific purpose connected with that location.

More imagination was needed with some of our questions and we felt it showed that even those with ideas that are 'alternative' to conventional history were often using logical methods to justify, seek out or prove so-called conspiracies. And what is imagination anyway, what is the source of inspired thinking such as imagination? Adrian Incledon-Webber, the current Vice-President of the British Society of Dowsers, has a view that dowsing is indeed only 'limited by the extent of your imagination'. Perhaps if more trust and imagination was acknowledged and included in the traditional scientific method, especially results, would we actually make more progress? And what is progress anyway, it depends on your point of view.

Session 2 – Oak Island

Note: In preparation for this session, when looking at websites for Oak Island, including examination of a suggested diagram for the shaft with descriptions of the various layers, I had an immediate insight about the possible treasure chest at a certain depth. This was that it was a sort of decoy or red herring. The chest was above the entry level of water tunnels and the blue clay layers seemed lower down than this. Steve immediately saw that the blue clay was an attempt to waterproof the lower levels; why do this, what is being protected lower down? For us, these were good examples of creative, synchronistic thoughts. Empirical modern treasure hunters seem to spend some time trying to find out what is here. It does not seem that much thought has gone into why certain things may have been done in a certain way. Ultimately some creative, imaginative, thought put to this may actually assist in discovering what is at the bottom of the shaft - a kind of 'try to get into the minds of the people who did this' approach. This is what we have tried to do in some way with our dowsing/enquiry.

As the session progressed, we found that there was a natural chamber at the bottom of the manmade shaft, already present before the shaft was dug, and this chamber was enlarged by the action of men using gunpowder. The shaft is constructed where a natural fault or fissure already existed. This would appear to have taken place during the Elizabethan period and was certainly more than 350 years ago (i.e., pre-1661, which is post-Elizabethan). The shaft that was dug and constructed was made in such a way that those who wished to find material treasure would be successful as there was some, but this was placed above sections where blue clay was found - as the blue clay would help make lower sections waterproof, where the real treasure (knowledge recorded on scrolls in lead-lined, mercury-filled caskets) was. This 'treasure' included documents written or prepared by Bacon and contained early Christian, Hermetic and cabalistic teachings as well as Templar ones (which could be based on all of the other three sources?). The shaft, the material treasure, and real 'treasure' were metaphorical of the individual's and humanity's journey through life to this point in recorded history. The messages here are multi-layered, but the individual will find what they seek, and if they think they have found what they are looking for, many will go no further!

At this point in the session we were getting ready to move from the Oak Island sequence and I was giving a reminder of why the group were asking questions about Bruton Vault when the word 'duplicates' came to mind; at the same time Elaine got a flash of the expression 'hidden in plain sight'. At the same time Steve became very quiet with his eyes shut and took us back to Oak Island with a very clear picture he was now holding in his head of the 'treasure' at the bottom of the main shaft, which had popped into his mind's eye:

Several scrolls, 6 to 8, weighted down on top with bars of lead, in mercury, in a lead-lined casket. Approximately 18 inches by 9 inches, by 15 inches in size (showed with his hands) and the lead lining about quarter of an inch thick. At this point he became emotional with tears in his eyes and a feeling of connecting with the craftsmen who had lovingly and with purpose made this. Steve is a craftsman working with wood on bespoke individual items and spends much time lovingly crafting each piece. Somewhere in the world of energy did this touch his heart and was a connection made with the energy of the craftsmen who had made this casket?

We ended by dowsing a picture of the inscribed stone found at a depth of 90 feet in 1803, and determined that what we were looking at was not an accurate copy of the original one. However, we then dowsed 'did the original stone found in the shaft have an accurate inscription upon it?' and all got a 'YES' response. The inscription is a code which is multi-layered so the 'code-breaker' will find what they seek. There is a second level or deeper reference within it, the knowledge in the main chamber.

Session 3 – Bruton Vault

The information at Bruton Church is not material treasure but knowledge, and is similar to the treasure/knowledge at Oak Island. In fact both locations were one of a number where a similar process or event had taken place where information had been placed for some sort of purpose, possibly to protect or save it for a future time. At Bruton this information was again contained in scrolls set in a similar lead-lined casket, with the weights holding the scrolls down in mercury. The casket was not in the ground but in a masonry wall 'above' ground, though there may be another casket or treasure buried in the ground to satisfy 'material' treasure hunters.

Regarding the question as to whether Bacon had tombstones engraved at Bruton Church, Williamsburg, to indicate the location of treasure/information, there was an idea that Bacon left instruction for it to be done, maybe to a group.

Conclusion of the Dowsing/Enquiry Session

No matter how carefully questions are worded there is room for interpretation based upon an individual dowser's life experience and understanding of a particular question. What are we picturing/creating in our mind's eye when a question is posed? How might this affect the so-called Baconian scientific paradigm as the same process must be at work there, and surely we then find what we seek? (Observers affect outcomes).

The rigid group dowsing of ALL using pendulum charts which were all identical, all drawn up at the same time with the same precise wording in an attempt to try to honour the scietific method did not allow a free flow of information access, and switching to open dowsing without the charts, and different tools if required, brought more of a flow to the session. Supplementary dowsing sessions were carried out as 'Yes but' and 'No but' answers could both be correct depending on the question. For example, 'Was Francis Bacon the son of Elizabeth I?' can be answered *correctly* either way, as he could have been not a biological son but been regarded or treated in a maternal way, as a stepson or the son she never had! Therefore 'yes but' and 'no but' are both accurate answers depending what the dowser/enquirer had exactly in mind at the point of the enquiry. From the Baconian point of view does this not mean that it is possible to get apparently contradictory answers to the same question or circumstance which are both correct?

From the point of view of trying to follow the scientific method in spirit, it very soon went 'out of the window' and the deeper we got into the session and the more open and individual the session became the more 'insight' and synchronicities we began to get. The more we moved out of the left brain and allowed the right brain to function the more fluid the dowsing and HSP began to flow. We felt that we were happy with the 'information' and 'feelings' that we had, and that a certain amount of this ultimately involved 'faith' and 'trust' in our results, two concepts which were uneasy bedfellows with the scientific method/modern scientific paradigm. Our faith and trust came from a feeling in the heart, not in facts and figures or provable, repeatable models. We 'know' we got some good information because it 'felt ' right and arrived in ways we 'trusted', beyond the normal five senses, and clearly there were magical moments when left and right brain were working in a truly integrated way.

Dave Patrick now resumes the narrative until the end of the chapter.
From the initial sessions held on 26th September, it was agreed that a number of loose ends and additional questions generated from those sessions required to be addressed.

A supplementary dowsing session was arranged for Sunday 31st October 2010 at the same location as before, with the same set up process.

There was a stated intent to dowse for the highest purpose and good, with permission, and to be open as before to information arriving outwith the dowsing session and by other means (HSP, etc.). Permission was also requested for me to join the group.

Having received detailed information from Mark about the first dowsing sessions, which has been condensed and summarized above, it was an entirely different prospect and subsequent experience being pitched into the dynamics of the group this time around.

The findings from this supplementary session have been incorporated into the information summarized in the previous sections.

Connecting the Dots

The dowsing conclusion that Francis Bacon may have visited Oak Island in a previous incarnation as a member of the Knights Templar is perhaps not such a fanciful one when considered in the context of Andrew Sinclair's book, *The Sword and the Grail* (2005 edition), which tells of a Scottish expedition led by Prince Henry St Clair landing in Nova Scotia in 1398 (although there was no suggestion that Bacon would have been St Clair himself, but a member of his group). During the following century, Prince Henry's grandson Sir William St Clair built Rosslyn Chapel, with its well-known Templar and Masonic associations; it was designed to represent Solomon's Temple, a significant influence both on Masonic traditions and Bacon's *New Atlantis*.

Coincidentally, the night after the first dowsing session at Milton, I was giving a talk in Dingwall with 'Family Constellations' facilitator and author of the book *The Science of Family*, Nikki Mackay (also a contributor to *The View*). Nikki offered to facilitate a family constellations session focused on Sir Francis Bacon's family with the small group in attendance (which included Mark). Examination of how these family entanglements may have affected Bacon showed a dominant male figure in the background who controlled and directed everything, with an energy directed at commerce and material matters. This seemed to have a profound effect upon the 'Bacon energy' which seemed very uncomfortable with this and almost 'did not want to be here and part of this'. It was speculated that this may have given him the impetus to write the *New Atlantis* treatise.

Returning to the nature of the specific sites under investigation, Bruton Vault and Oak Island, there appears little doubt that these sites are not accidentally situated, and form natural energy vortices. They are possibly part of an energy grid system which is only now being more fully understood.

It might be further speculated that these energy vortices form an important part of the earth's 'consciousness field' and are in some way linked to human consciousness, and that the evolution of the earth's consciousness and that of humanity are interdependent, at a time when energetic shifts are affecting both. Are these energy vortices portals into other dimensions of reality, accessible via altered states of consciousness? And are we reaching the point where these other dimensions of reality are becoming accessible to the wider population, not just initiates of secret societies?

From Ian Lawton's book *The Future of the Soul: 2012 and the Global Shift in Consciousness* (2010), in a channelled message recorded in the section *life on a more highly evolved earth* (p.80), it says in relation to those who resist the new energies:

> They will be trying to hold on to what is familiar, particularly in terms of material things, and when these are either taken away or not bringing them as much comfort, it will be a breakdown of sorts...They simply will not have accepted that there could be any wealth other than the material, ignoring the wealth of the mind.

Dr Christine R Page, in her book *2012 and the Galactic Center* (2008), relates the advice she was given by her spiritual teacher regarding the new consciousness, during the current times when humanity must learn to value and encourage the contributions of every individual, who each hold a unique part of the jigsaw, and where no one piece is more important than another, being a true reflection of the fifth world of ether (p. 17):

> As we move from the fourth to the fifth world, change is offered through the dissolution and transformation of the old...[only] five per cent [of people] will understand, recognizing the opportunity to be vanguards and light bearers of a new creative cycle, both for themselves and the world in general.

A New Atlantis?

In drawing this chapter to a close we may well ask: What would Sherlock Holmes have made of it, and would he have been able to draw any watertight conclusions? It is interesting to note that Sherlock Holmes, through the mind of his creator Sir Arthur Conan Doyle, was a master of deductive reasoning, whereas in contrast Bacon was noted for his inductive powers. Is it not now time to recognize the need for both, just as right and left brain thinking must integrate into whole brain thinking. Synthesis is the key. Where Conan Doyle and Bacon did share a common passion was in their vision for a fairer society, shown by their lifelong interests in the support of truth and justice.

Our search for 'treasure' has shown that although material objects may be involved, the real wealth is in the knowledge and wisdom which has been safeguarded throughout the centuries. This takes us back to Grace Cooke in the 1930s when she went hunting for 'treasure' with members of the Polaire Brotherhood in the French Pyrenees, where this treasure for Grace (or Minesta, as she was more commonly known) was found to be spiritual in nature rather than material (see *Arthur Conan Doyle's Book of The Beyond*, ed. Colum Hayward, 1994, pp. 141–47).

Perhaps now is the time, in the lead-up to 2012 and all that that may entail, for all these factors we have spoken of to coalesce, to allow us to transcend the conditions and challenges which have bedevilled us throughout history, with other mysteries of the past like Rennes-le-Château and Rosslyn Chapel also having their secrets revealed.

For human consciousness to evolve does society now need to face up to the excesses of 'scientific' materialism, epitomized by greed, power and corruption, the effects of which are destroying the planet, fracturing our families and communities, poisoning the food chain and damaging our health?

Earlier Ursula Seiler referred to the 'true New Atlantis, namely America'. If we consider Birgitta Jónsdóttir's article (see her chapter below, pp. 270–78, entitled *Transformation of Politics*), perhaps the modern-day 'true New Atlantis', in terms of developing a transparent, fair and just society, is being created in Iceland instead.

Is Iceland, not the United States of America, becoming the crucible of the emerging Golden Age?

> *'When you have eliminated the impossible, whatever remains,*
> *however improbable, must be the truth.'*
> (Sherlock Holmes in *The Sign of Four* by Sir Arthur Conan Doyle)

Footnote

Of necessity the amount of information we have been able to share in this chapter regarding the dowsing sessions held on 26 September and 31 October 2010 is limited. We intend to distribute more detailed information about these sessions in articles placed in various specialist (e.g. dowsing magazines) and general media publications. Collaboration on a book project to develop this research further is another possibility.

A Word on Dowsing and Related Activities

Dowsing may be regarded as a method beyond the five senses used to access information and is an innate ability that all humans have. It has been around for a very long time; it was used by ancient Chinese Geomancers and written about by the fifth century BC historian, Herodotus.

Essentially, dowsing involves the person concentrating with intent on a specific purpose or task whilst allowing the mind to relax. By tuning in and holding an implement such as an L-shaped rod, pendulum or stick-type device, minute muscular contractions in the dowser's hands causes what is held in them to respond in certain shapes or movements. This seems to occur because the item being held has an energy field around it and this has now become part of the energy field of the dowser; effectively the item becomes an extension of the dowser, a sort of antenna. What we are seeking, be it information or object, also has an energy field or signature, and by relaxing and tuning in we try to access that part of the energy field, its vibration or frequency. When we do it interacts with our own energy field, which includes the extension/antenna we are holding. This extension amplifies our energy field/physical responses to what we are seeking.

In an article in the April 2010 edition of 'Dowsing Today', the publication of the BSD, Billy Gawn likens dowsing to an 'information retrieval system', and we may 'complicate the process through the introduction of a tool' as this produces a crude semaphore system which we need to interpret (hence dowsing being a matter of opinion). To begin to dowse is a wonderful experience but to do nothing but dowse with some sort of tool following guidelines ultimately begins to feel like a Baconian method! It is probably quite restrictive, which was why in our dowsing sessions for the book we stated the intention to be open to information arriving through other methods other than the dowsing itself. I would see dowsing as one way of using high sense perception, which is accessing information other than with the five senses. We can use dowsing to access information (looking for water, lost objects and people, diagnosing health issues, for example) or we could use it to confirm what we already perceive we have accessed from the universal energy field.

It is all a kind of 'spiritual physics' really. As was mentioned to Mark by another BSD member some years ago, 'from quantum physics to faeries it is all the same thing'!

References/contacts
'For human beings to develop do we need to start to feel what we know (link intuition with knowledge)?' Sig Lonegren statement at BSD conference 2009.

Mark Harris: www.rainbow-energies.com; mob. 0782 444 9011

Dave Patrick: www.thevitalmessage.com; mob. 0780 302 4461

British Society of Dowsers: www.britishdowsers.org; email info@britishdowsers.org tel 01684 576969

Hamish Miller Books, Penwith Press, PO Box 11, Hayle, Cornwall TR27 6YF. www.hamishmiller.co.uk: email penwithpress@talk21.com

Adrian Incledon-Webber, Dowsing Spirits and Dowsing Academy; tel. 01249 8188807; www.dowsingspirits.com

MacManaway, Dr Patrick, *Energy Dowsing for Everyone*. London: Southwater (2004)

Brown, Elizabeth, *Dowsing: The Ultimate Guide for the 21st Century*. London: Hay House (2010)

For further information on global energy grid systems a good example to check out is the Becker-Hagens Grid (see http://www.bibliotecapleyades.net/mapas_ocultotierra/esp_mapa_ocultotierra_12.htm , http://www.crystalinks.com/grids. html and http://divinecosmos.com/index.php/contact-us/privacy-policy/68-the-shift-of-the-ages-chapter-12-becker-hagens-the-global-grid-solution).

Remote Viewing
There are a growing number of books available on Remote Viewing. A couple are suggested here for anyone wishing to gain an initial grasp of the subject, learn some powerful practical tools and techniques, and find out about its history and evolution.

McMoneagle, Joseph, *Mind Trek: Exploring Consciousness, Time and Space through Remote Viewing*. Charlottesville, VA, USA: Hampton Roads Publishing Inc. (1997) Joe McMoneagle was recruited into the US Army's secret, psychic-spy unit, Star Gate, as Remote Viewer #001 (Star Gate was terminated, and documentation associated with it declassified, in 1995).

Atwater, F. Holmes. *Captain of My Ship, Master of My Soul: Living with Guidance*. Charlottesville, VA, USA: Hampton Roads Publishing Inc. (2001)

Includes CD-ROM with video clips, workshops, declassified intelligence material, remote-viewing examples, and recorded out-of-body experiences.

CODES, CODING AND SYNCHRONICITY

Peter Welsford

Part I: The Francis Bacon Society (founded 1886)

Mente Videbor (By the mind I shall be seen)

SAID TO BE the oldest literary society in the country, the Francis Bacon Society has struggled on in its own particular way with a small, discreet group of members, many of whom live overseas, intent on promoting the Bacon cause ever since the Society was created by Mrs Pott in 1886, having headquarters in Canonbury Tower (once the home of Francis Bacon) – by kind permission of the current Lord Northampton and his ancestors.

Dedicated leaders such as Sir Edwin Durning Lawrence, Commander Pares and Thomas Bokenham (an ex-Bank of England official) 'carried forth the banner' so to speak, as dedicated researchers, writers and speakers – the Society having held periodic talks in the University of London Library (Senate House), the Nevern Square home of Mary Brameld, the current Vice President, or the Garden Room in Canonbury Tower, Islington, London.

The principal objects of the Society have always been to encourage the

Peter Welsford FCA., a former Treasurer of the Scientific and Medical Network England, is a researcher and writer interested in the science of phenomena and hence, hidden harmonics, super-strings and space time in higher dimensions. Earlier in co-operation with Colum Hayward there was published 'The Golden Key' by the Psychic Press, being communications from Edward Percy Welsford his father through Grace Cooke, by automatic writing to his grandmother. As Editor of *Baconiana,* the in-house Journal of the Francis Bacon Society, he studied for some years under the direction of Thomas Bokenham and is currently the Chairman of the Society.

study of Bacon's works as philosopher, statesman and poet; his character, genius and life; his influence on his own and succeeding times; and the tendencies and results of his writings. Together with the general study of the evidence in favour of Bacon's authorship of the plays commonly ascribed to Shakespeare, and to investigate his connection with other works of the Elizabethan period.

During the last decade the Society has hosted around forty talks by notable speakers including Peter Dawkins (Francis Bacon Research Trust), Dr John Henry (Edinburgh University), Mark Rylance (Shakespeare's Globe Theatre), John Michell (RILKO), Dr Edi Bilimoria (Theosophical Society, Science and Medical Network), Dr John Alabaster (Author), Francis Carr (Authorship Newsletter), Nick Young (ex-Shakespeare's Globe Theatre and a council member), Mark Finnan (Actor/Author, Canada) and Petter Amundsen (Norway) (Oak Island Mystery), Susan Sheridan (Actress/Author), Sylvia Francke (Anthroposophist/Author), James North (Oxford University and a council member), Karen Attar (Rare Manuscripts, University of London Library), Dr Sally North (the Society's librarian and webmaster), Colum Hayward and Mary Brameld (the White Eagle Lodge) and other visiting speakers from overseas, with well-attended meetings.

It has been generally stated that a profound study of Bacon's works and his life and times can lead to further contemplation, possibly on a more intuitional level, of the esoteric purposes behind the English Renaissance. In his own confident words, he has 'taken all knowledge to be my province'. His life has been said by many to be as much a curtain-raiser for the present age of scientific achievement, as it was a pattern of how men should live and work unselfishly, putting the good of the group, the nation and humanity before their own interests – and above all glorifying God.

Those wishing to learn more of the background to the Society are here referred to the website, www.baconsocietyinc.org, where the latest of the periodic, *Baconiana* Journals are available online, together with a useful, comprehensive Index from 1886 to 1999 listing many authors and articles from the Journals and with photographs of past Chairmen and some officers of the Society.

It is obvious to the world at large that Baconians in academia, and the nucleus of those represented by the Society in particular, have failed over the years to convince the general public of the case for his 'concealed' work – more particularly recently, at the Shakespeare Authorship Trust

Meetings, now held annually at the Globe Theatre. Is the Bacon 'secret' due to resistance by vested interests of the media and/or, is it the general mindset of the public to what still remains a taboo subject, for some mysterious reason?

Summing up the problem,Susan Sheridan the actress, a staunch Baconian, currently reminded us at a recent meeting: 'May I put forward a concern of mine ... that one of the Bacon problems lies in the fact that we BELIEVE it so strongly, we have FAITH and these sentiments are not academic. Proof is what is needed and no matter how many times we see Francis Bacon encoded in the plays and find connections with RosiCross, academia won't accept it as proof – indeed it makes things worse for us!

'Fundamental evidence is what is needed.'

For that matter, even a bunch of original, soiled manuscripts in Bacon's handwriting, hidden somewhere in an old, oilskin bag would still not provide adequate proof for this purpose, as someone will probably shout out loudly: 'Forgeries!'.

It so happens there are several initiatives to hand, any one of which may surprisingly, either individually or collectively provide just the sort of proof that is needed here.

Be that as it may, the Society sees itself quite proudly continuing to act as the major custodian of a vast amount of material and information, directly related to Bacon and the Authorship question, while at the same time participating and co-operating in any worthy initiatives that may help solve the riddle.

Vivitur in genio, caetera mortis erunt (One lives on
in one's genius – other things pass away)

Part II: The Shugborough Hall Decode - 'Et In Arcadia Ego'

[O.U.O.S.V.A.V-V]
[D. M]

An article about to be published in *The Research Into Lost Knowledge Organization* (RILKO) Journal deals extensively with the latest findings surrounding the Shugborough Monument, recently decoded by Mr Buff Parry, a

Canadian professional cryptanalyst, as published by The Times in 2006 and appearing on BBC News on March 17th of the same year.

The Shepherds' Monument, Shugborough Hall, is an eighteenth-century copy of Poussin's 'Les Bergers d'Arcadia' reversed, mirror image fashion with the motif: 'Et In Arcadia Ego', a photograph of which originally appeared in the international bestseller *The Holy Blood and The Holy Grail* by Henry Lincoln et al, dealing principally with the mystery of Rennes le-Chateâu and the strange parchments discovered by Saunière the French priest.

Buff Parry was referring to the marble tablet in the grounds of the Shugborough Estate, near Stafford (the old Bishop of Lichfield's palace) owned by the Anson family, (ancestors of the Earl of Lichfield) and it was reported that he said: 'it is a message that the Grail is buried nearby'.

It was also reported in a Press Release in 2006: 'His two-year study of a mysterious code inscribed in the estate's Shepherd's Monument comes after research by code experts from Bletchley Park in 2003. They claimed that the code was a message from a twelfth-century Christian sect'.

According to Press Reports on BBC News and *The Times* in March, 2006:

Mr Buff Parry believes a Holy Grail stone was captured in France and brought back to Shugborough in 1746 by Admiral George Anson. Shortly afterwards the family commissioned the tablet which they encoded with the stone's location.

Parry believes the D and M stands for 1500 in Roman Numerals and refers to the 1,500th verse of Genesis.

The lack of a full stop after the final V means that part of the code should be read from right to left, spelling VVA – a word which means 'bloom' or 'offshoot' in Hebrew.

Other letters refer to the name Joseph, leading to the phrase 'The Bloom of Joseph', as in Genesis verse 1,494. He said that in the bible the phrase means 'the stone the builders forgot'.'

He said: 'I believe it is very likely that at least one of the stones will be eventually found here.'

Prior to the event followed by this public announcement, the Francis Bacon Society had come across a copy of a book called *The Burial of Fran-*

cis Bacon and His Mother in the Lichfield Chapter House by Walter Arensberg (1924), an American philanthropist who spent many years researching this subject both here in Lichfield Cathedral and also in America, where he founded the American Francis Bacon Foundation before eventually leaving his vast collection of paintings to the Philadelphia Museum of Art.

Using the same ancient cipher method as that of Francis Bacon (previously established in *Cryptomencytices of Selenus*, by Trithemius), Arensberg extensively decoded works of Shakespeare, principally in the play *Cymbeline*, where he arrived at the conclusion that the burial place of Francis Bacon was in the Chapter House in Lichfield Cathedral.

In his book in particular, he had referred to the burial of Francis Bacon and said that there were several identifiable symbols including 'Aeneas' as expressed by Virgil the poet, 'The Golden Bough' and 'The Ring of Francis Bacon' for example, which he interpreted as pointing to the whereabouts of the grave he had found encoded within *Cymbeline*, having certain 'value for unit' correspondences.

Later, he visited the authorities in the Cathedral in an attempt to persuade them to continue with his investigations but to no avail.

The problem for us was that initially, he had found an anagram in *Cymbeline* (Act II, Scene IV, lines 78–95), where letters spelt out FRANCIS BACON, but it was clear from the refutations of Col. and Mrs Friedman, the professional cryptologists, as published in their book *Shakespearean Ciphers Examined*, that this decode was invalid since the letters chosen were random. Thereafter according to the Friedmans it mattered not that his other 'anagrammatic acrostic method' might be kosher, the damage had been done!

However, in attempting a completely fresh and therefore an alternative decode of the Shugborough Monument coded letters, now in the light of Buff Parry's work, we felt it essential that we should find a way to overcome this problem. But how to do it?

Determined as we were to find a solution, the search was on! Later it transpired that a Mr William Mudie had discovered a credible way to show how Bacon had encrypted his names in some of the Shakespeare Plays he had found, in the First Folio. This disclosure first appeared in 1929 but had perhaps conveniently been overlooked by the Friedmans in their indictment of the Shakespeare ciphers, as published in their book in 1957.

Armed with this fresh information and as an alternative decode of the letters:

[D.O.U.O.S.V.A.V-V.M]

we came upon interesting results which in no way contradicted Buff Parry's extensive work but instead produced parallel encryptions.

For example: STONE is an anagram of TONES or energies (harmonic frequencies), of a terrestrial and ethereal (or *celestial*) nature, where *Proserpina* or *Spirit*, in *The Wisdom of the Ancients* by Francis Bacon is also mentioned, in the introduction to Arensberg's book.

In it he relates The Philosopher's Stone and '*The Stones too hard to come by*' (p.16) to a line from *Cymbeline* (Shakespeare) corresponding to the Masonic symbolism of the stone that was rejected in the building of the Temple, which became 'the corner stone'.

Hence, it became quite clear that in our search for Truth, 'The Key' to the Grail is 'A Stone', where the final decode of The Shugborough Monument lies within the Code:

D O U O S V A V-V M = 4 + 14 + 20 (= 38), + 14 + 18 + 20 + 1 + 21 + 12 (86) = 124:

THE GOLDEN KEY = PROSERPINA, each the count of: 124 = A GOLDEN STONE.

This not only leads to wider interpretations through correspondences with words, phrases and symbols connected with Bacon's myths and allegories but also points the way in the future towards quantum solutions into higher dimensions – something Bacon had actually predicted when he spoke of 'Action At A Distance'.

Then armed with this new knowledge our attention was recently drawn towards the writings of Carl Jung, the Swiss psychologist, himself said to be a later incarnation of Francis Bacon, and with what appeared to be excitingly synchronistic results, pointing us towards considerations of 'alchemy' which we found that Carl Jung himself had investigated quite scientifically.

Study the laws of nature (Francis Bacon)

Part III: Codes, Coding and Synchronicity

Man is a portal through which one enters from the outer world of the gods, demons and souls, into the inner world – from the greater world

into the smaller world. Small and insignificant is man; one leaves him
soon behind, and thus one enters once more into infinite space, into the
microcosm, into the inner eternity.

VII *Sermones*, by Basilides, a Gnostic
teacher in Alexandria (117–138 AD)

In *Memories, Dreams and Reflections*, Carl Jung wrote:

'When I began to study Alchemy I realized that it represented the historical link with Gnosticism.... Grounded in the natural philosophy
of the Middle Ages, Alchemy formed the bridge on the one hand into
the past to Gnosticism, and on the other into the future, to modern
psychology of the unconscious....'

In *Synchronicity, an Acausal Connecting Principle* (p. 145), Jung describes
synchronicity as:

The coincidence of a certain psychic content with a corresponding objective process which is perceived to take place simultaneously.

The coincidence of a subjective psychic state with a dream or vision
which later turns out to be a more or less faithful reflection of a 'synchronistic', objective event that took place more or less simultaneously,
but at a distance.

The same, except that the event perceived takes place in the future and
is represented in the present only by a phantasm or dream that corresponds to it.

He also wrote: 'Since the remotest times men have used numbers to
express meaningful coincidences, that is those that can be interpreted' and
'There is something peculiar, one might even say mysterious, about numbers...which seems to indicate that number is something irreducible...
numbers are said to have an archetypal foundation.' (p. 54).

In *The Gnostic Jung and The Seven Sermons to The Dead* we read:
'Gnosticism is neither a philosophy or a heresy, but a religious experience
which then manifests itself in myth or ritual'; and on p. 27 he talks of a

Rosicrucian enlightenment.

The 'dynamism of the fullness of being' (p.105) and in the glossary he refers to 'Abraxus' as the state of being described by Basilides in VII Sermones, as *the figure of the union of opposites,* and Gnosis as *spiritual knowledge arrived at intuitively.*

It is to Basilides, a teacher of Gnosticism in Alexandria, that Jung attributes the authorship of the document itself, through the mediumship of *automatic writing* on his part, similar to that of Grace Cooke and Hugh Randall-Stevens, in 1925.

From the book *The Master R (Lord of our Civilization)* by Michael Taylor, we had learnt about Francis Bacon's other incarnations, including Carl Jung himself (1875–1961).

Whilst we were reconsidering the recent decode, originally by Walter Arensberg, of the Shakespeare play *Cymbeline,* there was produced a paper about 'Jupiter's Label', as having later been decoded by William Mudie in an article in *Baconiana* (No 92, January, 1939), due for publication as a footnote in an article about the Shugborough Monument decode, referring to the Burial Place in Lichfield of Francis Bacon.

In this footnote there is described a legitimate method whereby Bacon's signatures appear, not only in 'Jupiter's Label' from *Cymbeline* but also the bookplate to the First Folio, as well as in 'To The Reader', the endplate to the Folio and, thirdly, in the Stratford Monument inscription, thus linking all three together..

At the suggestion of Dr Regan, an FBS member, as to whether there might be distinctly meaningful links between Bacon and his incarnations, apart from the creation of the First Folio of Shakespeare's Plays, the search was on for any fresh Key Words in gematria (the letter/number count system used), like the count of: A FRANCIS BACON RING (=147).

By 'modernising' the spelling within the label, of 'Peace and **Plentie**' (as distinct from Plenty*, see below) then the count is 139, same as: A FRANCIS BACON KEY (139).

However, starting with the word: BASILIDES (Jung's inspiration) and a count of 77, immediately there came to light: MEAN RING (77), A BRANCH *SEED* (77), and then MEAN <u>AYRE</u> (77) the link with Jupiter's Label, third line: 'Tender <u>AYRE</u>'.

The word: *SEED* figured again, as in the web search on the internet into BASILIDES, in his Gnostic philosophy he had repeatedly referred to:

A UNIVERSAL *SEED* (a count of 147). So might other links to these words be found here within Jupiter's Label?

Yes indeed! A UNIVERSAL SEED (=147), same count as: PEACE AND PLENTY (147)* (see above) where both sentences remarkably, follow Mudie's sequential, hence 'legitimate', rule, as each are themselves 'hidden' within the words of 'Jupiter's Label'!

Searching for more KEY words, such as **'THE GNOSTIC'** and **'INNER ETERNITY'** lurking within 'Jupiter's Label' also proved positive, as they followed the same, legitimate rule, thus providing the much sought for links between Basilides and Francis Bacon!

Here then are several encryptions, strongly suggesting that there are more than circumstantial, new correspondences disclosing the natures of Basilides (Jung's Gnostic inspiration), Francis Bacon in the renaissance with his Shakespeare Plays and last but by no means least, that of Dr Carl Jung, the psychologist, a Francis Bacon incarnation.

Have these links been provided for us *synchronistically?*, we might well ask ourselves.

'Jupiter's Label', appearing in Cymbeline:

Although the original decode by Arensberg used in his book was initially flawed as it is composed of a random selection of letters, nevertheless he found it a useful 'signpost(?)', pointing him to the play *Cymbeline*, by Shakespeare, which he went on to decode extensively by the anagrammatic acrostic method, as presented in his book *The Burial Place of Francis Bacon and his Mother in Lichfield Cathedral*.

On the other hand, in *The Self-named William Shakespeare* (1929) by Alfred Mudie, there is described *the secret signature of Bacon* to be found in **'Jupiter's Label'**, also appearing in *Cymbeline*, where the letters necessary to conform to a regular as distinct from a random coding, can be seen as 'sequential', i.e., in a consistent order or sequence.

This method was reported in an article under 'The Cryptographers Corner' in *Baconiana*, (Vol. 24, no. 92, January 1939).

Mudie provides other examples, for instance in the first label or bookplate 'To The Reader' (1623) and the Stratford Monument 'Stay Passenger...' conforming furthermore to the strict rule that the first and last letter of an encryption must equally well appear as the first and last letter in 'Jupiter's Label'. In the example below, for instance, the 'F' (of Francis) is the first F underlined and the last letter 'S' underlined, of ... St. Albans.

Hence, the first F of ... Francis ... to ... Saint Albans ... last s, contains the passage...

Thus by applying this legitimate method to 'Jupiter's Label', Mudie finds the following names firstly, **Francis St Albans**' (see below) and secondly, 'Saint Albans, Saint Albans', *the signature of Bacon, secretly hidden in Cymbeline,* thus indirectly and independently validating Arensberg's initial decryption four years or so after the event.

'Jupiter's Label', appearing in *Cymbeline*:

When as a lions whelp, shall to himselfe unknown,
Without seeking finde, and bee embraced by a peece of
Tender Ayre: And when from a stately Cedar shall be lopt
Branches, which being dead many years, shall after
Revive, bee jointed to the old Stocke, and freshly grow,
Then shall Posthumus end his miseries, Britaine be
Fortunate, and flourish in Peace and Plentie.

Result = **Francis Saint Albans**.

Time brings forth the hidden truth
(Francis Bacon)

VI · ALCHEMY OR SCIENCE?

TOWARDS A NEW HARMONIC FRAMEWORK

Richard Merrick

THERE WAS a time when most people believed the universe and everything in it was made of music. The early Hindus were perhaps first to embrace this concept in their musical philosophy of *shabda*, a Sanskrit word meaning 'sound' or 'speech.' Their Vedic texts, written in the form of sacred hymns, were said to embody the divine knowledge of *sruti* or 'what is heard'. As this idea was adopted into Buddhist, Jainist and Tibetan teachings, it was known as the Audible Life Stream, Inner Sound, Sound Current and the Word. Spreading through much of the populations of India and China, many today still claim: 'the Sound Current vibrating in all creation can be heard by the inner ears'.

Richard Merrick was the founder and CEO of Postfuture, a pioneering rich-media communications provider for companies like Best Buy and Microsoft. Under his leadership, the company grew from a tiny start-up in 1999 into the top digital communications company of 2004 and fourth fastest-growing technology company in Texas. Prior to this, he was the technology founder and elected CEO of 7th Level, a global CD-ROM game publisher and Internet technology company known for such award-winning titles as *TuneLand Starring Howie Mandel* and Monty Python's *The Quest for the Holy Grail*.

Merrick's work spans many areas of digital media, including search engines, graphics operating systems, multi-media authoring applications, interactive games, voice-response Web agents and dynamically personalized Internet communications. Throughout his career he has been invited to speak around the world on the future of digital media and cited as an expert in leading publications.

He is now a pianist and composer, graphic artist and independent researcher into the physics, history and social ramifications of harmonic science. He received his BA (magna cum laude) and MSCS degrees from the University of Texas at Dallas.

The ancient Egyptians also celebrated the idea of a musical universe by employing harmonic proportions in the design of their pyramids and burial chambers. In the book *Egyptian Sonics*, acoustician John Stuart Reid found evidence the Egyptians had developed an advanced sonic science by the Fourth Dynasty, circa 2520 BC. His acoustical experiments in the King's Chamber of the Great Pyramid demonstrated that certain resonant frequencies would create vibratory patterns corresponding to some twenty hieroglyphs, suggesting that Egyptian writing may actually have its genesis in this early science of resonance.

Inheriting their wisdom from the Chaldean mystery school in lower Mesopotamia (modern day Iraq), the Hebrews developed their entire language around the harmonic properties of numbers and geometrical proportion. Their alphabet was based on the geometry of numbers, or *gematria*, from which the Torah was encoded. The Jewish people and later Gnostic sects then based their laws and social customs on these universal principles of harmony and balance.

In the fifth century BC, the Greek philosopher Pythagoras united all of these teachings into one, founding his own mystery school to study the harmonic properties of nature. Discovering that different musical intervals corresponded to simple whole number proportions, he and his followers developed a unified philosophy of harmony in numbers, geometry, astronomy and organic forms. Finding the same harmonious patterns everywhere they looked – the seed patterns of fruit, orbits of planets and shape of the human body – an ancient scientific method known as *musica universalis* was established to guide the study of nature.

As this method was applied to the study of form, the Greek philosopher Plato identified five perfect solids and developed a natural philosophy of archetypes to go with them. From this came Euclid's *Elements*, describing the mathematics behind such archetypes, complete with rigorous logic and formal proofs. In the Hellenistic period that followed, Archimedes of Syracuse developed an early form of calculus known as *infinitesimals* while Ptolemy charted the periodic motions of the heavens. Behind all of these advancements in geometry, mathematics and astronomy could be found the guiding light of Pythagoras and his scientific method of *musica universalis*.

But this golden age of Greek science was not to last. With the Roman conquest in 146 BC, the study of nature became less important as the

Romans focused on vast engineering projects to support their conquest of Europe. Beginning with Constantine in the fourth century AD, much of the pre-Christian knowledge was lost with the torching of the Royal Library of Alexandria by Archbishop Theophilus. Were it not for the work of Arab scholars, who had earlier translated and preserved many of the ancient works, all knowledge of the Greeks' science and mathematics would have been lost.

With the fall of Rome and the beginning of the Holy Roman Empire in 962 AD, the Dark Ages had begun. It was not until the European Renaissance in the fourteenth century that most of the important Greek works would be rediscovered and an interest in harmonic science would return.

Copernicus with his Sun-centric theory of the solar system was the first glimmer of a return to harmonic principles in astronomy. Then came Johannes Kepler's *Harmony of the World*, proposing that Platonic forms in some way governed the spacing of the planets. While this turned out to be an oversimplification, he did accurately explain other phenomena of the solar system, such as the difference between maximum and minimum orbital speeds of each planet will approximate a harmonic proportion.

Around the same time, a prominent English physicist, astrologer and Rosicrucian mystic named Robert Fludd publicly debated Isaac Newton against adopting a purely empirical method for science. In *De Musica Mundana*, Fludd argued that the Pythagorean model of the universe was essentially correct and should be used to guide the study of nature, since the cosmos is indeed a kind of celestial monochord of vibratory energy from which all things arise. But in spite of this last attempt to hold onto *musica universalis*, Fludd's harmonic ideals fell from favour and a new unguided science was born.

The Enlightenment or an Endarkenment?

Beginning first with Galileo, then Sir Francis Bacon and Sir Isaac Newton, a new 'scientific method' was proposed and adopted in the seventeenth and early eighteenth centuries. It was a method that presumed no guidance from harmonic principles. Instead, it was presumed that observations and experiments alone would lead the world to truth and enlightenment.

Bacon was the first to propose the new empirical scientific method, designed to shield the mind from false notions that could distort the truth. Calling such notions 'idols', he proposed four kinds that must be avoided:

those common to a given race, those peculiar to an individual, those resulting from the misuse of language and those resulting from the abuse
of authority. All together, he argued that avoiding such idols would lead
inductively to the discovery of forms and models that accurately describe
natural phenomena and their genesis.

Since the study of nature through musical patterns and proportions
had long been a central component of theology, the Greek harmonic science that had sparked the Renaissance was abandoned. Musical theory and
practice, tightly controlled and protected by Church canon law since 1234,
was now considered a false idol to be avoided. In academia, music became
just another field of study in the 'humanities', taking its place alongside
art, history and philosophy.

Yet in hindsight, the wholesale removal of a harmonic foundation from
the methods of science may have seriously impeded scientific progress.
Some argue that this decision led to a disorganized and fragmented study
of nature, resulting in the tentative, incompatible and rather dogmatic scientific formulae known as the *Standard Model*. The truth is the rejection of
harmonic science may have opened the door for the cause of science to be
swayed by even bigger idols than Sir Francis sought to remove.

Today, acceptance of contradictory theories has led to wildly different
models for even the most common phenomena, not the least of which
are gravity, the structure of the vacuum and human perception. Without
a unified foundation, the language of science has become increasingly ar-
cane, heavily barnacled and decidedly obtuse, a veritable Tower of Babel,
making it difficult for anyone outside of a given field of specialty to comprehend and integrate much of the scientific research now available.

At the same time, there is a rising chorus of scientists around the world
who complain of unreasonable and unfair barriers to the publishing of
their work. Journal review boards, controlled by older generations bent
on defending their life's work, often reject studies that do not conform to
already-accepted models, even in the face of compelling evidence showing errors in such established models. But, this is not all that now haunts
Bacon's scientific method.

New idols must be worshipped by science that did not exist prior to
the Industrial Revolution. These are the idols of economics and politics.
Markets now demand a continuing flow of new technologies to fuel the
global economic engine, redirecting the focus of university education

and research away from the search for real understanding. To make matters worse, more and more of our best scientists are being recruited right
out of college by the military-industrial complex to build more powerful
weapons and devastating war machines. It seems that Bacon's idols have
become bigger and more powerful than he could have ever imagined.

So, even as the worldwide standard of living has risen from waves of
innovations in productivity, entertainment and creature comfort, we are
really no closer to an agreement on how the major components of nature
fit together than we were three hundred years ago. There is no understanding of how the quantum microcosm contributes to the development
of life; no agreement on what causes gravity; no interest in the geometric
properties encoded in DNA (or life in general) and no explanation for what
caused life to evolve along the particular path it did, to name but a few. And
while we can tell through MRI imaging which parts of the brain are acti-
vated by different stimuli, there remains no accepted model for how the
brain actually thinks or how conscious self-awareness could emerge from
inanimate matter.

Welcome to *The Endarkenment*, an age where the quest for the big picture has no currency – a time when seeking enlightenment in the study
of nature has become not only irrelevant, but laughable. A time when
field specialization and isolation have brought us to an artificial and overly
complex view of things where we no longer see *or even care* about how the
pieces fit together. We embrace the differences and eschew the commonalities. We think we get it, but we really don't.

The time has come to reevaluate and update our methods of science.
We must seek a new approach where natural study can once again be guided by laws common to all fields of study. This method must be powerful
enough to overcome Bacon's false idols while loosening the strict dogma
of the Standard Model. It is time to reintegrate the fields of science and, in
so doing, begin the process of reintegrating our fragmented society.

But to do this, we must first reconcile ourselves with the past. We must
find a way to mend the worldviews of Pythagoras and Planck, Plato and
Bohm, Euclid and Lisi. Only through reconciliation can we hope to find
our way forward.

A New Harmonic Framework

First off, let's agree that the ancients were essentially right – all things are in vibration. From the smallest particle to the whole of the cosmos, everything we see comes from the resonance of electromagnetic waves and the formation of atomic particles. This is the harmonic framework of our physical reality.

It all starts with spirals. As pressure builds, vortices form; as vortices form, closed cycles appear; and as these cycles stabilize, energy crystallizes into harmonic forms. Repeating at every level of reality, the fractal formations of galaxies, solar systems, planetary systems, biological-botanical systems, molecular systems and atomic systems all emerge from layer upon layer of coherent vibration. Yet each system is part of a whole, sharing a common source of energy and descending from a set of universal laws. These are the laws of the ancients – the laws found inside a periodic *standing wave*.

A standing wave occurs whenever vibration is trapped inside a container and reflects back upon itself, becoming stationary as it oscillates in place. This occurs because the energy in the standing wave travels in opposite directions, adding together into a single, coherent waveform. As this process begins to stabilize, whole-number harmonic frequencies emerge to piggyback on the fundamental frequency of the container. This natural process, known as *resonance*, quickly generates an entire *harmonic series* of wave frequencies that share the energy of the fundamental.

*The **Harmonic Series** is a series of wave frequencies produced as a single wave vibrates and subdivides in halves, thirds, fourths, fifths and so on, inside a container. This natural process generates the whole number set of harmonics $h = \{1, 2, 3, 4, 5, ..., \infty\}$. Also known as 'overtones' in music, harmonics are responsible for the various timbral qualities of an instrument.*

Like the musical tone of a simple reed flute, all matter results from the same physics of resonance that brings harmony to music. While the container for a flute is its pipe, planets resonate harmoniously into place from the hot plasma contained inside the gravity bubble of a star. Similarly, living things resonate into harmonic forms inside the container of their cell, egg or body. The atoms that make up those living cells then resonate inside their own microbubble of space, bonding harmonically into larger molecules, compounds and mesoscopic structures. The quantum world beneath is no different, emerging from spiralling 'torsion' fields that form spherical standing waves whose harmonic intersections form the nodes we call particles.

But resonance alone is not the whole story. There is something else quietly at work inside these standing waves that makes coherent resonance possible. This is the phenomenon known as *harmonic damping*.

If standing waves are the stuff of the visible world of structure, harmonic damping is the invisible force of stability, order and balance. Discovered in the 1930s by Soviet physicist Lev Landau, plasma waves were found to exchange energy at 'avoided crossings' called 'adiabatic transfers'. Known as *Landau-Zener Theory* or simply *Landau damping*, this idea quickly spread to become the cornerstone of quantum mechanics and has since been applied to explain such phenomena as superconducting, superfluidity and extraordinarily coherent states of matter like Bose-Einstein condensate.

As it occurs in the very special case of standing waves, the principles of Landau damping explain how wave energy transfers across gaps called *damping wells* to form harmonics. In particular, the damping wells in standing waves exist at fixed locations identified by the natural constant known as the *golden ratio*.

*The **Golden Ratio**, documented in the third century BC, but known thousands of years earlier, occurs when a line is divided in such a way that it can be nested infinitely into itself at the same proportion. We can easily visualize this as the proportion between line segments in a pentagram, commonly expressed as: $\phi = (1 + \sqrt{5}) / 2 \approx 1.618033$ and its inverse $1/\ldots = (\sqrt{5} - 1) / 2 \approx 0.618033$. In a variety of studies, the golden ratio has been found to represent the maximum damping location in standing wave phenomena.*

This is not a trivial point. The Landau damping effect of the golden ratio can explain many properties found throughout nature – from the average spacing of planets to the branching patterns of life to the lattice alignment of atoms in crystals as they spin in the same direction. It is because of this effect that rectangular speakers and auditoriums are often built near golden ratios of 0.62 x 1.62 x 1, in order to suppress wave reflection and echoes. Indeed, it is the damping effect of the golden ratio that enables standing waves in all mediums to nest deeper and deeper within themselves, creating endless fractal formations.

Landau damping theory also suggests that as standing waves form within a container, those frequencies near the damping well of a golden ratio or its inverse will be suppressed while those furthest away will remain as whole number harmonics. Thus, we find that the golden ratio is responsible for creating the space between harmonics and carving out the slack needed for harmonics to coexist within the same space. We can define this 'anti-harmonic' or fractional set of frequencies using the infinite set of numbers in the *Fibonacci series*, a subset of the harmonic series.

*The **Fibonacci Series**, named after Leonardo 'Fibonacci' of Pisa but first documented by the Sanskrit grammarian Pingala in the Chandah-shastra around 450 BC, represents a 'mountain of cadence' that 'grows' by adding adjacent pairs of numbers starting with 1 + 1. This growth process continues to produce the infinite series {1, 1, 2, 3, 5, 8, 13, 21, 34, 55, 89, 144, ...}.*

The relevance of this series to standing wave formation is apparent when each adjacent pair of ascending Fibonacci numbers is taken as a proportion, creating numbers closer and closer to the golden ratio.

For instance, the adjacent Fibonacci proportions 13/8, 21/13 and 34/21 are roughly equal to 1.625, 1.6153 and 1.6190, respectively. As the process continues, the Fibonacci series approximates the golden ratio of about 1.6180339887 by spiralling closer and closer to it, but never actually reaching it. In this way, all of the Fibonacci frequencies are increasingly damped and suppressed from the standing wave as they converge ever nearer to the golden ratio, leaving only whole-number harmonics in the space between (Fig. 1).

Thus we see that Fibonacci proportions in a standing wave are just as important as whole-number harmonic proportions. They produce a silent spiralling background field in the waveform that stabilizes the process of resonance, enabling the formation of 'sympathetic' harmonics. And, at the center of these deadening Fibonacci vortices lies the golden ratio and its inverse – two infinite and constant damping wells present in every standing wave cycle where energy is exchanged. Without this natural ordering property at every scale of nature, standing waves, their harmonics and physical structures of all kinds would simply cease to exist.

We now find in the containment and reflection of waves the universal method by which energy self-organizes into coherent particles out of

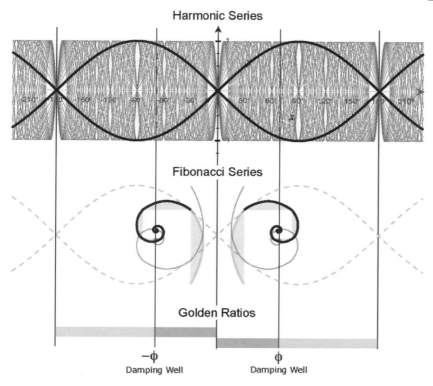

Figure 1. Harmonic damping stabilizing a standing wave

chaotic spread spectrum energy. The golden ratio – often considered of little real importance to science – is actually what keeps atoms from flying apart, yet simultaneously bonds them together. At the cosmological scale, it is the golden ratio that sets the size, spacing, orbital frequency and other attributes of the planets within the Sun's resonating current sheet. And in life forms, the golden ratio is responsible for every crevice, curve, hole and flexible joint as organisms self-organize from the atomic realm up. It is this one constant of nature that makes it possible for the resonant structure of our bodies to articulate, move and do work.

When organized around a central polar axis, standing waves composed primarily of water and carbon-12 resonate together into the familiar shapes of life, first exploding outward as spheres but then spiralling back inward as the damping force becomes too strong. Trapped inside a gravity bubble of space, compressed by atmosphere and water, living cells have little choice but to resonate into a multitude of nested cardioid forms (Fig. 2).

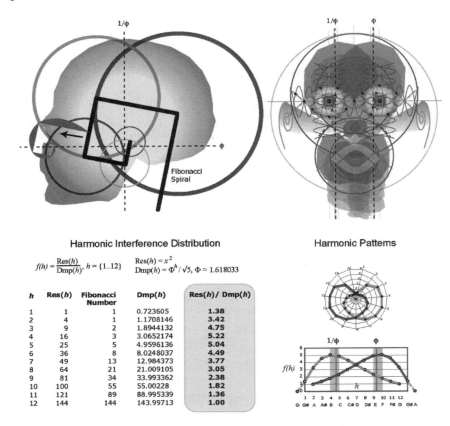

Figure 2. The universal harmonic pattern of life.

That's it – harmony is everywhere and in everything. It is the simple balance of resonance and damping intrinsic to spacetime, there from the very beginning. This is the physics of a standing wave that offers a new framework for science, if only our methods would allow it.

Towards a Harmonically Guided Science

Early natural philosophers had no need of Bacon's scientific method to protect them from undue influence and bias – they were innocent from the beginning. Their societies looked with fresh eyes at the planetary movements in the sky, mineral crystals on the ground and geometry of life all around them, seeing only commonalities. Wherever they gazed, they found the truth staring back at them – the universe truly is made of music.

In those days, the tools of science were drums, gongs and flutes. The scientist's method was to sprinkle sand on a drumhead, intone a simple chant and then watch wide-eyed as geometric patterns appeared on its surface. Taken as the first symbols of language and ideas, the physics of a standing wave was the model upon which early civilization achieved its coherence. Just as we now celebrate music as the universal language of culture, the study of resonance and damping was once revered as the universal language of science.

It is through this simple and most beautiful worldview of our forebears that we might now envision a new future for science. Perhaps it is time to bring back harmonic study to our schools, such as took place long ago. And while we are at it, perhaps we should consider adding harmonic principles back into the scientific method, recalibrating all scientific research to the universal model of a standing wave. Maybe it is even time for the return of a new field of harmonic science – a field whose job it is to look for the commonalities and reconnect the fragments of modern science into a meaningful whole.

Let us envision an educational system where every student takes at least one year of general harmonic studies. One obvious benefit is it could help guide more students toward science through their love of music. At the same time, the scientifically inclined may find greater passion for their work as it became infused with the values of art.

But no matter their field of choice, might we expect these students to develop a more integrated worldview from harmonic theory and a musical archetype for the universe? Would our youth not begin to see the broader impact of their decisions, bringing more ethical and socially responsible solutions to market? Surely they would, and it could change the world.

With harmonic principles central to a new scientific method and integrative field of harmonic science, the study of nature would certainly become more efficient and less likely to follow dead-end paths. New generations of scientists, guided by harmonic models, would seek deeper causality in the phenomena they study, more often finding their answers in adjacent fields. When this is not enough, a new field of harmonic science could pose questions, recommend avenues of research and encourage research across fields to solve key problems.

As astronomers came to embrace harmonic processes again, we could expect many of the competing cosmological theories to be put aside as models grounded in harmonic laws take centre stage. Quantum mechanics, itself already founded on harmonic principles, would at last become the foundation of astrophysics. Soon, astronomers would feel free to discuss the true musical properties of the universe, triggering a domino effect into other fields.

With the Standard Model adjusted to guide research toward integration, the life sciences would experience a revolution not seen since Charles Darwin. Biologists would feel compelled to recognize and study the role of atomic resonance in guiding evolution, therein realigning anthropological and genetic models with quantum and cosmological models. Beginning as only a trickle of information to the outside world, the message would eventually get out that life is just an enfoldment of the same harmonic processes at work all around us. A new vision of life as a beautiful musical crystal could suddenly blossom into the social consciousness, elevating self-image and bringing a new sense of interconnection and responsibility back to society.

As medical scientists also came to accept the human body as the resonating liquid crystal it really is, increased research into bio-currents and directed wave resonance treatments would surely come, bringing unimaginable medical breakthroughs to replace many of the drug therapies so heavily promoted by today's pharmaceutical industries. Change would also come to the cognitive sciences, refocusing research on brain resonance and non-local quantum effects, establishing new models of perception and a more natural approach to machine intelligence.

No field of science would remain unchanged. Reconciliation with ancient harmonic wisdom could lead to revised interpretations of history, a rereading of the archeological records and new social theories proposing harmonic physics as the central theme behind the development of social order. The economic and political sciences would change as well, gradually shifting Western institutions toward less polarized, more moderate policies. This, in turn, could bring a surge of R&D funding to alternative and yet-undiscovered energy sources to relieve the world's oil dependence. The ecosciences would flourish beyond anything we can imagine now.

If we are to have a true understanding of nature and achieve a sustainable civilization, a harmonic framework must be reintroduced into our schools, our science and our society. Continued avoidance of harmonic principles resulting from long gone theological associations is no longer warranted and has indeed become a clear impediment to progress. The sooner this is recognized and rectified, the sooner science can begin fixing the really big problems that will ensure humankind's survival.

FRANCIS BACON AND PSYCHICAL RESEARCH

Leslie Price

THAT FRANCIS Bacon was an inspiration to natural science is a truism. But he has also been an encouragement to the extension of science into the paranormal. The creation of the Royal Society, which celebrated its 350 years in 2010, has its more limited counterpart in the formation in London of the Society for Psychical Research in 1882.

Psychical researchers recognized that they were actually going beyond Bacon. We can see this in the aspiration of their leading thinker, F. W. H. Myers, in the Epilogue to his magnum opus *Human Personality and its Survival of Bodily Death* (1903).

> The influence of the evidence set forth in this book should not be limited to the conclusions, however weighty, which that evidence may be thought to establish. Rather these discoveries should prompt, as nothing else could have prompted, towards the ultimate achievement of that programme of scientific dominance which the *Instauratio Magna* proclaimed for mankind. Bacon foresaw the gradual victory of observation and experiment—the triumph of actual analysed fact— in every department of human study;—in every department save one. The realm of 'Divine things' he left to Authority and Faith.
>
> I here urge that that great exemption need be no longer made. I claim that there now exists an incipient method of getting at this Divine knowledge also, with the same certainty, the same calm assurance,

Leslie Price was founder editor of *The Christian Parapsychologist* (1975), *Theosophical History* (1985) and *Psypioneer* (2004). He is a former librarian of the College of Psychic Science, of the Churches' Fellowship for Psychical and Spiritual Studies and of the Society for Psychical Research. He has organized small conferences on psychical research, Christian parapsychology and theosophical history.

with which we make our steady progress in the knowledge of terrene things. The authority of creeds and Churches will thus be replaced by the authority of observation and experiment. The impulse of faith will resolve itself into a reasoned and resolute imagination, bent upon raising even higher than now the highest ideals of man.

Myers had briefly been a Christian when young, but ultimately his faith owed most to Neoplatonism, to psychology, and to the finer aspects of Modern modern Spiritualism. In this passage, he challenged religious authority in a way that Bacon never dared when, after all, men were still being executed for the wrong religious beliefs. (Elizabeth I, for example, hung three Congregationalists.)

The claim that 'there now exists an incipient method of getting at this Divine Knowledge' is a remarkable one. In the early days of the SPR, Myers was briefly a fellow of the Theosophical Society, but soon rejected its occult claims. But he did revere the mysticism of Plotinus, greatest of the Neoplatonists, whom he quotes three times in his Epilogue. Some admirers of mysticism would deprecate the suggestion that the merely paranormal should be linked with it, but just such a continuum, from the subliminal to the supraliminal, was a central theme of Myers.

One psychical researcher went so far as to acclaim Myers as a new Bacon. This was Sir Oliver Lodge, the leading figure in the SPR after Myers died. In his SPR presidential address of 1903, Lodge noted the significance of Bacon for science.

> 'Scientifically he was an amateur: but he was an enthusiast who with splendid eloquence, with the fire of genius, and with great forensic skill, was able to impress his generation, and not his own generation alone, with some idea of the dignity and true place of science, and to make it possible for the early pioneers of the Royal Society to pursue their labours impeded by persecution and to gain some sort of recognition even from general and aristocratic society.'

Lodge went on to make a more specific claim, on the eve of the posthumous publication of Myers' *Human Personality*.

> Has it struck you, it has often struck me, that in the history of the psychical sciences we too have had a Bacon, and one not long departed from us? Is it possible that in the two volumes which to-day or tomor-

row may be emerging from the press, we have a book which posterity will regard as a Novum Organon? History does not repeat itself, and I would not draw the parallel too close. It may be that posterity will regard Myers as much more than that, as a philosophic pioneer who has not only secured recognition for, but has himself formulated some of the philosophic unification of a mass of obscure mental and barely recognized human faculty, and has thrown a light on the meaning of personality which may survive the test of time.

There have been speculations in esoteric circles as to how the spirit of Bacon might have reincarnated – Sir Oliver was not a reincarnationist, though he was a long-time defender of pre-existence. In any case, as noted above, the spiritual affinities of Myers lay mainly elsewhere than in science as conceived by Bacon.

An objection may be made to the suggestion that Bacon was in some sense a forerunner of psychical research. Perhaps the most controversial scientific discovery in Bacon's time was the motion of the earth round the sun. Bacon was opposed to it, though it may be doubted if he understand the mathematics involved. If Bacon was reactionary in relation to such a dramatic astronomical development, might he not also have been dismissive of the much less respected psychic field?

We can take comfort from one or two references in Bacon which suggest he would be sympathetic to psychical research. Dr Alan Gauld, in a private communication, draws my attention to

> the part of Book Two of *The Advancement of Learning* that deals with the History of Marvels (Historia naturae errantis). He states that he has found 'no sufficient or competent collection of the works of nature which have a digression and deflexion from the ordinary course of generations, productions, and motions; whether they be singularities of place and region, or the strange events of time and chance, or the effects of yet unknown proprieties, or the instances of exceptions to general kinds.' While distancing himself from works that are intended to 'give contentment to the appetite of curious and vain wits', etc. he goes on: 'Neither am I of opinion, in this History of Marvels, that superstitious narrations of sorceries, witchcrafts, dreams, divinations, and the like, where there is an assurance and clear evidence of the fact, be altogether excluded. For it is not yet known in what cases,

and how far, effects attributed to superstition do participate of natural causes; and therefore howsoever the practice of such things is to be condemned, yet from the speculation and consideration of them light may be taken, not only for the discerning of the offences, but for the further disclosing of nature'.

It was doubtless hoped when the two-volume *Human Personality and its Survival of Bodily Death* was published that humanity was at the beginning of a psychical revolution comparable in its advances to those of the scientific revolution. A century later we can see that these problems have proved more intractable. Our grandparents could confidently publish books like *The Facts of Psychic Science* (1925); Conan Doyle could dedicate his *History of Spiritualism* (1926) to Sir Oliver Lodge, F.R.S., 'a great leader both in physical and in psychic science'. But in fact, no such science has developed.

So far as the Spiritualist movement was concerned, a research tradition persisted until the outbreak of the Second World War. Infra-red viewing, for example, was an acceptable tool in the 1930s at the British College of Psychic Science, the International Institute for Psychical Research and the London Spiritualist Alliance. But after the war, Spiritualists attempted little research, and no less a leader than Percy Wilson actually warned of the dangers of infra-red.

The Theosophical Research Centre was also active between the wars, and had access to its own clairvoyants, but the austerity after 1939 contributed to a gradual fading of this line of investigation.

The Myers spirit was also somewhat eclipsed in mainstream psychical research or, as it was often called abroad, parapsychology. Laboratory-based experimental investigations of a limited statistical kind became prominent. J. B. Rhine, author of 'Extra-Sensory Perception' (1934) was the leader of this approach, which could be almost contemptuous of the investigation of spontaneous psychical phenomena.

At present there is renewed interest in Myers himself. Trevor Hamilton has published a well-received biography which not only places Myers in the firmament of Victorian intellectual leaders, but also traces his post–mortem influence as a significant communicator through mediums. His discussion of the research methods used by Myers and his colleagues is of interest to all students of science.

In addition to a number of shorter centenary assessments of Myers and his main book, a massive examination appeared in 2007: *Irreducible*

Mind: towards a psychology for the 21st Century by Edward F. Kelly, Emily Williams Kelly, Adam Crabtree, Alan Gauld, Michael Grosso, and Bruce Greyson (Lanham, MD: Rowman & Littlefield). This is, among other things, an examination of how far the psychology of Myers has been substantiated by later research. It deliberately returns to the wider concept of psychical research championed by Myers.

In his Introduction (p. xxiii), E.F. Kelly sets out the methodological principles of the book, the first of which is humility. He continues:

> Second, we emphasize that science consists at bottom of certain attitudes and procedures, rather than any fixed set of beliefs. The most basic attitude is that facts have primacy over theories and that beliefs should therefore always remain modifiable in response to new empirical data. In the forceful words of Francis Bacon 'The world is not to be narrowed till it will go into the understanding.... But the understanding to be expanded and opened till it can take in the image of the world as it is in fact (p. 276.) [*New Organon*, 1960 edition]

There are several institutional developments which are significantly contributing to the wider penetration of psychical research. The Parapsychological Association, a professional body of researchers, was admitted to the American Association for the Advancement of Science in 1969. The Scientific and Medical Network, founded in the UK in 1973, originally a semi-secret group, includes psychical research in a wide range of areas it studies on the borders of science, and is an important bridge body between these areas, the academic world and the public. The Society for Scientific Exploration is a professional organization of scientists and scholars who study unusual and unexplained phenomena also includes psychical research; references to Bacon in its journal are not infrequent. The inclusion of psychical research with other scientific areas would be welcome by those parapsychologists like Ian Stevenson who deplored the separative nature of many psychical research organizations, which cut them off to some extent from mainstream science.

There are grounds for hope then, that the vision of Myers a century ago of a new science of the spirit may be realized in the century ahead.

AETHER AND BEYOND

Michael I. Finesilver

THIS SHORT piece can be no more than a sketch of a subject which, by its very nature, is fluid, indefinable and endless. Given that, a useful way to introduce the concept seems to be to approach it from various directions – historical, artistic, cultural and scientific – in order to gradually build up an impression. The aether or ether, is said to pervade the whole universe, and is sometimes referred to as the fifth element or *quintessence* – from which emerge the four traditional elements, fire, air, water and earth. It is also said to be similar to the Indian concept of *prana* and the traditional Chinese concept of *chi*, implying vitality and perpetual change.

The *aether* is of a pre-physical era in the evolution of the cosmos. So thinking about it and trying to attune to it requires a different kind of consciousness from the point-centred outlook of individuals in the physical–material world. This is easy to say, but not so easy in practice. For example, instead of singular, exclusive *points* of view, aether awareness involves an all-round, all-inclusive *plane* of view.

But then treating such a major adjustment as simply an intellectual

Michael I. Finesilver is a Londoner with an Honours Degree in Psychology from Manchester University, followed by a long spell in the music business as an independent writer, freelance producer and studio proprietor. He finally opted out in 1999 to focus on his work on aether, which has always been quietly evolving in the background.

He went on to produce an audio CD, entitled 'Aether: Knowledge is Power', compiled from a series of over a dozen interviews with a wide range of contributors; they included scientists, engineers, biologists, doctors, healers, clairvoyants and esotericists. A book, 'Aether: The Transcript', was also published from the same source material. Many of the quotations in this chapter are transcriptions of those interviews.

exercise can result in a superficially mystical, fantasy-like state of mind – which may be pleasant for a while, but will lack a sense of grounded connection with the earth and will probably soon dissipate.

A certain amount of acclimatising is required. Also, just to peep out longingly from the materialistic box-world will not satisfy the truly curious mind. Going beyond involves growing out of our present limitations – like adolescents, no longer dependent and relishing our independence, yet beginning to realize there's a whole lot more to being an adult than merely indulging in individualistic pursuits.

The aether's 'beyond-ness' is experienced in its presence as the invisible, dynamic reality behind and also permeating the physical realm of matter and discrete objects. By inferring this vital presence from physical clues, some coherence can be brought to the scientists' fragmented world of building blocks, particles and abstract units of quantity. In this respect, the aether is a transition state between that realm and the unity, not uniformity, of pure consciousness. What follows includes several quotes, mostly the spontaneous responses of some independent scientists and academics to questions about the aether; they are drawn from recordings made in 2004 and later transcribed.

Other names for the aether

Awareness of the aether under different names, and ideas about it, go back into the farthest reaches of human history. Aether comes from an ancient Greek word, and one of its many meanings is: 'the substance that permeates the cosmos from which the stars and planets were made'. It also signifies 'a blazing', the heavens, shining light and the upper atmosphere.

Sambhoga-kaya, an ancient Tibetan term, refers to the intermediate stage in the emerging of the cosmos. From the nothingness or unity state emanated radiant light, which then evolved into this physical universe. Indian and Chinese culture have various names for different aspects of the Aether. In the Hebrew Old Testament it's referred to as the 'cosmic waters'.

Aether is alluded to in hymns which speak of inspirational light, fire and radiance... and in the literary works of Milton, Keats, Wordsworth and Shelley. The influential Renaissance philosopher Marsilio Ficino wrote, 'the force of the World-soul is spread ... through all things through the quintessence, which is active everywhere, as the spirit inside the World's Body'. *Quintessence*, which literally means the fifth essence or element, is another ancient term, recently re-introduced in modern physics. It refers to the subtle, indefinable, universal something that pervades the whole cosmos.

Albert Einstein, in 1920, explicitly affirmed the existence of the aether. He said, 'There is nothing in Relativity that discards an aether'. One eminent physicist, David Bohm, seemed very close to the idea of the aether when he proposed a non-physical realm of potential manifestation. This he called the implicate order, which exists as the middle level of a three-level system. And another well-known contemporary scientist and writer, Paul Davies, has suggested the concept of a *quantum ether*. So with numerous signs of the aether being acknowledged again under various other names, and despite various authoritative dismissals over the years, the aether has never gone away.

Levity and gravity

Sir Isaac Newton knew and wrote about the aether and was the first Western scientist to identify gravity and put it on a scientific and mathematical basis. As a man deeply interested and involved in spiritual and occult knowledge such as alchemy, he also covered a lot more ground than the Western science establishment has been prepared to acknowledge. And this included his writings on the polar opposite of gravity, the universal expansive force, known in earlier times as levity. Gravity and levity are the two polar opposite forces of the aether, and thus of the universe.

Nick Thomas, an independent scientist and mathematician who has written for *Encyclopaedia Britannica,* writes: 'You can have this notion of a force in the cosmos that's drawing away from the centre rather than towards it. And there's a lot of evidence that such a force exists in the cosmos now'.

We can appreciate levity directly when we see heat rising as in a flame or when we get a sense of elevation in our upright posture.

It was around Newton's time that the *Accademia del Cimento* in Florence, then a world authority on scientific matters, issued a paper entitled *Contra Levitatem,* which decreed that science should no longer recognize levity as meriting equal rank with its opposite, gravity. The historical context was that of a newly-emerging discipline of scientific enquiry which was trying to be ultra-objective, unlike religion, and focused solely on the physical, as opposed to anything which was reminiscent of mysticism or the Church. And the idea of levity, as the opposite of gravity, was felt to draw people away from a physical earthbound mentality towards a more transcendental, aethereal state.

At a stroke this denial of the principle of polarity prevented any balanced scientific enquiry into the nature of gravity. And it helped distort Western science into making a false distinction between the physical, as what is 'real', and the non-physical, thereafter to be considered 'unreal' and so not worthy of scientific investigation. So although, in its historical context, it can be seen to have had some justification, its consequences have echoed on way beyond their useful time.

Four Aethers

Within its wholeness, the aether can be seen to consist of four distinct grades or qualities. These are known as the *Warmth Aether*, the *Light Aether*, the *Tone* or *Chemical Aether* and the *Life Aether*. First described by Dr Rudolf Steiner, they correspond to the four traditional elements, *Fire, Air, Water and Earth*, and fit in with several other four-way views of the world, such as the traditional *humours*, *temperaments* and the compass directions.

Four Aethers

*tone aether, aka chemical/sound/number/colour aether
Note: it's only a diagram!

Nick Thomas writes: 'It's the aether that gives us life. It's the aether that gives us vitality. It's the aether that makes us healthy or ill. Or at least, it has a huge role to play in all of that. And if we have no idea what the aether is, then obviously we're going to judge ... things in a false way'. *

Consciousness and Materialism

The ancient Eastern concepts of *Akasha*, and the Akashic Record which refers to a kind of cosmic memory bank, are part of the consciousness aspect of the aether. Included in this would seem to be what some call the Platonic world, a realm of ideal, archetypal forms such as the perfect circle and square — forms which don't exist in physical Nature. It's named after the Greek philosopher, Plato, who lived in a much less materialistic era than ours.

The problems of Western science seem to have arisen primarily from it having been corrupted by the belief system known as *materialism*. This proclaims that matter is the ultimate reality – despite physics simultaneously stating that matter is actually condensed energy, while energy itself remains a deep mystery. It was eminent physicist Richard Feynman who said: 'Science fails to admit that it has not the slightest clue what energy is'.

A Harvard Professor of Genetics, Richard Lewontin, eloquently highlights one of the main self-inflicted problems of Western science by confessing: 'We take the side of science in spite of the patent absurdity of some of its constructs, in spite of its failure to fulfil many of its extravagant promises of health and life, in spite of the tolerance of the scientific community for unsubstantiated *'Just So'* stories, because we have a prior commitment, a commitment to materialism...'

Consciousness, meanwhile, remains the ultimate mystery for materialistic science – its Holy Grail, some would say. Materialism portrays the emergence of matter from consciousness *in reverse*, ending up with a picture of a haphazard, meaningless, fragmented universe. In this respect, aether awareness is not some kind of ultimate body of knowledge. What it does is extend and clarify our experiences, setting them in a greater context, enhancing every area of our lives.

*An understanding of the Four Aethers was first outlined by Rudolf Steiner and subsequently developed by the following authors: Dr Ernest Marti (*The Four Ethers*, Schaumburg Publications, 1984), Guenther Wachsmuth (*The Etheric Formative Forces*, 1932), and N C Thomas ('The Four Ethers' (unpublished paper)

The false 'luminiferous' ether

In the nineteenth century, science in the United Kingdom, the leading industrial country, represented the classic age of machine-minded thinking. Scientists then tried to identify a subtle but material aether as the medium through which electromagnetic light waves travel. But the quest to establish this kind of aether failed and the whole notion of an aether was abandoned within orthodox science. For aether is not a finer kind of physical substance, like a more subtle version of air, but is of a wholly different order of existence, which functions according to different principles.

Quantum and the Non-Quantifiable

At the start of the twentieth century, the *quantum* idea, in simple terms, put an artificial lower limit on 'smallness'. It said that below a certain microscopic scale there can be no further measurement. Whatever exists below that scale must be continuous, i.e. not consisting of separate bits. So it effectively served as a kind of limit beyond which there could be no more quanti-fying.

Max Planck, professor of physics and founding father of Quantum Physics, said: 'If we wish to arrive at a concept of what we call aether nowadays, the first requirement is to follow the only path open to us in view of the knowledge of modern physics, and consider the aether **non-material**.'

That seemed definitively to put any serious consideration of the aether beyond the scope of materialistic physics, which probably explains why Richard Feynman, Nobel laureate and physicist, later famously said: 'I think it is safe to say that no-one understands quantum physics.'

However, we can see the apparently bizarre and irrational findings of Quantum Physics making some sense when looked at as a kind of visionary revelation – unintentional, of course. For it does link our present day micro-detailed awareness with the ancient wisdom-knowing of humanity, mostly ignored in the Western world for the last few hundred years. This is the view we gain from the threshold of the physical and the aethereal.

Presently, Western science offers only an inelegant patchwork of stopgap theories and models in its attempt to fill the great gaps resulting from the denial of the aether, and each only hints at a part of the true aether. Among these are the *quantum vacuum, morphogenetic fields* and the *Zero Point Field*.

Professor of physics, Ian J. Thompson: 'There's another kind of process in physics which has often also been identified with aether. And this is the idea of 'zero point motion' – the fact that in a vacuum there are many things which *appear* to be happening or potentially happening, but not *actually* happening. And so there's this idea of 'zero point motion' or 'zero point energy', which is the energy in the vacuum. And this has often been thought of as the aether.'

Nick Thomas: 'There's supposed to be this seething mass of zero point energy. And then people imagine that there's some sort of 'field' that explains all.... I take this seriously. I suspect that there is... a true boundary between the physical and what we're calling the aetheric. And they actually are not dualistic. They are part and parcel of each other. They work with one another hand in glove. And if you restrict your perceptions to purely physical things then you hit a boundary which is called the *zero point* energy. That's the boundary where what's really going on is what we're calling the aether – rightly calling the aether.'

Light and Aether

Professor Arthur Zajonc, author of 'Catching The Light', has asked a question that has a bearing on Light and Aether: 'The figure of sound is borne by the air. What bears the fleeting figure we call light? One thing has become certain, whatever it is, it is not material.'

That non-material 'something' has been the subject of much speculation. And the current idea in physics of a universally present, so-called *dark energy* – which implies that it's invisible – indicates a rather desperate groping for something very much like the non-material aether. So we can now clearly distinguish two kinds of light: First, there's the primary, invisible, pure, aethereal, cosmic light. And then there's the secondary kind of light, physical light – visible because it's Light Aether interacting with matter – whether gas, liquid or solid. And this gives us the familiar colour range of the electromagnetic spectrum.

Light, as the colour spectrum, visible to our physical eyes, was the subject of much disagreement back in Newton's time. And his theory is still the one favoured by the science orthodoxy. But a very different theory of light was proposed by the German poet, playwright and scientist Goethe. His theory was that you have darkness and light and when the two interact with one another in a real way you get *polarity*. What a prism does, according to Goethe, is to make dark and light interact with one another, and then you get the colours that you see in a prism.

Michael Watson, an independent scientist, has spoken about Life Aether in contrast to electricity.

'The aether is not just an abstract force like electricity is. It's got this mobility inside it which electricity doesn't have. Electricity's got one set of rules which are written down by Maxwell and it always behaves along those lines. Aether doesn't have that. It's got myriads of different rules. The aether is a reactive thing. Just like living organisms are, which are an embodiment of these aether forces.

'You look at life and you see how it works. It reacts to the environment. (It's not a passive force like electricity, which reacts only in one single way.) It can react in a variety of different ways, and this is the aetheric force. And because it's self-organizing, because it's reactive, it is the essence of what we call 'life'....

'If you're looking for the Chinese meridians, the acupuncture points, you get a physical instrument, a voltmeter, and you go along there and you prod an acupuncture point and you think, Ah, there's a point. You find a meridian ... because the meter indicates it.

Now, you're left with a division of the ways here: If you're a physicist you say, the meridian exists but it's none other than electrochemical potential.... But, you see what happens. *In the process of detecting the chi energy, you've destroyed it – converted it into electricity.* So, if you ask a physicist to detect one of these vital processes, he'll get his instruments out and the instruments will kill the goose that's laid the golden egg. All physical instruments, no matter how sensitive they are, extract energy from something. Kill it. So, you're dealing completely in the world of corpses. And you can forget the Aetheric. Einstein was a Master of the World of Corpses.'

The *Tao*

The ancient Chinese Taoist understanding of the cosmos seems closely resonant with the Western idea of the aether. It also seems to eloquently describe much of what the quantum physicists are struggling to grasp, using the sterile language of mathematics and such paradoxical terms as 'quantum mechanics'.

'The Tao ... is a seamless web of unbroken movement and change, filled with undulations, waves, patterns of ripples and temporary 'standing waves' like a river. Every observer is himself an integral function of this web. It never stops, never turns back on itself, and none of its patterns ... are real in the sense of being permanent, even for the briefest moment of time we can imagine.... In a strong wind clouds change their shape fast. In the slowest winds of the Tao the mountains and rocks of the earth change their shapes very slowly – but continuously and certainly. Men simply find it hard to observe the fact.

'Each human being himself is woven out of a complex system of totally mobile interactions with his environment.... It is only useful convention which justifies even our seeing a man, a tree, a rock, as a 'thing' instead of a set of surfaces, each of which represents changes and transformations as they go on.... This immense web consisting of rolling change does not itself change. It is the 'uncarved block' devoid of any definable shape, the 'mother', matrix of time, including both 'being' and 'not being', the present, future and vanished past – the Great Whole of continuous duration, infinite space and infinite change.'   (excerpts from *Tao* by Rawson and Legeza,1973)

Not without risk

The power of the aether is of a scale way beyond our normal human capacity to comprehend. However, that has never stopped certain people trying to grasp it – for all manner of motives, good and evil. There is, then, considerable risk in raising public awareness of the aether. But perhaps now, the dangers of irresponsible misuse are outweighed by the perils of leaving this powerful knowledge in the hands of a few – to exploit for their own purposes.

Nick Thomas: 'You have a technology at your fingertips which can be used for good or evil. Because it depends upon you as a personality. Therefore there's more involved than the aether. One of the aspects of that is that your feelings are also involved, which are not aetheric – they're *above* the aether. If you know how to bring forces to bear to make somebody better, you also know how to bring forces to bear to make them worse. It's always two-edged. And the aether is no exception to that.'

The cleverest con

Suppose your life and thinking are already being subtly manipulated on the aethereal level, and higher, in ways not beneficial to you. And suppose this includes your being successfully persuaded that there is no aether or aethereal level ... or anything beyond. Then you'd have little or no chance of countering any such manipulation, either as an individual or collectively. If this were the case, wouldn't it be just about the cleverest confidence trick we could fall for?

So don't expect to find this view being presented in a balanced way by any mass media corporations or by any orthodox science journals. The reasons for this merit some thinking about....

Nick Thomas has said: 'We know there are forces that lie behind our life for the good, and there are also forces that lie behind our life for evil. And if one becomes conscious of where and how those kinds of forces are active, then one can rise to whatever level one's capable of in trying to meet it. And since there's no discernible level at which all this ceases to be relevant, the questions remain open-ended.... I do think that aether awareness is actually against certain special interests which are, at a very high level, manipulating to some degree, human beings.'

Aethereal money

Money is essentially aethereal, an idea, a concept. It flows, circulates, enables and transforms. And it takes form as a wide range of tokens, which we gain or lose for all kinds of reasons. So, money can remain an abstract, aethereal idea – as numbers stored in computer memories – or it can be converted into action, cash or other material things. This materializing of an aethereal idea, and vice versa, can be seen as demonstrating the interchangeability of energy and matter, as established by Albert Einstein.

Awareness of the 'missing something'

In our language, various terms have been substituted for the missing Aether. For example, we speak of an 'air of celebration', a 'highly charged atmosphere', someone having an 'air of grace' about them, or a radio station being 'on air'. We speak of the 'chemistry' between people which is really the alchemy of qualities, which is itself actually about aethereal processes.

Then there's the 'thrill' of anticipation or excitement as we await the indefinable, magical 'X factor' in a performance. All these physical–material terms are used poetically to describe our experiencing of the aethereal realm.

The search for the 'missing something' has been given form in stories

of quests – some portrayed in highly popularized epic movies and novels.
These have dealt, for example, with superhuman forces and powers, the
blurring of the boundaries between real and imaginary worlds, ideological conflicts, and love lost and found. The stories of Western medicine and
science – from alchemy to our present dilemmas – can similarly be seen
as quests.

Awareness of the Aether is what's crucially missing from our present
Western science and culture. And this 'absence' is at the heart and root of
many of our problems, great and small. Meanwhile, there are any number
of industries and professions providing an endless supply of substitutes –
for the insatiable demand, the worldwide addictive hunger, for that missing fulfilment, meaning and magic.

Knowledge is power

If ideas and thoughts are real, the aether is real. Through raised aether
awareness, we can transcend such artificial divisions as *sacred* or *secular*,
consciousness or *matter*, *subjective* or *objective*. We then find that these pairs
of opposed ideas are actually complementary – within the wholeness that
is the aether.

If knowledge and information bring empowerment, ignorance and
disinformation bring disempowerment – which inevitably leads to dis-
content, fear, insecurity, greed and so on. And the power of propagating
information and ideas through the aether is now being appreciated and
exploited as never before – for all manner of motives.

Aether: the essential medium of communication

With the Internet now a kind of materialization of the aether, virtually
all existing information is becoming accessible to all humanity – in varying degrees of good or evil intent, and of accurate or distorted presentation. Given this whole scenario, appreciating the dynamics and qualities
of the aether enhances our powers of discrimination. For once we've seen
through lies and deceptions – whether other people's or our own – there's
no going back to a state of unknowing innocence.

So humanity now has the potential, at least, to decide whether or not
to continue being kept in ignorance, and consequently, whether or not to
continue being exploited as a disposable resource, unaware of much bigger power games being played out.

And beyond the aether, infinitely more awaits. Available, it seems, is power and subtlety of a scale presently unimaginable. So with our aether-based overview, we find we now have a choice. We can allow ourselves to be imprisoned in an immature 'us-versus-them', divided and ruled world – or we can transcend this and evolve into a more mature level of consciousness, enriched by our awareness of the aether.

Beyond the aether

The 'bigger picture' context outlined here shows a major shift in consciousness going on worldwide. This is evidenced in, for example, the increasing emphasis on the software of life rather than the hardware, on cyberspace, the internet and global telecoms, on wars about 'hearts and minds' rather than blood and guts, on electronic money and so on.

Venturing beyond and out of the materialism box is to begin a journey of discovery through the aether – towards a 'place' where higher levels of consciousness can be accessed, yet with feet still firmly in contact with Earth. On this journey, however, there are no easy short-cuts for the impatient. But much that has been lost during the long descent of consciousness into matter can be recovered, such as an intuitive sense of the wholeness, continuity and fluidity of this ever-evolving cosmos. All of which goes way beyond the machine-mentality models, concrete or abstract, of current science.

End Notes

Some of the material in this chapter is to be found in *Aether: Knowledge is Power*, an audio CD-ROM, most of the contents of which are obtainable in book form (and as an e-book) entitled *Aether: the Transcript*. (from www. aetheraware.org). A new work, about progressing beyond the aether, is being prepared for release in 2011.

A few pioneers in aetheric technology

Here are a few of the committed, courageous scientist-seekers who have explored unorthodox paths in the quest to better understand the nature of life – as distinct from the non-living – on Earth and in the wider cosmos. In so doing, they have risked incurring hostility and rejection, for example their reputations being attacked, their work being ridiculed, and in some cases severe persecution when they seemed to pose a threat to some established positions. So we have to beware of any reported judgements of them and their work – either favourable or unfavourable – and focus on what they were actually investigating... with whatever limited resources they had at their disposal at the time.

John W Keely 1837–1898

Controversial designer of a motor claimed to require no external material power supply. But it only worked when he was present to operate it. In that pre-Quantum era, orthodox science did not yet have the notion that the very presence of this or that person subtly affects set-ups of very delicately balanced forces.

Nikola Tesla 1856–1943

Genius-pioneer-inventor in early electricity developments, originated alternating current technology and much, much more.

Rudolf Steiner 1861–1925

Science-trained, multi-disciplined educator, first distinguished different levels or grades of the Aether, particularly the Four Aethers. Expounded the idea of the living Earth long before 1960's Gaia theory.

Viktor Schauberger 1885–1958

Pioneer in water research and the polarity of implosion and explosion, acknowledged water as the blood of the living Earth.

Louis Rota 1886–1952

Discovered a 'universal current' of non-electromagnetic Earth energy which he thought controls the manifestation of matter

Wilhelm Reich 1897–1957

Medical doctor and natural scientist, discovered Orgone energy which he likened to the then discredited Aether.

Dr Ernst Marti 1903–1985

Swiss medical doctor, made a lifelong study of the Aether, developed understanding of the Four Aethers in *Das Aetherische*.

George Adams 1894–1963

Scientist, mathematician, wrote *Physical and Ethereal Spaces* (1933,1965)

George de la Warr 1905–1969

Engineer, in the 1940–50s developed a camera which photographs emanations from living bodies for diagnostic applications with results comparable to recent MRI scanning.

Sir Oliver Lodge, FRS (12 June 1851–22 August 1940) was a leading British physicist, inventor and writer, who supported the idea of an aether, investigated its properties and wrote about it in *The Ether of Space* (1909)

A few books, among the many concerning the Aether

Adams, G. *Physical and Aetherial Spaces*. London: Rudolf Steiner Press.(1965)

Lehrs, E. *Man or Matter*. London: Rudolf Steiner Press (1951). ISBN: 0854404309

Marti E. *The Four Ethers*. Schaumburg, USA: Schaumburg Publications Inc. (1984) ISBN: 978-0935690026

Wachsmuth, G. *The Etheric Formative Forces in Cosmos, Earth and Man*. London: Anthroposophical Publishing Co. (1932)

Bailey, A A. *Telepathy and the Etheric Vehicle*. London: Lucis Press (1950) ISBN: 085330116 6

Finesilver, M I. *Aether: Knowledge is Power*. UK: Pathway Initiatives (2006) ISBN: 9781900034111 (CD-ROM 8 hours of audio MP3s)

Finesilver, M I. *Aether: the Transcript*. UK: Pathway Initiatives (2006)ISBN: 9781900034104

SCIENCE, SUBJECTIVE EXPERIENCE, AND OUR POWER TO DISCRIMINATE: A CONVERSATION

Colum Hayward

O NE OF THE things the essays in this book may have done is to make our view of Sir Francis Bacon a little more complex. It has concentrated on some features of his work that do not lend credence to the crude 'Bacon is responsible for a science that is truly monstrous' charge, which has been levelled against him by voices of both left and right. 'It was … Francis Bacon who led us into the labyrinth, who stole the fire from the gods' (see above, p. 69) is not really a fair view given what we know of Bacon today. Bacon had his own contemporary detractors to deal with, as passages like the following suggest. He anticipated ignorant attack in claiming in the *Advancement* that the organization of science should come from the government of the state.

> And as for the disgraces which learning receiveth from politics, they be of this nature: that learning doth soften men's minds, and makes them more unapt for the honour and exercise of arms; that it doth mar and pervert men's dispositions for matter of government and policy, in making them too curious and irresolute by variety of reading, or too peremptory or positive by strictness of rules and axioms, or too immoderate and overweening by reason of the greatness of examples, or too incompatible and differing from the times by reason of the dissimilitude of examples; or at least, that it doth divert men's travails from action and business, and bringeth them to a love of leisure and privateness; and that it doth bring into states a relaxation of discipline, whilst every man is more ready to argue than to obey and execute.

In spite of these difficulties, Bacon was instrumental in convincing the men of politics to regard science as a domain worthy of attention. Yet we also need, I think, to recognize the remoteness of Bacon's thinking, how alien it is, as well as its surprising modernity, before we can understand or accuse him. We all too easily regard someone as 'modern'.

Given the argument that has been made about Bacon as the progenitor of a 'mad' science, I was interested to run what I could of Bacon past Scott, a friend who is also a government official outside the UK, and who had not previously read much at all of the philosopher. He responded,

> Looking into Bacon, it seems like he was basically advocating inductive reasoning in many aspects of life: from fact, to axiom, to law. This Baconian reasoning became a fundamental aspect of the scientific method, and in this way he was a founder of modern science. In his *Novum Organum*, he talks about freeing human reasoning from four idols, which are roughly the decisions based on animalistic groupthink, decisions based on rhetorical deception, and decisions based on or in preservation of social hierarchies. These are elements of social decision-making, still very much in play in modern life, and especially in modern power structures.
>
> Thus, Bacon seemed to be lobbying against the same thing I am constantly having to fight. His advocacy of science in policymaking was perhaps not so much government-sponsored scientific exploration, but rather a government-condoned scientific approach to government. He wanted, in some sense, the philosopher king – only a more democratic version of it. I cannot criticize this view, I agree with it – and I blame what are popularly thought of as the dangers of 'science' as really being failures of society to adopt this Baconian, scientific approach to governance. When science sets us wrong, it's not because it has produced an inherent evil, it's because we have not thought analytically about how best to employ our new scientifically derived knowledge. In self-governance, we seem to give priority to the four idols, even to this day.

Many of those who rail at science are actually failing to recognize how science could support them. That science needs ethical controls seems to me axiomatic; the questions are about where those ethical controls come from, politically and intellectually. This we can come back to; for the moment, let us stay with the simple statement we have from Bacon, that *all*

things are open to scientific enquiry. That was the most truly 'modern' statement Bacon made. I asked Scott whether he felt that it is true, that all is
indeed open to science. It will be immediately obvious that my friend is
a scientist in the philosophical as well as the practical sense. After some
caveats about things that are very real to us, but fall into the realm of the
subjective – aesthetics was an example – he continued:

> I don't see much limit to science as a method of inquiry, nor did Bacon
> as far as I can tell. All other aspects of the world are subject to scientific
> inquiry, and in my mind ought to be if we seek truthful understanding.
> All substitute methods of inquiry are false. At best they can be heu-
> ristic, but when they too quickly become axiomatic, all turns to dross
> (e.g., much of political science). In my opinion, for a healthy, learned,
> successful, happy, and just society, science need be applied everywhere
> possible – and that is what I have set out to do, more or less. I think,
> from what little I've read, Bacon felt the same way. Thus, it is very
> hard for me to cede that there are any real limits to science *per se*; the
> limits to the application of science in human endeavours are limits of
> ego, or limits of comprehension. But to speak of that sort of limit is
> simply to dismiss all non-scientists as either poorly trained, or worse,
> self-centered apes that haven't yet stood upright! I am willing to say
> that I may be wrong, but on a philosophical basis I am pretty close to
> being a 'true believer.'

That's the bald statement of 'science is my philosophy', but he came
to a rather more interesting position after some further reflection, and a
talk with another, who

> disagreed that science could be used to approach any problem: ethical
> questions were high on his list. At first this seems correct: there is no
> doubt that there exists a body of questions that are intimately tied up
> with society as a purely human-to-human interaction. Like art, these
> would be free (almost) of the natural world. Why am I a pacifist? Is
> abortion wrong? Or, more interestingly, suicide? I realize on thinking
> of these questions how little I really care about whether someone un-
> known to me takes their own life; I care a great deal if someone takes
> someone else's life.

For ethical questions that affect the lives of others, my rule-making axiom of choice has been the Categorical Imperative. Let us assume for a moment that the Categorical Imperative is sufficient to address all questions of human ethics. We could ask whether, by science and observation of humans in groups, we could arrive at the categorical imperative empirically. If yes, then even these questions are, at least in principle, the domain of scientific method. That may be too purist an argument, true to my own thinking though it may be. I must admit that in reality there are a great number of emotional motivators behind much, if not most, of what I do; I spend a lot of time fitting my actions into rational frameworks consistent with a scientific approach. But should I see these as limits of science, or as limits of my self-discipline?

The questions here have strong relevance to Bacon, because while it may not be clear in Bacon's own work that he believed science could give answers to ethical issues, it is not very far beyond the work that Thomas Hobbes was doing, as an heir of Bacon, in seeking to establish a basis for human psychology in mechanical science. Hobbes starts from the presumption that humans fail at self-discipline so reliably that the only hope to escape Bacon's idols, what Hobbes calls the State of Nature, is to cede their natural rights to a sovereign authority. Kant, on the other hand, charges humans with individual moral duty, and provides the Categorical Imperative as a basis for making those decisions. In Kant's language, an imperative is a commandment of reason from which all duties and obligations derive. There are hypothetical imperatives, but the categorical imperative is one 'that asserts its authority in all circumstances.' The first statement Kant makes is perhaps the clearest, 'Act only according to that maxim whereby you can at the same time will that it should become a universal law.' So what my friend is asking is whether science can actually deliver us the Categorical Imperative? And, perhaps more poignantly, whether we as a species can rise to the challenge of abiding by the Categorical Imperative on our own?

At this point in our correspondence, I felt I wanted to make a rather stronger statement about the subjective. I pointed out the various directions our argument might go, and wrote to Scott thus:

We are, of course, talking about a number of different things. We are asking the question, 'is there any limit to the number of phenomena and principles that we can subject to scientific enquiry?', which is what you are mostly writing about so far. We were also asking, or I was, 'what limits do we have to put around science that fit with our ethical assumptions?' ('do we permit ourselves unrestricted experimentation on animals?', for instance). We are also asking (I hope we are), 'is there an area of human activity that science cannot encroach on?'.

Taking the last question, the simple answer is surely that anything that is subjectively felt is unavailable to science, by definition. And of course the subjective has all sorts of limitations. It may be useless opinion, for instance, but while science can examine its content (for at that moment it becomes objective, if we choose to take up the challenge) in its subjectivity we can only respond by saying or asking ourselves whether it matches up with our own subjective experience. In the simplest terms, the content of the conversational line, 'It's a hot day', is measurable, but the experience described is not. Yet we may agree on the warmth of the day, and do no insult to science by agreeing. The aesthetic judgments of your email a while back, and your friend's example of ethical judgments, are not substantively different from this, just more complex.

You are, to some extent, seeking to extend the argument for science a bit further when you ask, 'We could ask whether, by science and observation of humans in groups, we could arrive at the Categorical Imperative empirically'. Here we are either crossing the subjective–objective divide, or else we are saying there is an objectivity we have not yet quite discovered. Game theory, I suppose, is seeking to do this, but will it always be something of a hybrid?

Let me put forward my own attempt to push the boundaries a little, in the other direction. The proposal is that subjective experience has a substantive value, and where it is subject to deep and controlled exploration, it can have a high rate of substantive value. Thus the writings of Tolstoy, for instance, are more than things we enjoy; they hold a record of experience which, although it is Tolstoy's own, we not only subjectively relate to it, but our sense of value has an objective quotient, even if to measure it would be all but impossible. Included in the value I give the experience there may well be aesthetic and ethical components; but I cannot explain the richness away that easily: there is some respect in which my own experience of life is easier to understand because of Andrei and Pierre's feelings about war, or Anna Karenina's experience before she throws herself under the train. My life has a richness because of the writings of Tolstoy; Tolstoy maybe helps me even to objectivize my feelings. Yet the experience is anything but objective, and yet it is certainly true.

Scott wrote back, and made some observations about the subjective before moving on to what I had said about game theory. He then returned to the Categorical Imperative.

I think you put our three questions very well. Questions one and three are complementary: Are there phenomena that science cannot observe? And are there areas of human activity that science cannot encroach on? It seems to me possible that scientific methods can be applied to any observable phenomenon, but they cannot tell us everything we seek to know about the observed. As you rightly say, science fails at the subjective, and the subjective is itself valuable to human experience. The same curious mind that causes us to ask the scientific questions how and why, also craves information about human experience: What is it to feel the dry heat of the Sahara, the oppression of nineteenth-century Russian class structure, or to ascend with Mallory into asphyxiation? The subjective enriches our life by connecting it to other lives we cannot, or have not, personally lived.

I wondered for a while whether it were possible to say science could tell us everything we needed to know to make rational decisions. While failing to relay to us subjective experience, it can—at least statistically—predict the outcome of a course of action. Is this enough to make rational choices? To govern one's life, one's people, or one's country? I suppose the answer is no, because we seek to govern not only the world outside, but also our experience, and our experience includes connecting physical outcomes with subjective experience.

Game theory is, as you say, only a hybrid. A way of ordering what are fundamentally subjective valuations of different outcomes. The same is true of the entire field of economics in which value is based on a deeply individualistic measure of utility. So yes, there are limits to science, and social sciences are more simply scientific observations about subjective values and not themselves a replacement for subjectivity.

Which brings us to the really interesting question: what about ethics? In a sense, ethics is about making choices that affect not your own, but somebody else's experience. That may explain why the Categorical Imperative is such a powerful tool. Since the moral man has no ability to optimize his choices to maximize another, anonymous, person's set of preferences, the best proxy he has is to use his own preferences on the presumption that, both being both human, the two sets of preferences are similar. The key, as Kant points out, is universalization. I interpret this as an appeal to judge only actions with outcomes that affect others, and to make evaluations of those outcomes using only the most fundamental of human preferences. In other words, we are to exclude idiosyncratic preferences and ignore outcomes that are uniquely our own.

If science does not give us the subjective, but human experience necessarily includes the subjective, and ethical decisions are about weighing experiential outcomes, then logically science is insufficient to answer the ethical choices we face. Insufficient because it cannot link outcomes with experiences, but still important because science, not subjectivity, is what links actions with outcomes. So both science and subjectivity are needed.

An interesting paradox arises, however, if we accept the Categorical Imperative as a sufficient basis for ethical judgments. The universalization clause narrows considerably the range of subjective experiences that can be considered. Only those preferences of man that are fundamental to all humans are valid considerations. The Imperative specifically excludes matters of taste or preference that are idiosyncratic. The question arises, then, whether these core preferences common to all men can be scientifically observed in the population. If so, and if, as I posited earlier, the Categorical Imperative itself can be derived by observation of societies – as arguably Kant and others before him have done – then we have derived a way of using the scientific method to answer every valid ethical question.

It seems, however, that as humans we are far better at evaluating the experiential using our own subjective experience as a reference than we are at evaluating experience based on learned, science-derived knowledge. This may explain why the scientific method has not come to dominate man's approach to ethical decision-making or self-governance, lending some credibility to Hobbes. A daily read through the newspaper will demonstrate forcefully the pollution of decision-making by personal preferences, which manifest as nepotism, greed, and contentious ideology. I think Bacon understood this, and would have accused men who avoided science being intellectually lazy. But it is easy to be an apologist for the nonscientific man. Our subjectivity is the human condition, and the human condition is the product of our subjectivity.

It seems to me that some important statements can be taken out of this reply. One is the acknowledgment that 'as humans we are far better at evaluating the experiential using our own subjective experience as a reference than we are at evaluating experience based on learned, science-derived knowledge'. I might be seeking to make a more positive use of the statement than my friend intended if I say that it seems to me a reminder we keep crucially aware of the way we refer to things subjectively. 'Awake', as Buddha said. The other is actually a question, not a statement, and it is one I would link a little more closely to the one just quoted than perhaps my friend intended. It is the question, 'Are there phenomena that science cannot observe?'.

My problem is with what we might call deeper subjective experience, the experiences we have that seem to go beneath even meaning, but which may have the effect of changing our lives. Some of them we may call mystical experiences, but let us not for the moment so narrow the definition. Here is something I wrote to my friend on the subject, quoting from memory (and since this article is recorded conversation, I will risk my memory once again):

I am put in the mind of the exchange in their essays between Matthew Arnold and T. S. Eliot, which you will recall from our conversations many years ago. Arnold, claiming that religions would perish but poetry linger, stated 'poetry is at bottom a criticism of life' – a statement which itself seeks to give poetry some sort of objective valuation (I actually don't subscribe to this, in Arnold's terms, much as I admire him). Eliot, perhaps with a measure of wilful incomprehension, described the experience thus:

'At bottom? What we call 'the bottom' is a long way down. The bottom is the bottom.... We bring back little from our rare descents, and that little is not called criticism.'

I can't subjectively know that my 'at bottom' is the same as Eliot's 'at bottom' but I employ imaginative trust that we are at least moving around the same underwater region. I relate myself to what he says, and like Tolstoy's fiction, it is useful to me. What I pick up from my own 'rare descents' brings me insight, joy, a sense of presentness, heightened self-awareness, and very often something which words will not contain for me. To give an example from Eliot's own poetry, the lines

So, while the light fails
On a winter's afternoon, in a secluded chapel
History is now and England

rarely fail to put me in a place of psychic awareness – I mean that in the strict sense, not the Spiritualistic. I would make a claim that the best of my own meditative experience – and certainly some of the experience related by others – has substantive value to me. In this the word 'fiction', which I have just used, has no relevance whatsoever, nor does the current 'God' debate (which is about something dualistic, whereas my subjective experience is unitary).

Let me go further. Just like poetry, the value of our meditative experience can be our own, but it can also be valuable to others. This is in no way about scientific truth – it cannot have that sort of value – but it does have an external value (I suppose my definition of 'external' here is something that can be traded – i.e., shared, passed on, exchanged).

Science, of course, can measure brain activity while I am having my profound thought. It may well detect surprising levels of activity in unexpected parts of the brain. It may detect significant levels of particular types of brain wave. As the result of quite recent work, it may even go so far as to detect me actually 'growing' areas of my brain through doing this sort of inner work, the phenomenon of neuroplasticity, and it is rewarding to me that it is precisely meditation that has caused the phenomenon of neuroplasticity to be accepted. Science can't, of course, ever measure nor ever will (as far as we can yet conceive) detect what are the thoughts I am having. Nor may they be ones I can myself verbalize.

At this point, our correspondence looked like being cut short by more pressing concerns for policymakers, yet my own interest continued. I am making, after all, a claim that there is a type of awareness, which I would like to call a knowledge – a *gnosis* is perhaps the best word – that is immensely valuable to us all, cannot be measured (which is what science does) in ways that carry any useful relation to the way I relate to it, and yet can in some way be transmitted and received between individuals.

The problem is that once there is an acceptance of this *gnosis*, we are usually remarkably short on the rules of discrimination that help to sort out the true gnostic perception from the bit of highlighted special pleading that the next man or woman offers me. I actually think my friend's phrase in the context of the Categorical Imperative is rather helpful, although he intended a different use for it: 'exclude idiosyncratic preferences and ignore outcomes that are uniquely our own'. It does, however, only refine the question, not answer it. What would be real criteria, by which we might recognize true *gnosis* (in the sense I have used the word) and separate it from subjective experience which however colourful, or dramatic, or poetic, or enjoyable, is not, in the sense implied by *gnosis*, 'true'? (Ah, I use a very challenging word there, one that would require a whole book to defend.)

Well, here are some possibilities.

The first is that the echoes of what we hear from another, what they offer us as '*gnosis*' in this special sense, should reverberate inside us in a way that gives us a feeling we have always known it. That is like saying we have innate understanding, and I suppose that is just what I do mean.

The second is that it should have breadth of reference, by which I mean something not hugely distinct from the line I quoted from Kant earlier in this chapter, about preparedness to see our maxim as universal law.

The third is that it has longevity, in the sense that there are parallels with what people have long found useful to them in leading their lives. This is what the Theosophists, borrowing an Upanishadic term, called 'the ancient wisdom'.

For I need to be able to separate the teachings of the Buddha, which arose out of deep and long meditation, from the latest New Age faddist's, in some way. In fact, mysticism has for long had criteria with which to judge the level to which it may be applied; it is more self-regulating than self-appointed gurus often allow themselves to think. An early Indian text, *The Crest Jewel of Wisdom*, tells us that 'Knowledge is gained by discernment, by examining, by instruction' – in short, by a very objective view of subjective experience. Its author adds 'dispassion' in another paragraph:

'First is counted the Discernment between things lasting and unlasting. Next Dispassion, the indifference to self-indulgence here and in paradise. Then the Six Graces, beginning with Restfulness. Then the longing for Freedom'.

I shared these texts with my friend, and needed to amplify for him what were the Six Graces. They are (1) Restfulness; (2) Self-control; (3) Withdrawal; (4) Endurance; (5) Faith; (6) Meditation. Restfulness is defined as 'the steady intent of the mind upon its goal'. Self-control is 'a steadying of the powers that act and perceive'. Withdrawal is 'the raising of the mind above external things'. Endurance is 'continuing without self-pity'. Faith is 'honest confidence in the teaching and the Teacher'. Meditation is not simply practice, but 'the intentness of the soul upon the pure Eternal'. Within the context of inner experience, each one of them seems to me a way of raising the purely subjective into something which, though scarcely objective, is something entirely free of 'idiosyncrasy'. I continued,

> These are prescriptions from 500 BCE, but they have not lost their usefulness within the vocabulary and enterprise of twenty-first century mysticism. They are criteria within a context, but there will be other criteria for other areas of study. Maybe even Bacon's alchemical writings are among these. It may be that in the period we are entering, with its wider range of phenomena to explain, the objective will be more difficult to attain; these sorts of criteria will become more important. Or shall we really, as you suggest, be able to put every possible judgment to scientific test?

In the end, Scott rose to the challenge after all, but generously gave the last word to Wordsworth. In what follows, I actually agree that the Six Graces are remarkably close to scientific method. That was precisely the point I had intended from the beginning; that whatever we do, it needs concentration and discernment, of many different types, before we are sure it is something we can hold to. We came to some agreement that the 'Six Graces' rather well described scientific method, despite some initial misunderstanding about the word 'faith'. I had needed to point out that I felt the author of the *Crest Jewel* did not mean faith in the Christian sense, but rather faith applied to what one is doing. Scott agreed that science was, *in this context at least*, a faith-based activity, inasmuch as 'faith is critical to scientific process: faith in our senses, and what we observe is in fact true. That faith is the principal axiom of science'. Scott put in a lively challenge, with which I concur, that the mind remain healthy and alive, and not sink into the negative aspects of faith, in any way. And thus in the Wordsworth quotation, which comes from the poet's *Preface to the Lyrical Ballads* (1798), we found some sort of shared repose.

> Truth is both enduring and beautiful, but beauty and age do not make a thing true. Scientific truth can only be posited if there exists a test that has the possible outcome of false. If it is not falsifiable, it cannot be said to be either true or false. It is merely opinion.
>
> In the early Indian text, *The Crest Jewel of Wisdom*, you note that 'Knowledge is gained by discernment, by examining, by instruction'. I should say discernment and examination, done systematically, is called science. As for the six graces, restfulness (systematic methodology), self-control, withdrawal (objectivity), endurance (persistence), and meditation (analysis) – all these are part of science.
>
> Religions are systems of thought that lay claim to the domain of truth. Of the six graces, the one common to all religion is faith, for without it the religion might be shown to be an aesthetic construction void of any 'true gnosis'. But with faith, comes persistence, sometimes longevity too, until the mind gives into quiescence, at which point it finds a path to self-deception, or succumbs to madness.
>
> Science and aesthetic constructions can co-exist, but they should not lay claim to the other's territory. As Wordsworth said:
>
> 'The knowledge both of the Poet and the Man of science is pleasure; but the knowledge of the one cleaves to us as a necessary part of our existence, our natural and unalienable inheritance; the other is a personal and individual acquisition, slow to come to us, and by no habitual and direct sympathy connecting us with our fellow-beings. The Man of science seeks truth as a remote and unknown benefactor; he cherishes and loves it in his solitude: the Poet, singing a song in which all human beings join with him, rejoices in the presence of truth as our visible friend and hourly companion. Poetry is the breath and finer spirit of all knowledge; it is the impassioned expression which is in the countenance of all Science.'

VII · THE *NEW* ATLANTIS : 1

THE GOLDEN AGE

Kathleen Pepper

*I tell you, you are capable of achievements and experiences beyond your
wildest dreams. You are standing even now at the edge of a Golden Age, the
beginning of a Thousand Years of Peace, which could lead to a grander glory
for the human species than your heart can now hold the knowing of.
This can be your gift to the future. This can be your
destiny. You need but choose it.*
(From *The New Revelations*, by Neale Donald Walsch)

What is the Golden Age?

MYTHS AND legends from all parts of the world refer to a past gold-
en age, where life was peaceful and harmonious. People still long
for a golden age, which represents the height of a civilization, the height
of our ideals. The Hindu tradition looks forward to a future age, *Satya*

Kathleen's professional background is in education and management.She has
been teaching about yoga and meditation for over thiry years. She trained
yoga teachers in her safe, gentle and harmonious approach for the Friends
Of Yoga Society International. She has written two books, *Essential Oils and
Meditation* (2007) and *Hand in Hand with Angels'* (2010), both for Polair Publishing. She is a qualified spiritual healer in the London White Eagle Lodge team.

Kathleen is the Director of her own centre in yoga and therapies, called
KEYS, which she runs with her husband Roy. She teaches professional development workshops for yoga teachers and workshops about angels at the
College of Psychic Studies in South Kensington as well as in her own centre.
Kathleen is convinced that the approach to new spirituality can empower
people to make changes in their own lives and in the world as a whole. It's
time for a new Golden Age.

Let us hold the vision and work towards it.

Yuga, which is a Golden Age where people live up to their divine qualities and are self-ruled by the knowledge of Divine Law. In Hindu writing,
the world evolved from a golden egg and a well-known yoga meditation
symbol uses this imagery. At the present time, we are living at the end of
an age, that is, an astrological age. What do we mean by the term age,
when referring to periods of time? Most people know about the Age of
Pisces and the Age of Aquarius, which are astrological ages. Each lasts
approximately two thousand years. We are leaving the Age of Pisces and
preparing for the Age of Aquarius. Nearly everyone knows that the term,
New Age, refers to Aquarius, which became familiar to most people from
the 1960s musical, Hair.

At present, according to ancient Indian tradition, we are living in a
time called *Kali Yuga*, the Age of Iron, or Dark Age. It is certainly true that
the twentieth century was probably the most violent and destructive of
eras. It saw two devastating world wars as well as the Holocaust and the
invention of weapons of mass destruction like the atom bomb. Other wars
and confrontations were also common. The Mayans call the present time
'the time of no time.'

In 1987, there began a period of twenty-five years following an event
that came to be called 'The Harmonic Convergence.' On August 17th,
1987, people all over the world meditated on earth healing and it is said
that their unified energy of intention caused a new spiritual era to dawn. It
is considered that this event changed the history of the Earth forever. Ancient prophecies of the Hopi, Lakota Sioux and other Native Americans, as
well as the Maya, foretold a time of twenty-five years, August 15th – 17th,
1987 to 2012, when a spiritual initiation would enable humanity to expand
their consciousness into a time of spiritual transformation. This twenty-
five-year period that we are in seems to be a time of unparalleled spiritual
interest. Books about spirituality, angels, spirit guides and self help abound
on the shelves of bookshops and libraries.

Other traditions look forward to a period when the human race will
become more spiritual. The Lion Shamans, guardians of a rare family of
white lions in South Africa, look forward to a time of renewed spirituality
and responsibility towards Planet Earth and have much to reveal about past
Golden Ages as well as looking forward to a future one. They consider that
the white lions, thought to have been a legendary species, have recently
been born again, although threatened. White lions have become a symbol

of high value, gold. Africa, of course, has long been one of the sources of gold. The environmental threats we currently face seem to be associated with a decline from the mythical Golden Age already discussed. In fact, some of the Lion Shamans regard them as heralding coming earth changes. Protecting these rare animals becomes a symbol of caring for the earth.

Rare white species of animals are considered to be signs of a returning time of spirituality, a Golden Age. In North America, white buffalos have been born. Like the lions, these animals are not albinos. Their eyes are blue, not pink. A search of the Internet will reveal other news items about white birds and animals that have recently been born and indigenous peoples consider them to be spiritual signs.

The Symbolism of Gold

Gold has long been sought as a rich source of wealth. It is regarded as the King of metals. It represents value, and kings, queens and the priests of many traditions regarded it as a symbol of their power and authority. People have given their lives in the search for it, as in the Californian Gold Rush of 1848 –55. Apart from its monetary importance, gold is associated with divine principles and values. Phi, 1.618, is the golden ratio, found in many plants and in our human proportions. It is constructed using the Fibonacci sequence of numbers – 0,1,1,2,3,5,8, 13, 21, etc. Phi-based relationships are also found in the relationship of the planets in the solar system. The Golden Rule is to treat others as you would like to be treated yourself. A Golden Anniversary represents the wisdom accumulated through aging and the later years of life are often known as the Golden Years.

People have often attempted to create a golden age or golden city. Perhaps the first such attempt in historical times was Amarna, established by the Egyptian Pharaoh Akhenaton. Unfortunately, in spite of his high ideals, after about twenty years, this experiment was abandoned after his death. All traces of Amarna vanished under the desert sands until archaeologists rediscovered it recently.

There is a legendary hidden city or country that is said to exist somewhere between the Gobi Desert and the Himalayas called Shamballa. It is well known to the Tibetans. The capital is said to be surrounded by mountains of ice that shimmer like crystals. The king's palace is likewise said to be made of gold, diamonds, coral and precious gems. The inhabitants practice meditation and have advanced mental skills and superhuman powers, as well as advanced technology. Legends say that as the outside world becomes more violent, there will be a war and the city will be revealed. The king of Shamballa and its inhabitants will be victorious in the war and a Golden Age will be ushered in.

In relatively recent history, Sir Francis Bacon expressed his ideals about a Golden Age, in his book *The New Atlantis*, published in 1626. His images were of an ideal land, where 'generosity and enlightenment, dignity and splendour, piety and public spirit' were the general expectations of society. He wrote about his vision for a future of human discovery and knowledge and established the ideals of the modern research university. This vision is something we now call 'Baconian Method.' It is interesting that Bacon's world is a world of science.

The environmental threats that face the present world show how far humanity has fallen from the ideals of a mythical Golden Age. Alchemy, the supposed study of turning base metals into gold, is the highest form of spiritual enlightenment. It is often said that we cannot change the world until we succeed in changing ourselves. The highest form of alchemy is in changing the 'base' metal of our human everyday selves into the spiritual alchemy of enlightenment. Alchemy is a symbol of transformation. We can all be alchemists. Through the difficulties of our earthly lives, darkness can be transformed into light, into the gold of spirit. In any culture and tradition, there are people who achieve the highest of which humanity is capable. In recent times, we think of such great scientists as Einstein, or of Gandhi or Mother Teresa. History is full of people who have overcome great difficulties to discover divine qualities in themselves. What are these qualities?

The Age of Enlightenment, during the eighteenth century, established a set of values that questioned the traditional ways of working and overcame dogma as the way of thinking hitherto used. The power of the church began to decline. Such values were liberty, divine justice, freedom, victory, themselves divine gifts that help people to overcome fear and suffering.

Challenges to Overcome

Perhaps the greatest challenge is to realize that we are spiritual beings having a human experience. Generations of conditioning have created in us feelings of guilt and the expectation that the best way of learning and developing spiritual qualities is through suffering. This is the greatest challenge to overcome. We may instead be pro-active about change, and learn our lessons not through suffering, but through joy. From our earliest years, information and 'education' are pumped into the left brain, the intellectual and analytical centre of our nature. The right brain, our creative and intuitive side is stunted and undeveloped. We need to find the balance between the mind and heart, our soul and spirit. The great World Teachers of the Ages from time immemorial are on our side and have left us the signposts in their teachings. Gandhi, the great teacher of the twentieth century, reminds us, 'You must be the change you want to see in the world'.

We are reminded that as soon as we start the spiritual journey we draw to us all that we need to achieve it. We can start to clear out the low vibrations of our fearful emotions and this challenge is like a graduation test. We need to reconnect with the highest expression, pure love. When we are separated from our spiritual nature, we fall away from pure love, from our intuitional guidance. We can all change ourselves, heal ourselves, love ourselves and change the world. The time of no time, this twenty-five-year period from 1987, is a window of opportunity. Each day, we can spend some time in meditation and tune in to our spirituality. Spirituality should be an everyday event, whether it is five minutes before going to work or a longer period of time when it is available. Love is the fundamental basis of our spiritual transformation.

Many people talk about having no time, or ask where the time goes. Sometimes we hear the present time referred to as the End Times and some people delight in discussing destructive prophecies. It is easy to be pulled into negative and destructive thoughts and ideas by what we hear or read. We can keep our own power by being independent and not allowing ourselves to be drawn into this kind of negativity. There is no time like the present and perhaps we are living in the best time to be alive. Spiritual teachers like White Eagle remind us that the focussed thoughts of one person can be more powerful than the negative thoughts of ten thousand. When enough people achieve spiritual transformation, the alchemy of finding spiritual gold, then we can be the forerunners of the next Golden Age. Then perhaps the earth herself, Gaia, will also be transformed from a dark planet to a truly brilliant planet of golden light.

References

Cote-Robles, Patricia Diane, *What On Earth Is Going On?* New Age Study Of Humanity's Purpose, Inc., 1997; 0-9615287-5-3

Pepper, Kathleen, *Hand In Hand With Angels,* Polair Publishing, 2010; 978-1-905398-21-8

Pinchbeck, Daniel, *The Year of The Mayan Prophecy,* Piatkus, 2007; 0-7499-2760-7

Tucker, Linda, *Mystery of the White Lions*, Hay House, 2010; 1-4019-2721-9

Neale Donald Walsch, *The New Revelations,* Hodder & Stoughton, 2002; 0-340-82588-X

TRANSFORMATION OF POLITICS

Birgitta Jónsdóttir

I have seen signs
the end of the world
as we know it
has begun
Don't panic
it might look terrifying
on the surface
but inside every
human being
a choice
to go under
or act
Earth is calling
Sky is calling

Birgitta Jónsdóttir is a poet, artist, internet pioneer and an activist. Currently she is serving as a member of the Icelandic Parliament, representing the Movement, an experimental horizontal movement she helped create in February 2009. She was elected as an MP in April 2009 on behalf of this movement; its chief goal is democratic reform beyond party politics of left and right. She has been an activist and a spokesperson for various groups, such as Saving Iceland and Friends of Tibet in Iceland. Her greatest achievement in parliament was to spearhead the IMMI proposal. The Icelandic Modern Media Initiative (IMMI) is an Icelandic law intended to make the country a haven for freedom of information, speech and expression. It creates a supportive and attractive jurisdiction for the publication of investigative journalism and other threatened online media. It was adopted unanimously by the Icelandic Parliament on June 16th, 2010.

God is calling
Creation is calling
wake up, wake up now
Generate the capacity for love
for compassion in your heart
Now is the time
to yield to the call of growth
to the call of action
you are the change makers

Sleepers of all ages
wake up
wake up now

THE TWENTY-FIRST century will be the century of the common people – the century of YOU: of US.

The ideologies of the old school of politics, media, monetary systems, corporations, and all known structures are in a state of transformation. They are crumbling. Now is the time for fundamental change on all levels, we have to seize this moment. Because this is THE moment. We are living in times of quickening – times when the power of belief, the power of thought, will move reality in the direction of our dreams. So we need to know what it is we want. We need to know what sort of future we want to live in, what sort of future we want to manifest for the future generations. For it is our responsibility to leave a legacy of hope, not desolation.

It is rare that generations and so many individuals get such an opportunity to transform the world as we know it. The big question is, how do we transform it? We can start by turning the pyramid of power upside down.

It is obvious that we are running out of planet. Many people have lost the vital connection to the environment, most of humanity doesn't comprehend cause and effect of lack of sustainability anymore. Many of us feel lost, displaced and lonely. All the structures we thought would take care of us, be it systems, ideologies, religion, politics or institutions are failing. Big time!

I know we can get sustainable change in our world if we use the concept and methods of the corporate globalization to our advantage to push for changes that benefit everyone on our planet in a joint effort locally and globally.

Iceland is in many ways an ideal place for experimental work in this regard, being a country with only 316.000 souls living there yet our society is among the most developed in the world. With a tiny bureaucratic body compared to similar societies, we can move radical change much quicker through our system.

Many people who think alternatively look to Iceland as a country that could become the core place for change because of how developed it is and yet it is in a state of transformation. A country that was ranked three years ago as the most developed nation in the world according to UN standards, had a colossal fall and now has the same monetary figures as Zimbabwe. At times of such turn around of fortune – nations need to look deep into the fabric of society and that is what has been occurring in Iceland. People are confronted by the lies – the total confrontation of the maya – the grand illusion being lifted. Time to either become brutally honest or swallow the lie. The lie was so grand that it is impossible to ignore it. Thus the soul searching has begun. People have started to face the fact that our society is lacking the needed ethics for us to carry on as we have been doing.

At times of shock people first get numb, then angry and then they either cover up the hurt or they transform through healing and deeper understanding of what brought the grief about.

There are groups now within Iceland looking to transform the monetary system – move beyond fractional reserve banking into more sustainable models. There are groups looking into making Iceland the first country to only run cars on methane gas. And then there is of course the project that made a model for how we can change the way we make laws in our world. The IMMI project.

The global ruling elite knows how to make secrets. Tax havens are a symbol of that. Tax havens pull together all the best laws from around the world to create a shield of secrecy so clients can elude paying taxes and perform shady dealings within that shield beyond the legal framework within their own countries. To avoid accountability and integrity. We decided to use the same model in a reversed order. To create a transparency haven.

So we went on a quest to find all the best possible laws from around the world that ensure freedom of expression, information and speech. By basing our laws on legislation that has already proven to be strong enough to withstand attacks from those that want us to live in a world with less flow of information about the darker side of politics, international corporations, war and oppression.

Information doesn't have any borders any more. We live in a world where the super powers want to put global censorship laws on the Internet. We have to be a step ahead of them.

I joined forces with the global transparency movement because I feel it is so incredibly important that there is a place in our world where whistleblowers and sources can feel safe to drop important documents that governments and corporations want to hide from us.

The Icelandic Modern Media Initiative (IMMI) can make it possible for investigative journalists from around the world to publish their stories if they are under treat to be placed under gag orders and prior restraints in their own countries, everyone should have free access to information, in our world there should be no gag orders, no prior restraints, no falsification of our historical records on the Internet. IMMI can provide a shield against that.

We should have a haven in our world for those that are willing to risk their lives to blog or write news about things in their own world, even if we might not be able to save them from the risk they take, we could at least make sure that their stories will not be taken down from the Internet, no matter what.

My hope is that IMMI will transform into the *International* Modern Media Initiative, because every day the freedoms we want to protect with it are eroding at an alarming rate. Without freedom of information, you don't really have democracy but dictatorship with many heads. As things are progressing, it looks like this dream IMMI International is becoming a reality. MPs, NGOs and journalists from around the world who understand that if we lose the battle of freedom of information on the Internet we will also lose it in the real world, will join hands in the establishment of the IMMI foundation.

The twenty-first century will be the age of us, the common people, where we will understand that in order to live in the reality we dream of, we have to participate and help co-create that reality.

Here is our first task: If there is something we have to make sure stays under the guardianship of nations, not corporations, then it is the following: water companies, energy companies, social welfare, education and health systems.

We have made everything so complex and grand, perhaps it is time to return to more simple ways, more self-sustaining ways. We can do that by learning from each other, by helping each other locally and globally and by remembering that we as individuals can change the world, and now is the time to step forward – take on that challenge and be the change maker. Don't expect others to do it, your time has arrived to make a difference!

To follow my intuition as a politician makes more sense to me then the rivalry and manipulations of the left and right ideology. The right and wrong ideology of the old world has simply outgrown itself. No longer do we have strong parliaments with a direct link between the general public and decision makers. We have so called professional politicians that are far removed from the reality most of us live in.

Parties and politicians are often in an unhealthy marriage with corporations and corruption is thriving in the political arena all over the world. Many governments and politicians talk about transparency yet the process of politics and laws is shrouded in secrecy.

When everything collapsed in Iceland in 2008 I sensed that within this crisis was to be found an incredible opportunity for change. As a result of an attempt to have the grassroots groups work together on larger issues and of course to join hands in protests and pressure for change I helped create a political movement in the form of the Movement Party in February 2009. Its chief agenda was to bring forth democratic reform, such as people being able to call for national referendums, be able to vote for individuals not only parties, and sever the ties between corporations and politics.

We also are aware that no matter who you place in a corrupt system in thrones of power, even fine individuals get corrupted with power and the fear of losing power. In order for profound change to be possible those of us inside parliament have to behave like activists by changing the traditions and revealing the unwritten rules of power.

Information will set you free. Now once we have the information what are we going to do with it? What sort of world do we want to live in and are we ready as individuals to put the time, energy and effort into creating the blueprint of the future?

As we will become increasingly aware in order to live in the reality we dream of, we need tools to be able to do that.

Yet again an Icelandic experiment might be an answer. All nations have done this at some point. We are going to re-write our constitution. Usually it is the elite that writes the constitutions; we however have managed to make sure that the general public will take part in both the dialogue about what should be in our constitution and to vote on each new constitutional law before the parliament has its final say. This is fundamental in order to ensure that the constitution writing will be a part of a broad dialogue and consensus on what we agree on as a nation should be the foundations of our society. If this experiment works for us I strongly recommend that all nations will follow suit if your constitution is not something you know by heart and has a real meaning towards the future. Perhaps we can, once that process is over, make a constitution together for the world.

The concept of gross national happiness (GNH) was developed in an attempt to define an indicator that measures quality of life or social progress in more holistic and psychological terms than gross domestic product (GDP). I think every constitution on our planet should include something about the importance of happiness among its nations. I hope ours will.

The real value I see in the rewriting of constitutions is the dialogue between people about what sort of society they want to live in. Constitutions is something that needs to be looked deeply into since the fabric of our world is in a state of change and the constitutions don't usually reflect who we are as nations anymore. Of course there are exemptions – the most important thing about the agreement we make about our social structure is that it is in tune with the direction we are heading in and that we know this living document by heart or we can be assured that those in power will breach the laws that are written in the constitution.

Small nations might not have much weight on the scale of world powers – yet they can play important roles as nations who work for peace, human rights and sustainability. They can be that annoying fly in the tent of the consciousness of greater nations. They can be bold where others dare not, and set the standard of the direction for important issues. We are living in interesting times where the impossible can become possible just like the fact that I of all people am now a lawmaker.

If I could become an MP in the Icelandic Parliament, anyone can become a Member of Parliament. In March 2009, I was a temporarily unemployed, single parent who had the simple goal of figuring out how I as an individual could help create a sustainable future for the next generations. Needless to say, no one really believed I could be where I am today. Yet it is not a Cinderella story but a story I co-created with my society. I have somehow managed to not only plant seeds of change in my own country but been blessed with being able to do the same all over the world.

Most people have realized that left and right politics don't have any meaning any more. To create a political movement based on a common agenda of the pressing issues of basic human rights and democratic reform is so important right now.

In order for the common people like us to co-create our society we have to have the democratic tools to do that. People need to get into parliaments to change the laws so we all can have the power that is rightfully ours, to impact our society and apply real pressure on those in power to work for us, not the elite. The single most important tool is national referendums that nations can call for about important issues.

Political parties have become like thrones of worship. Political cults, with professional leaders who most of the time are willing to sacrifice the principles of the parties' agenda for a secure place of power. It is called compromising. Yet the compromising is based on pressure from lobbyists from the special interest groups called corporations. Corruption and manipulation has become the norm. If people belonging to these parties criticize the course their leaders are heading into they get dishonoured and expelled from the club. People vote for these cults generations after generations because they belong to these cults. Born and bred into it and find it as difficult to leave them as for others to leave their religions. Yet if we examine the history of the parties we realize that they have always served special interests as soon as they get into power. Very few have managed to get out of the power game untarnished. Simon Bolivar said: 'If you want to know a person, give her power'.

My political movement's chief aim has been to inspire ordinary people to take on political responsibilities. We don't want people with political training, we don't want professional politicians and we above everything else don't want to be a political party. We have a horizontal structure and have no leaders. We share the responsibility of leadership and try to bring together people from all levels into action and collaboration. It is not easy, and we have made mistakes, but we acknowledge the fact that we are human and prone to make mistakes, especially when we are doing things we have never done before.

We have to remind ourselves at all times that no matter what our fellow MPs tell us we should be aware of the fact that power corrupts and disconnects people from the reality other citizens live in. Thus no one in our movement has the right to work as an MP for more then eight years.

We created the Movement eight weeks before the elections; we had no money, and no one knew us, yet we got more then 7% of the vote at the general elections in 2009.

Many people don't understand why I made myself available to run for a seat in the parliament. I have never carried much respect or trust for the trinity of power in Iceland or elsewhere. I think most courts are corrupt, I think parliaments have been taken over by lawyers and the ruling elite is like a mockery of democratic principles to me. Why in the world would someone like me want to enter the belly of the beast? I have never aspired to become a politician and I find politics to be overrated and too much trust thrust upon people who are frail and simply human yet attributed some demigod qualities. The general public tend to want the politicians to be perfect and at the same time they are supposed to be a reflection of all qualities of society. It is a paradox. Human elements of mistakes and frailty are of course something that should be expected from the politicians. What is lacking now in the political landscape is trust. People no longer have trust in politicians or parties. That is because there is a lack of integrity and humbleness in that field. Politicians have forgotten that their role is not to govern but to serve.

I would never have chosen to become part of the theatre of the absurd within the parliament if I had not seen a real need and chance for profound fundamental change. It is important to have people there who understand the way people in power use times like this to pass unethical laws and those who pull the strings of the politicians from the corporate world who are willing to go to any lengths to maximize their profit at the cost of the general public. At times like this someone has to report from within, even if at times it nearly feels like an impossible task.

I also like to see myself as someone planting seeds of change in thought and traditions, by being clear about the fact that even if it is tempting to sell out to get your vision through – it is never an option. Integrity is the single most important element to make the places of power invested in. I have no idea if I will be successful or not, but it is worth the try.

One of the reasons why it is so important for groups to get representatives into places of power, is that it is a lot easier to get media attention on your causes, and it is handy to be able to confront or talk with ministers and other MPs about important issues without delay. I have already many success stories in this regard, especially when it comes to helping asylum seekers in dire need for their case to be looked into.

When I was working as an activist one of the hardest challenges was to get the attention from both the media and the people in power to the cause, getting some changes implemented was nearly impossible. Now that I am getting a better understanding on how things work within the legislative body I have a much better chance to help other activists and the general public to get attention and even legislative changes and resolutions on issues they are concerned about.

What might seem impossible now might be quite possible tomorrow because we are experiencing very rapid changes on all levels. So I encourage you to start to make the blueprint for the future you want to live in, to be passionate about your cause and to believe that everything is possible, today's failings might turn into tomorrow's successes.

But the most important part is if you have a chance to work within the belly of the beast to not become like them but to listen to your heart, to listen to your intuition and to be impeccable with your word. And finally not care at all if you lose that place of power.

THE BIRTHING OF A GOLDEN AGE IN OUR TIME

Steve Nation

FRANCIS BACON is widely acknowledged as the visionary who laid the foundations for what has become the scientific method, a core element of modern civilization. Yet the esoteric, Rosicrucian heart of his writing and thinking has remained largely hidden and out of view in modern Western thought, as if it were irrelevant to the issues and concerns of the age.

Bacon lived at a time when the world was experienced as including dimensions of interpenetrating levels of Being, a matrix of relationships with numinous presences. The intelligent, thinking culture took note of heavenly realms. Our age is very different. Material progress has been the dominant concern. We have interpreted what we see in the world and ourselves in almost entirely humanistic terms. As a generalization, it can seem as if all the higher reaches of Mind and Heart where the sacred mysteries are to be found are repressed and deeply embarrassing to any intelligent sense of what it is to be human in the twenty-first century. And so it is that Bacon's contribution to the development of experimental science is honored, while the broader metaphysics of his thinking are considered, if they

Steve Nation worked for almost twenty years at the London office of World Goodwill and Lucis Trust. Together with his late wife, Jan, he is co-founder of Intuition in Service and the United Nations Days & Years Meditation Initiative. Since 2002 he has coordinated an annual global meditation Vigil for the United Nations International Day of Peace. He writes a monthly newsletter available by email, *Please Hold in the Light,* as well as a regular column for UK journal, *Caduceus.* Steve is actively involved as a Board member of: Lifebridge Foundation; Lucis Trust; Triangle Center, New Zealand; Darjeeling Goodwill Animal Shelter Trust, India. He and his wife, Barbara Valocore, co-facilitate the 'Spiritual Caucus at the United Nations' in New York. He lives in the Catskills region of the Hudson Valley, NY, USA.

are considered at all, as irrational fantasy.

Yet clearly this is too simplistic a view of our times. While the domains of magic, alchemy and mysticism have been largely repressed, a new vision of wholeness is sweeping through consciousness and, as a consequence, the hidden worlds of the esoteric are again being brought into our awareness and are beginning to find a space in serious intelligent thinking and discourse. Bacon's vision of a Great Work, a historical process leading sequentially towards the dawning of a utopian golden age, in part as a result of the application of scientific method, is alive and deeply resonant. Increasing numbers see a momentous cultural transition occurring – marking a passage into a new epoch when sacred and profane, inner and outer, intuitive and rational, are seen to be part of one whole. As the theologian Hans Küng has reminded us, we don't yet know what names (like 'Reformation' or 'Enlightenment') or nicknames (like 'baroque' or 'rococo') the new epoch will come to be known by – but what we do know is that the wholeness paradigm is stimulating a massive reorientation of consciousness. In Küng's words, we are experiencing 'an epoch-making paradigm shift from modernity to post-modernity, in a change of overall constellation which has now also broken through into mass consciousness'. [Hans Küng, *Global Responsibility, In Search of a New World Ethic. London*, SCM Press, 1991, pp. 19-20]

The development of the Western esoteric utopian view from the late nineteenth century through to the middle of the twentieth century can be traced through a host of writers and visionaries. I think particularly of Helena Blavatsky, Annie Besant, Alice Bailey, Rudolf Steiner, Helena and Nicholas Roerich, Grace Cooke and the White Eagle phenomenon, Western Buddhists such as Lama Anagarika Govinda and Christmas Humphreys, the Christian vision of Teilhard de Chardin, the Sufi writings of Hazrat Inayat Khan, and the Hindu visionary Sri Aurobindo. All of these diverse thinkers were directing attention to the merging of an inner esoteric view of consciousness with the vision of a historical evolutionary process leading to human and planetary unity. Today, they are the sources of inspiration for millions worldwide and have given inspiration to a wide variety of networks and initiatives.

My own background is with the teachings in the Alice Bailey books, where the numinous presences of the theosophical tradition are seen to be stimulating and nurturing a vision of right relations among people of all cultures, professional and academic disciplines and faiths. True esoteric work for we human beings with feet of clay is seen to be concerned with a process of bridging between and integrating higher and lower, inner and outer dimensions of consciousness – in the Eastern language of Theosophy, Bailey writes of this fundamental process as 'building the *antahkarana*'. One of the immediate tasks is to foster group consciousness, particularly amongst those individuals who are naturally inspired by the oneness vision and who are working actively (in inner, esoteric and outer, exoteric ways) to build a more just, equitable and unified world. Another is the awakening of the intuition – direct apprehension of reality. Meditation, a core discipline in the building of the antahkarana, is also a way of service – working within group fields of mind and heart to see beyond veils of illusion where separateness rules, invoking and radiating energies of Light, Love and Divinely Inspired Purpose into the collective mind and heart. Meditation as service is a way of enhancing all that is being done in thought and outer activity to give birth to a world centred around the principle of Oneness or Living Synthesis.

In the utopian vision outlined by Alice Bailey, evolution (guided by Great Ones on the inner side of life and an integral aspect of a wider occult process whereby our Planetary Logos is itself undertaking an initiation) is leading to an increasing realization by human beings of two great principles: First, the fact of the One Humanity and the One Life; Second, the sacredness and significance of the individual – honouring every human being as a unique expression of the divine. The modern mantras, 'Unity through Diversity', 'Think Globally, Act Locally', 'Local is Global', 'Human Rights and Responsibilities', are a perfect reflection of these principles.

There is plenty of evidence to suggest that these two principles are indeed fundamental forces, increasingly driving the processes of history and the evolution of consciousness. Oneness is different from sameness or uniformity. The phrase 'living synthesis' is perhaps nearer to the mark. Organic, living systems tend to be rich in diversity, and full of apparently contradictory elements. Living synthesis suggests the many parts fitting together in such a way that they retain their awareness of individuality and difference within an overarching sense of being part of a greater Whole. The part is precious – facing its own evolutionary challenges and possibilities. Yet these 'individual' challenges are arising within the context of the wider environment of interdependent systems and ecologies (the environment of thought, of events, of local, national and global issues and concerns, for example). From the esoteric perspective these ecologies include dimensions of consciousness stretching from all the creatures and kingdoms of the natural world, including the human, through to the higher levels of luminous mind where Ancestors, Saints, Rishis and Great Beings such as the Christ and the Buddha are to be found, and on to those centres of awesome mystery, the Earth itself and all the planets and stars of the universe.

In social affairs and the human psyche, living synthesis describes the awakening sensitivity to wholeness, interdependence, universality. I am not suggesting, as we sometimes hear in New Age circles, that we are living in an age of enlightenment or that Love and Light are the dominant energies of our time. Clearly this is not the case. Yet what is happening, it seems to me, is that there is now a dominant dynamic in psyche and society in which the instinct of separation and identification with the separated self is being balanced by and in a state of tension with the newly emerging notion of wholeness. There is evidence of this dynamic in all fields of experience, of thought, of arts and sciences and it is through this dynamic that a new world is being born. As a species we are being initiated into a new yoga of synthesis as we learn how to respond to the growing sense of universality. We are learning this on an individual level as well as a group and collective level.

The idea that the intelligent mind is today awakening to synthetic thinking processes is fairly self-evident. Let's take one example that is a basic aspect of our lives: the impact that the wholeness vision is having on medicine around the world. In part we see this in an on-going dialogue between complementary, indigenous, traditional and allopathic disciplines. Of course there are lots of powerful forces opposing a living synthesis approach to medicine, and more often than not it is these that attract our attention. Yet I believe that we can see these opposing forces as outside of the main thrust of the new. They are what Hans Küng has called 'counter-movements and deviant trends'. The entrenched power of the drug lobby, for example, and all of the prejudices of inherited thinking from medical establishments naturally resists new paradigms. What we see now is a dynamic tension between synthesis and separation. Yet the fact is that new approaches to inter-disciplinary thinking, medical anthropology, cross-cultural studies, whole new fields of medicine like studies of human electrical fields, brain and consciousness research, pain clinics, the use of ultra-sound, the study of systems like the immune system – these are where the paradigm of interdependence and wholeness thinking are fostering an entirely new understanding of the nature of the body and the mind-body interface. Diseases demanding a wholeness and trans-disciplinary approach are constantly challenging the post-modern medical world. Think of HIV/AIDS, of lifestyle diseases and the avian flu. The minds of researchers and the economic forces that fund research are being challenged to investigate the way in which many different factors interact and combine in totally unexpected paths to manifest in new diseases.

Within this holistic paradigm in healing, esoteric therapists working with subtle energy fields are now widely available. Within hospitals and medical practices, acupuncture is increasingly offered and there are numerous examples of spiritual and energy healers being included as part of a team of practitioners.

In the emerging global community it seems amply clear that the tension between living synthesis and national self-centredness is at the heart of international relations. Just look at the issues that are so central to the economic, political and social affairs in all nations: environment, climate change, financial regulations, world trade, human rights, minority rights, race relations, the relations between men and women – in all of these issues there is a massive conversation taking place reaching into the sitting rooms of most homes. It is a conversation that plays itself out in national politics as well as law, business and economic life, the arts and so on.

We are living in an age of interdependence. This is no longer a matter of ideology or belief or dream. It is a fact. The problems we face are very much problems of our interdependence: global poverty affects all; world trade issues are fundamental to the economic debates in all societies; climate change is a topic of heated discussion in national and even local legislatures. These issues reflect the fact that the agenda of human affairs is being set by our collective response to issues of living synthesis – it is not surprising that the response includes a strong measure of resistance to the processes of dialogue, multilateral agreements, participatory planning and consensus-building. The tension between separation and synthesis is a logical and to-be-expected part of the process. Yet the simple physical realities of, for example, climate change, the spread of deserts, global terrorism and global crime are such that ultimately societies have no choice but to adapt to the circumstances of a world of unity in diversity.

One of the great symbols of the way in which the vision of wholeness is conditioning the agenda of global affairs is the discussion, politicking and negotiation around the United Nations Millennium Development Goals. During the period leading into the Millennium celebrations of 1999/2000, when the oneness spirit received such a stimulation (think of the dawn ceremonies watched by millions around the world, or the joy of the celebrations in the opening of the Sydney Olympics) government leaders met at the UN for a historic Millennium Summit. At this gathering they signed a solemn declaration – a promise to the people of the world that, acting together as a global community, governments and peoples would together achieve eight clearly-defined goals by the year 2015. The significance of these goals cannot be overestimated – they defined exactly what was achievable (politically and humanly) during the coming fifteen years in the universal human rights agenda of the United Nations. The Goals include cutting by half the numbers of people living in extreme poverty, empowering women, ensuring every child receives basic primary education, reducing infant mortality by two-thirds, serious action to reverse the spread of HIV/AIDS, malaria and other diseases, specific targets to ensure environmental sustainability and a compact of cooperation between the economically wealthy nations of the north and the developing nations of the south.

It is easy to look at this process in the short term and be very skeptical – on current trends the Goals will not be met. But this is a grand process with many steps, and stages. Never before has there been this worldwide attention to what can be achieved and what is the best, most pragmatic, evidence-based way to achieve simple goals. Never before have there been major single-issue efforts like the malaria campaign or the focus on clean water and sanitation. And never before has there been such a diversity of approaches – small-scale, local, people-centered initiatives; multilateral international programs, government projects, and private business efforts - all designed to meet measurable and achievable targets.

In the language of esotericism, it seems to me that this new process consciously fosters will and purpose and brings the principles of living synthesis into incarnation. We need to remember that it is in the process, in the discussions and muscular negotiations between governments, civil society, local government and business that people change and the world changes. It is through deep processes like this that a civilization centred on interdependence (a true sense of global community) is being born.

The initiatory issue, the field of consciousness around which a New World is being born, concerns the care, the attention, the focus given to the process of meeting these goals (in small local settings as well as national and regional settings) by us, the peoples of the world. A collective will emerges out of the pioneering concern and altruistic caring by individuals. As the goals become alive in the thinking of more and more people, so will governments be forced to stronger actions and so will people's organizations be empowered. It matters that we care about this process and these Millennium Goals – that we allow them into our heart. From Alice Bailey's perspective, the key issue is the awakening of the Oneness vision among the masses of the people of goodwill and the mobilizing of their action. This is the labor (with all the accompanying trauma and pain) of the birthing of a new, reoriented human consciousness. It involves every one of us. It is the Great Work of our time.

Among the most interesting signs that the initiatory process within humanity is underway is the emergence of focused, global meditations for world service. These are becoming so widespread a new phrase has been coined: 'subtle activism'. Just look at the network of activities for globally synchronized inter-faith meditation, prayer, ritual, dance and celebration on the United Nations International Day of Peace, September 21st. Millions are involved. Nothing like this has ever occurred in the history of the human family. It is a sign of the rise of the esoteric consciousness. Even at the United Nations itself there is an interesting collection of consciousness-focused activity. A group of representatives of Non-Governmental Organizations (NGOs) affiliated to the UN has, since November 2000, been meeting twice a month at UN Headquarters in New York to *spend time together as a group in silent reflection, share insights, and explore ways of using this inner focus to serve the highest potential of the UN.* Friends around the world are encouraged to link in subjectively, wherever they are physically, with the silent focus held at the UN. Another Committee of NGO's affiliated to the UN in New York is the NGO Committee on Spirituality, Values and Global Concerns which, among other things, co-ordinates an annual Week of Spirituality, Values and Global Concerns at UN Headquarters.

Naturally these global initiatives to serve through the power of thought encompass a vast array of degrees of attention, intention, and intuitive sensitivity. Yet through practice more and more of us are developing inner skills – and are feeling a sense of responsibility to get training in meditation to help us to grow in our own appreciation of, identification with, and ability to serve the ancient verities of Goodness, Beauty and Truth.

One of the most interesting signs of this concern to get training in

esoteric work is the emergence of academic initiatives to incorporate con-
templative arts in higher education. The pioneering work of the Wrekin
Trust in the UK is well known, as is the Temenos Academy. HH the Dalai
Lama has hosted a number of high-level scientific gatherings exploring the
interface between orthodox and esoteric realms of mind and matter. The
Center for Contemplative Mind in Society, established in the US in 1991,
has a strong and active Academic Program with particular focus on Social
Justice, Law, Business and Philanthropy. Between 1997 and 2007 over 120
contemplative practice fellowships were awarded to scholars who included
contemplative practices in their university teaching.

These are just some of the signs helping us to see the evolutionary direction of history towards what might be referred to as a 'Golden Age'. Partly as
a result of the scientific method advocated by Bacon our views of this utopian
future tend now to be less idealistic, in a sense less sentimental, than they
were even just fifty years ago. We are entering an age when spirit and matter
mesh in such a way that human beings and communities are in a dynamic
relationship between the heights of the sublime and the desires of the world.
When the UN was founded, human and planetary unity was perceived as an
ideal, a dream, a hope, a vision, a possibility. Now we are more interested in
looking for evidence of the vision shaping human affairs – we want to see
where it is happening in the midst of the gritty reality of the world.

Alice Bailey tells the story of this initiatory, birthing process in humanity
in terms of a Coming One, a Wise Teacher who will inaugurate a new cycle
and whose life and being will embody a revelation that will be the guiding
light for civilization for thousands of years. This story of a Coming One
(historically expected under different names by all major faiths) is not presented as some psychic event to shock and inspire a change of heart. Alice
Bailey speaks more in terms of a process of emergence – a process we are
now in the midst of. It includes an awakening to the reality of the soul (the
Christ within, or the Buddha nature) amongst millions of individuals and
the psychological tensions and processes this brings about. It also includes
an overshadowing of fields of group consciousness in the service network
and of the whole vast net of all human beings who find a measure of their
meaning and purpose in the service of humanity. This is the collective Christ
consciousness spoken of by several seers (including Rudolf Steiner). In Alice
Bailey's view it is a fundamental element of the Second Coming. The result
of this ferment of transition will, we are told, culminate organically and

naturally in the emergence of a World Teacher for the New Age who will give a face to the Divine Presence in the world and whose radiation will initiate the emergence of the new global civilization of synthesis.

You might well ask why such a vision of the dawning of a Golden Age matters to us now, living in these transition times? The future is always in the process of being created. It is created out of the living realities of the present – in an individual sense as well as in terms of a culture. To see our times as part of the birthing of a completely reoriented humanity gives each one of us a meaning and significance for our lives. We contribute to the birthing of the new, through the choices we make, through the lives we live. We can see our own lives in immediate relation to the wider planetary process. All that is asked of us is to be engaged in the on-going work of bringing our higher vision into relation with our personal lives. It is not about some fantasy of becoming saints – but about seeing our lives as part of an evolutionary transformation happening throughout the planet. We are living the awakening of consciousness – the awakening is living through us (through all human beings in incarnation at this time). The feminist writer Sue Monk Kidd speaks eloquently of this process of awakening through the parable of a woman's experience of conception, labor and birthing: 'The parable tells us things we need to know about the way awakening works – the slow, unfolding, sometimes hidden, always expanding nature of it, the inevitable queasiness, the need to nurture and attend to what inhabits us, the uncertainty about the outcome, the fearful knowing that once we bring the new consciousness forth, our lives will never be the same.' [Sue Monk Kidd, *The Dance of the Dissident Daughter*, San Francisco, Harper, 1996. pp. 11-12.] The experience of being alive during the birthing of a new Golden Age is like this. If we recognize what is happening within us and in the wider world we can better understand what is happening, cooperate with the process – and we can begin to see it through the eyes of love – through the eyes of the soul, the eyes of the Angel.

Web References

www.intuition-in-service.org; www.gaiafield.ntet; www.idpvigil.com; wwwinternationaldayofpeace.org; www.spiritualcaucsun.org; www.csvgc-ny.org; www.wrekintrust.org; www.temenosacademy.org; www.lucistrust.org/cycle/

For a list of Polair's other titles, please go to
the website, www.polairpublishing.org, or
email info@polairpublishing.org.uk for a
catalogue

To note in particular:

THE VIEW
From Conan Doyle to CONVERSATIONS WITH GOD
edited by Dave Patrick
In series with this volume, THE VIEW celebrates Sir Arthur
Conan Doyle on his 150th birth anniversary
ISBN 978-1-905398-18-8

THE SHAKESPEARE ENIGMA
Peter Dawkins
The search for the true authorship of Shakespeare
brings rich understanding of the plays
ISBN 978-0-9545389-4-1